The Good Father

On Men, Masculinity, and Life in the Family

MARK O'CONNELL, PH.D.

SCRIBNER

New York   London   Toronto   Sydney

SCRIBNER
1230 Avenue of the Americas
New York, NY 10020

DISCLAIMER

This publication contains the opinions and ideas of its author. It is intended to provide helpful and informative material on the subjects addressed in the publication. It is sold with the understanding that the author and publisher are not engaged in rendering medical, health, psychological, or any other kind of personal professional services in the book. The reader should consult his or her medical, health, or other competent professional before adopting any of the suggestions in this book or drawing inferences from it.

The author and publisher specifically disclaim all responsibility for any liability, loss, or risk, personal or otherwise, which is incurred as a consequence, directly or indirectly, of use and application of any of the contents of this book.

Names and other characteristics of the individuals described in this book have been changed.

SCRIBNER and design are trademarks of
Macmillan Library Reference USA, Inc., used under license
by Simon & Schuster, the publisher of this work.

For information about special discounts for bulk purchases,
please contact Simon & Schuster Special Sales:
1-800-456-6798 or business@simonandschuster.com

Designed by Kyoko Watanabe
Text set in Granjon

Manufactured in the United States of America

1   3   5   7   9   10   8   6   4   2

Library of Congress Control Number: 2004052109

ISBN 0-7432-5801-0

To Miles, Chloe, and Dylan

Who bring me joy, who give me meaning,
and who quietly remind me about what really matters.

Contents

Children make fictions of their fathers, reinventing them according to their childish needs. The reality of a father is a weight few sons can bear.

Salman Rushdie,
The Moor's Last Sigh

The Good Father

1

A Father's Weight

"JUST A MINUTE, DAD."

Dylan, my eight-year-old son, kneels over a battlefield of knights, dragons, and fantastic beasts—each imbued with special powers that he has beneficently bestowed. I've asked that he leave behind the immense (though instantly reversible) carnage that surrounds him in order to do his homework. His answer tells me that the response I want won't occur right away.

By now I've heard "Just a minute, Dad" thousands of times—from Dylan, from Chloe, his older sister, and from Miles, their older brother. I've heard these words often enough to have acquired an ear for their music, for the very different meaning conveyed by each subtly different tone.

Sometimes "just a minute" means that Dylan hears me and will do what I ask, but I'll just have to wait a minute. This tone hints at a new order: By taking this minute's space he makes clear that his mind is emerging from mine, that his being is no longer seamlessly folded into my vision of who he is.

This version of "just a minute," with its embedded claim of selfhood, holds a hard and important truth: Time is passing. And lately Dylan's distinctive little-boy gait, with its quick patter of small feet moving across the floor, has taken on a slower and heavier rhythm. The simplicity of his smile and the pureness of his voice are still there, but a slight edge in his voice, a new curl at the corners of his lips, hint at the more complex emotions that lie ahead. His skin is still smooth and unblemished, but the biology that will change his body and mind from boy to man lies coiled within him.

Yet "Just a minute, Dad" is not always about respectful proclamations of emerging selfhood. And indeed, that's not its meaning this time.

This afternoon Dylan's "just a minute, Dad" is spoken inwardly, more to himself than to me. His eyes move away from mine, looking not so much to his battlefield but to the middle distance, away from what is happening between us. And when I find those eyes, when I try to hold them with mine, he looks away again, smiling a smile that hides more than it reveals. This "just a minute" is not about a *real* minute, instead it proposes timelessness; it asks that the game never end, and that homework never begin.

These days Dylan's messages are reassuringly familiar. Yet years ago, when Miles, my older son, would say "Just a minute, Dad" in this same reality-bending way, I often didn't know what to do. I knew my son hadn't really heard me, didn't really want to hear me. His opposition made me angry, though it was not a useful kind of anger. I didn't feel solid or rooted, like a man and a father who had been through this before; rather, I felt edgy, ungrounded, like a fatherless boy trying to be someone he had not yet become. I knew that I needed to do something in response to "just a minute" but I didn't know what. So either I'd let things go, or I'd find a frictionless way to coax Miles into doing what I wanted. And with this lack of contact I lost touch with him, and our relationship vanished into a fuzzy world of pseudo-niceness.

But over time, I began to do things differently. I forced myself to confront as well as to coax, to seek out my son's eyes rather than look away. At first my uneven efforts felt like paternal prosthetics; strategies and techniques aimed at working around those places where I felt no guidance from the memory of my own father. But, organizing myself within the exoskeletal belief that as a father it was my responsibility not only to love my children but also to use my power and position to help them grow, I began to find my footing.

These days the psychic landscape around "Just a minute, Dad" is less daunting. For one thing, I have learned that Dylan, like all children, needs his father's help. The private battle that lies on the floor around him is a valuable one to him; it is a place where his mind can play with truly important things—death, violence, triumph, and defeat—without flesh-and-blood consequences. But eventually he will have to move outward from it, to real-world struggles that require the backbone that accrues from having done homework, to jobs and relationships that are lived in real time, and to a life from which he does not avert his eyes, his mind, or his body. So I know, now, that I have to find him with my eyes, my voice, my mind—with my self. I have to lead him, through the friction of our contact, away from the infinite minute he proposes, and introduce him, again and again, to the finite minutes within which we all must live.

He doesn't need a heavy hand right now. But he does need a quiet and firm, "No, not just a minute, now. You've got homework to do."

Fatherhood and Authority

What does it mean to be a father? A good father? These days the answer is not so clear. Indeed, every week all manner of fathers, from the newly minted to those near the end of active duty, from men who are successful in many areas of their lives, to those who are struggling, come to my office with painful worries and confusions about their fatherhood and, by extension, their very masculinity. Often their concerns and doubts flow from a common source.

Consider Jeffrey, a forty-five-year-old father of two. Jeffrey came to talk with me about trouble he was having with his teenage children, who were failing at school, getting into drugs and alcohol, hanging out with a bad crowd, and generally spinning out of control. Jeffrey was at loss. "I listen to them, I love them, I took them to their Little League games and all that, but it seems like I've lost them," he said. "I don't see what more I can do." I could tell that Jeffrey cared about his kids, but I also noted that he seemed to be timid and helpless in the face of the chaos. Indeed, as he spoke he slumped his tall, thin frame ever deeper into his chair, averted his eyes, and spoke haltingly, a man tumbling into himself. I noted how defeated he seemed, and I wondered aloud, gently, had he ever considered tightening things up a bit? Perhaps some rules, a curfew, and a generally firmer attitude might help. Jeffrey became instantly more alert, but only because I seemed to have horrified him.

"I'm a father," he answered testily. "Not some kind of 'tough love' tyrant."

Jeffrey was struggling with what it means to be a father, and, what was more, with a dilemma that is familiar, indeed, I will argue, defining, to many men these days: What kind of *man* am I? And who could blame him for wondering? The world in which we live is replete with pill-form enhancements and strap-on accoutrements of male power—Viagra, bodybuilding magazines, advertisements for penis enlargement, hormone supplements, power tools, power suits, Hummers, and more. Yet all of these products are emblems of our confusion about masculine power, not viable paths toward it. There is tremendous pressure on men to be strong and powerful, but simultaneously there is overwhelming uncertainty as to how to do that, whether it is okay to do that, and, indeed, what exactly "strong and powerful" even means.

And nowhere is this uncertainty more evident than when it comes to the question of what role, if any, a father's masculine, paternal power, his *authority,* should have in the raising of his children.

Fatherhood and authority: These subjects have long depended on each other for their meanings. If there is such a thing as a bedrock paternal function, it may well be authority. And if there is such a thing as an archetypal representation of authority, it is a father. From the strong and usually (but not always) fair hand of God the father, to Oedipus usurping his father's position and thus breaking the rules that are the foundation of civilized life, to Lear's failure in paternal authority, all the way to the mileage the late Ronald Reagan got from his seemingly benign paternalism, fatherhood and authority have been intimately linked.

But what do the words "fatherhood" and "authority" really mean?

Let's start with "fatherhood," a word essential to all of us, yet one that evokes remarkably different feelings. For some of us, fathers are kind and protective. For some, fathers are loved and loving. For some, fathers are agents of discipline. For some, sources of strength. For some of us, fathers have been harsh, critical, and even violent. And, of course, for all too many of us, fathers have been absent.

This latter phenomenon is central to our modern relationship with fatherhood. As we all know, many families are currently without fathers, because fathers are either emotionally unavailable or physically missing by virtue of long work hours, divorce, estrangement, outright abandonment of mothers and children, and even death.

This epidemic of fatherlessness and father hunger has generated revived awareness of the importance of fathers. Indeed, many fathers have made a conscious attempt to be more involved with their children. But these well-meant efforts have been accompanied by, if not stimulated by, a cultural prescription for fatherhood and masculinity that, while in some ways valuable, is also incomplete and flawed. These days many men and women believe that to be a "good father" means to act in a way that could best be described as a caricature of a "good mother." Meanwhile, in a related development, many of the basic qualities we have long associated with masculinity are coming in for heavy criticism. Men's strength and stoicism are now seen as the root of numerous ills, and so men are exhorted to renounce these "archaic" aspects of their masculinity for such "feminine" attributes as empathy, connection, and attunement.

It's news to no one that this is a complicated and confusing time to be a man and a father.

And then, what about authority?

Webster's defines "authority" as "the power to determine, adjudicate, or otherwise settle issues; the right to control, command or determine; an expert; persuasive force, conviction," and, in earlier editions, "power [that is] derived from opinion, respect, or esteem," and "power exercised by a person in virtue of his office or trust." These definitions, with their emphasis on power and position, are consistent with Machiavelli's assertion that it is better for a prince to be feared than loved, and Weber's belief that the power of authority derives from its legitimacy. These familiar ways of thinking call to mind people and institutions invested with keeping the social order—judges, policemen, clergy, doctors, politicians, teachers, and others—and they certainly call to mind the traditional image of a father.

But beyond these definitions, the word "authority," like "fatherhood," evokes a wide range of individual responses. To some it speaks of structure and order; to others it brings to mind discipline; to others, it conjures images of oppression and tyranny; and to still others, it elicits the urge to rebel.

And, as with fatherhood, there is evidence of a dramatic shift in our relationship to authority. Whereas most people once located themselves clearly within accepted, if sometimes begrudged, hierarchies, these days we consider the lines of these power structures to be fluid and negotiable. Teachers' knowledge, judges' judgments, politicians' motivations, the wisdom of the elderly, parents' right to discipline, priests' moral rectitude—all were once accorded institutional status, and we organized ourselves around and even underneath them. Now they, and many more, are subject to scrutiny and skepticism. Indeed, even authorities of a different order are being disenfranchised. I'm talking about the underlying realities that surround us—physical realities of time, space, our bodies, and so on, and more conceptual realities like science and God. In generations past we lived our lives within their immutable confines, and we understood ourselves to be subject to their relentless demands and expectations. But now we have developed schools of philosophy and cultural analysis that claim that moral truths are relative, that biological imperatives such as gender and life span are negotiable and contextual, and that scientific givens are really uncertain matters awaiting refutation by yet more perspicacious investigators. Now technology allows us to imagine that the inexorable march of time and the nonnegotiable reality of distance are not the obstacles that they once were.

Every day I see these disorienting shifts ripple through the men, women, and children who come to my office to talk. I see them in men like Jeffrey, who worry that they will become "tough love tyrants" if they discipline their children. I see them in men like Jake, a forty-two-year-old father of two, who said: "After being driven crazy for half an hour about whether my son was going to get dressed for school I'd had enough. I put my hands on his shoulders, I walked him to his room, and I told him not to say a word until he was dressed and ready. It felt great to me, and I could tell my wife was relieved too, because the kids' routine drives her nuts every morning. But that night we wondered: 'Was I too hard on him? If I make him do it, will he never learn to do it himself?'" And I see these questions arise not only in men, but in women and mothers. Consider Phyllis, a thirty-nine year-old mother of three, who told me: "I'm sick of the chaos. I know our children need rules and structure, and that happens when Hank [her husband] weighs in. I *know* I shouldn't say this, but his voice *is* different from mine—stronger and heavier. They hear it differently. But I worry. He's so big, sometimes I think he scares them."

Fatherhood and authority: two ubiquitous and important phenomena, often linked, whose meanings are, perhaps as never before, fluid and uncertain. These days fathers, mothers, and families are struggling with basic uncertainties regarding whether to shape children or leave them alone, whether to speak softly or firmly, whether to discipline or support, and whether the words "Just a minute, Dad" signify an emerging selfhood that needs to be respected, even promoted, or whether they communicate a stance that begs to be opposed and redirected.

In the end, fatherhood and authority, alone and in their convergence in a father's authority, are such deeply human and personal matters that they cannot adequately be understood by looking in *Webster's,* or by turning to even the most well informed of the experts. So if we are going to understand this issue in a useful way we'll have to go further. We'll have to find the meanings that help us apprehend things not just cognitively and semantically, but genuinely and experientially. Which means that we'll have to get personal.

Gary Palmer

When Gary Palmer first came to see me, neither he nor I could anticipate how much his story revolved around fathers, both his children's and his own.

Gary was a brilliant mathematician with a good job, a wife, and two children. In his forties, he was a study in contrasts. Handsome and well built, he could be engaging, particularly when he brightened with interest. However, he often retreated, and became boyish and unassuming. At times he went even further away, and would hide behind an ironic, nihilistic detachment.

Gary and I had something in common. His father had been older when he was born (mine was sixty-three when I came along), and, when he was a little boy, his father, like mine, had vanished (mine died when I was five). In Gary's case this absence involved nothing so straightforward as an outright death; rather, it was an emotional disappearance. What was more, the cause was a mystery. Maybe it was his father's frustration with his career, or maybe his unhappiness in his marriage. Maybe it was due to something so bedrock as a chromosome loaded for alcohol or depression. I often wondered whether Gary's father's pain had grown out of his having been a bomber pilot in World War II. He had flown many missions over Germany, and had never talked about the war. In any case, Gary's father had become depressed and discouraged. His once promising military career came to a dead end, and he gave himself over to drink and to unhappiness. As Gary told me, "My dad was like a ghost. I know he was important once, but by the time I came along, he was pretty much a shell of a man."

Gary had been a good kid—he didn't get into serious trouble and did well in school. Still, like most boys, he had his moments—of disobedience, of disrespect, of getting out of line. Occasionally his father would lose his temper with Gary, but he was never much of a dependable disciplinarian. Gary spoke of this shortcoming with regret. "I have a love-hate relationship with rules," he told me. "Aren't they amazing? Rules, I mean. I have a friend, another mathematician. He calls mathematical rules the Great Fascist." Gary became somber. "A father has to embody the rules. But to do that he has to be steady and fair. My father was in and out. Drunk, angry, and remote. I have a lot of anger at him, and at rules. I didn't take him seriously, and I don't take rules seriously either."

By the time Gary was a teenager he came and went pretty much as he pleased, having very little to do with his family. He remembered his father as a ghostlike presence during these years, floating around the edges of his life, physically there, but having no impact. And he also told me about a shift that took place, one that was to have great repercussions. Gary came to realize that he could think circles around his father. He later learned from his mother that his father had been painfully aware of this, feeling that he had very little to offer his gifted young son. But Gary, caught up in the heady intoxication of it all, wasn't aware of how his father felt. It simply seemed that outsmarting his father was a "cool" thing to do.

Like so many men these days, Gary had suffered a kind of fatherlessness, the costs of which could be seen in the reasons he first came to talk with me. Sure, Gary had a good job. But as I learned about his education, and his singular academic accomplishments, it became clear that he was bored and underchallenged. He could get done what he needed to get done in a very brief time, using little or none of his creative mind. He spent most of his time daydreaming—playing privately with mathematical and technical problems that interested him but which had nothing to do with his job.

And sure, Gary loved his wife, Margaret, and their two children, Jason and Catherine. Margaret appreciated him as a decent husband and father, which he was, and he felt that she was a good wife and mother. But he didn't feel passionate and alive with his family. "I'm there," he told me, "but I'm not *really* there."

Gary and I went to work—on his detachment, and on the lack of meaning and passion that characterized his out-in-the-real-world life. Along the way we learned a lot.

I say "we" quite deliberately.

I learned because our talks led me to think not only about Gary's father but also about my own. I recalled how mine had been a withering and dying man who occasionally burst forth with fits of hepatic encephalopathy—transient out-of-control behavior brought on by the effects of his chronic alcoholism. I thought about how this man, who had seemed to me to be part ghost and part home care patient, had affected my life. I came, in particular, to know more about the ways in which my own pattern of withdrawal and self-deception grew from my fatherlessness.

And Gary, I believe, also learned, as we fought things out, usually playfully, but sometimes more seriously (particularly when I took him on about his ironic detachment). And while I don't wish, here or elsewhere in this book, to imply that the only thing that matters in life is one's relationship with one's father, I think you will be able to hear how some of Gary's vulnerabilities, in particular his pattern of withdrawal and self-deception, grew directly from his father's absence.

I will fast-forward to a conversation that occurred some three years into our therapy, when things had begun to change, and when Gary, by dint of hard work and commitment, had become more effective in his career and more present as a husband and a father.

One day, when he'd been building a stone wall, the feeling of working with his blistered, dirty hands led Gary to a memory. "All of a sudden I can picture my dad's hands," he said, beginning to sob. "He was good with his hands. They were strong—kind of flat. It's so weird. I thought he and I were so different. Me the long-haired freak that I was back then—him a military man. It turns out that a part of me is just like a part of him. Why couldn't we find each other?"

Gary had begun to remember his father. He had begun to feel how much he missed him, and to recognize that he, like so many children, had been profoundly shaped by his father's absence. The fleeting sugar high of "outsmarting" his father had only obscured the fact that he had needed his father desperately. As he grew more able to tolerate his pain, Gary could see that he had, as a boy, retreated into the privacy of his own mind so as to armor himself against loss and disappointment. And now, as an adult, his private "mind play," his working problems and thinking creatively in a place no one else would ever know, merely continued what he had done years before. Like my son when he knelt among his knights and beasts, Gary played a game that existed outside of his job and family, outside "the rules" of consensual, daylight life. He continually fled to a place he could control, a place where he could not be hurt.

These realizations led to changes. Rules, Gary now could see, weren't the "Great Fascist" after all. They were, as he came to call them, the "Great Father," guiding embodiments of the daylight world of competitive and cooperative interchange in which we all must try to live. Gary now resolved to step back into this world. He got himself a job that demanded that he use more of his mind, and he worked on getting his innovative thinking a more public airing. At home, he pushed himself to talk more intimately with his wife, and to be more of a presence in his children's lives. His efforts made him feel anxious, exposed, and vulnerable, but what he was doing mattered to him, and he stayed with it. His life began to feel more alive and grounded, as though he was, to use his own words, "really there."

I found Gary's self-confrontation both inspiring and fascinating. It challenged my assumptions about the goals, and limits, of therapeutic "cure." His life-solution was essentially an existential one. He saw the problem, saw what it was costing him, and he took a risk. He didn't think of himself as "cured"; rather, he simply committed himself to challenging what frightened him. You can hear how he felt about things when, toward the end of our time together, he told me, "I think that what has changed is that I would rather know what I can really do, even if it means feeling the pain of finding out that there are things I *can't* do. I think that it's better to stay in the real world than to go into my head, even though in my head I can pretend that anything is possible."

A Father's "Weight"

Salman Rushdie writes: "The reality of a father is a weight few sons can bear." What does Rushdie mean by this "weight"?

One could certainly argue that a father's "weight" is a burden of pain. This pain may flow from a father having been actively hurtful and injurious, or, as is the case for so many men and women, it may be the legacy of bitterness, hunger, disappointment, and anger that results from a father's being absent. It may even be the weight of a father's own pain, transmitted to the next generation. All of these weights are heavy indeed.

To my ear, however, Rushdie has more in mind. The word "weight"—so open-ended and evocative—comes as close to the essence of a father's authority as any I have heard. I believe that Rushdie also alludes to a weight that is to be honored, a deeply human and necessary experience that flows from what goes right between a father and a child. I'd say that Gary's father failed him because he, like me in my early years of fathering, and like so many other men struggling to find a place for their masculine, paternal authority, had *no* weight, at least not for his son. Gary couldn't feel his father's love, but that wasn't the whole of it. He also couldn't feel his father's impatience, irritation, pride, ambition, and anger. He didn't have his father's rules to shape himself to, and to push off against. Without his father's impact, his gravitational pull, Gary spun off in space, untouched and ungrounded. Not only did he not know his father, he also didn't know himself very well. How could he? He had not been able to bump up against his dad, to use these collisions to test himself out against a man whom he valued and trusted.

So, working from the lesson that can be learned in Gary's father's failure, here is the first of many attempts to go beyond *Webster's,* and to communicate both a deeper sense of what is meant by the words "a father's authority" and also a preliminary understanding of why authority is such a core element of being a good father.

In a mode that can be quite different from that of a mother, a father conveys to his children, ideally in a way that can be emotionally metabolized, the often reasonable, sometimes harsh, always inescapable, rules, expectations, and inevitabilities of life. A father does this by teaching his children about the realities of time and limit. He does this by being a relatively nonnegotiable "other." He does this by using the right amount of power at the right time to help his children understand that the world does not lie in their omnipotent control. In these ways, all of which involve bringing his very being, his weight, into contact with the mind of his child, a father inoculates that child against retreating into the muffled, daydream world of fantasy, pretend, and self-involvement. And so a father teaches enduring lessons about living and thriving in the real world.

Gary and His Son

The gods visit the sins of the fathers upon the children. And then, as we all know, the children visit the sins of their fathers upon their own children.

As with so many men, Gary's sense of himself as a man was intimately and inextricably linked to his sense of himself as a father. As it turned out, much of our work became focused on his relationship with his son, Jason, who was eleven at the time we began.

Jason did reasonably well in school, and dabbled in sports and music but wasn't fully committed to any endeavor. I sensed that Jason was drifting, yet for some time I could not put my finger on why.

Eventually I realized that my lack of clarity reflected something about the father-son relationship. Gary was a decent man, and he was certainly an adequate father. However, just as his own father had with him, Gary stayed on Jason's periphery. Their relationship was without fight or struggle, in large part because Gary didn't weigh in with demands and expectations. For example, though Gary was himself a brilliant man, he didn't seem to be very interested in Jason's mind. Now some might say that Gary gave his son space to grow, but this wasn't the whole story. The fact was that Gary assumed that Jason's mediocre performance in school was a product of his being reasonably, but not exceptionally, intelligent, and he made this assumption without ever really getting to know his son's mind.

Over time I became troubled by the seemingly Teflon-smooth surface of Gary's relationship with Jason, and I increasingly called Gary's attention to the fact that father and son didn't scrape against each other very much. "You're being like your own father was with you," I'd say. "You can see what it cost you, and I imagine you can appreciate what it costs Jason when you do the same. What's going on that you keep your distance like this?"

Gary quickly acknowledged that something problematic was going on. He was not depressed, as his own father had been, and he had not retreated into alcohol. Nevertheless, he could tell that he was not all there. He seemed, at times, more like a pal or big brother than a parent. He didn't seem to realize how much Jason admired him and looked up to him. He didn't see himself through the eyes of his boy— as a big, strong, smart man, one who could use his fatherhood to shape his son's character and behavior. In essence, he lacked a sense of his own power and weight: his authority.

Once Gary realized that he was repeating what his father had done, he did what he did best—he resolved to change. He took Jason to his gym, and working out together became a regular routine. He involved the boy in building the stone wall, the one that had blistered his own hands and conjured memories of his own father. And he also became more involved in Jason's education. He challenged his son to get more from himself, sometimes by simply pointing out that Jason could do better. The two worked math and science problems together, and this gave Gary the occasion to show his son his own considerable talents (talents about which he had previously been overly modest). As things turned around (which they did quickly), Gary talked with his wife, and the family made a plan to send Jason to a more challenging school.

Two years after we began, Gary told me the following story about himself, and about a far more focused and content Jason: "I was working on the stone wall—you know, I never knew that I could be as happy as I am when I'm out there, in the crisp air, working with my hands, with the stone and the dirt. Anyway, Jason came out, and he worked with me for a while. He set several rocks. When he left, I went over to look at his work. It wasn't bad, but his rocks were a little loose. I thought, should I go chew him out? But I decided no, I'll wait till he comes out again, and I'll just talk to him about it. So an hour later, he came out to do some more work with me. I took him over to the rocks he'd set before. I showed him how they were loose, and I showed him how he had to fill in with more gravel to make them solid. He just listened. And after he'd worked for a while, he came over, and asked me to take a look at what he'd done. His rocks were in there really solid. I said that it was good, that was all. Just good! Neither of us said anything more. We just kept working—together. What else is there to say?"

As you can hear, Jason didn't need hard discipline, in the form of punishment and consequences. He wasn't that kind of kid. But Jason did need his dad's presence, his authoritative presence. Gary provided this in quietly forceful ways. He communicated to his boy not only his interest, persistence, and expectations, but also his own ambitions, struggles, and irritations. And in this way, he became the opposite of his own father's ghost. He became a man whose weight *could* be felt. He became a better father, and, as is always the case, in so doing he became a better man.

A Few Words on Method

There are many experts out there who fancy themselves able to pull the sword from just about any stone imaginable. They write in the popular literature about how to parent, how to love, how to discipline—about virtually all aspects of how to "be." Some of these experts are open-minded and thoughtful; quite a few are polemically driven. Some refer to research. Some of this research is reliable, some of it suffers from methodological flaws, and a surprisingly large percentage of it is influenced by ideological bias. Some of this popular work is worth knowing about, but the words "caveat emptor" apply even to the best of it. The expertise of others, no matter how smart, can never, by itself, lead us to better understand, and master, life's most deeply meaningful and personal experiences.

Moreover, as Ann Hulbert notes in her book *Raising America: Experts, Parents, and a Century of Advice About Children,* literature on parenting has undergone an endless series of pendulum swings, from one single-minded perspective to another. This certainly holds true for the surprisingly small subset of the parenting literature that pertains to fathering. On one side there is a "hard" school in which the father is king, and the rule is that children should have a clear sense of who gives the orders. On the other side there is a "soft" school, the aforementioned "fathers-should-be-more-like-mothers" school, in which men are exhorted to eschew what is seen as their traditional masculine roles for more "civilized" and "loving" attitudes like attunement, negotiation, and, as Susan Faludi puts it in her popular book *Stiffed: The Betrayal of the American Man,* "husbanding." Embedded in this division can be found a critical distinction. Is a father's masculine presence shaping, generative, and organizing, or is it oppressive, domineering, and even abusive? In other words, to introduce another important concept, is it *authoritative* or is it *authoritarian*?

While polemics do, at times, contain truths, in the end they are of limited value. For one thing, polarized thinking does not help us to embrace, and then work effectively with, our human natures: rather it seeks to simplify and control by disavowing one aspect of our essential selves in favor of another that is more palatable in the context of the given cultural moment.

Meanwhile another, related reason that we would be wise to be judicious in our use of the experts has to do with the critical matter of "authenticity."

The advice literature is based on the notion that what matters most is what you *say* and *do*; in other words, that to *act* a certain way is the same as to *be* a certain way. Well, it goes without saying that what you say and do matters a great deal. But it also needs to be said that saying and doing aren't the whole story. Words and actions, those things that are manifest and on the surface, often diverge from what is true beneath the surface. And when it comes to all manner of relationships, this divergence matters. When what you do or say accurately expresses what you feel, what you think—in essence, who you are—you are being authentic. When the opposite is true, you're being disingenuous. Authenticity is better. Wouldn't you rather be with someone who loves you deeply, even if he or she rarely tells you, than with someone whose affection is fleeting and superficial, even though he or she showers you with gifts, and tells you often and profusely how wonderful you are? Can't you usually feel which is more real? Our kids certainly can.

Gary read all kinds of self-help books. He and I went over ways that he could approach Jason. (I may be a psychoanalyst, but I'm not above offering advice and suggestion.) In the end, however, what mattered was that Gary was able to be himself in a way that both he and his son could feel, and use.

I raise the question of authenticity right at the start because it speaks to one of the central premises of this book: Fatherhood, like motherhood, indeed like most truly meaningful human endeavors, must be built from the inside out. If a man is to forge a solid relationship with his authority, indeed with any and all aspects of his fathering, he must learn to act from deep within his own self, that is, from all of the bedrock elements of his history, his psychology, and his constitution (including those parts of him that are relatively, and even distinctly, male). The advice literature can help with this in only a very limited way. "Answers," whether they be to simple and mundane dilemmas like how to get a child to leave a game of knights for the task of homework, or to those urgent and complex life crises that inevitably occur in family life, must be deeply personal and hard-earned; one arrives at them only by making the quite often painful journey of getting to know oneself, warts and all.

This book, therefore, aims less to "advise" than to begin a conversation.

For my part, I'll speak from a number of vantage points.

One is that of twenty years' experience talking, as a psychologist and a psychoanalyst, with fathers and mothers, indeed with all manner of men, women, and children. Throughout the book I will relate the stories and the struggles of my patients. When possible I've shared what I've written with my patients, not only to get permission to use their stories, but also for the sake of accuracy. When such interchange was not possible, I did my best to capture the essence of the persons, the relationships, and the issues involved. In all cases, the people and situations portrayed in these stories are heavily disguised.

I will also draw on the popular and academic literature on fatherhood and the myriad topics that relate: motherhood, gender, biology and neurobiology, discipline, authority, violence, aggression, sexuality, and more. I'll summarize the relevant debates. I have my own biases, and, to be sure, these biases will influence my distillations and interpretations of the literature. Nevertheless, I'll do my best to acquaint you with the field such that you can decide for yourself what you wish to reject, examine further, or embrace. Please keep in mind that theories of human behavior, from the most simplistic self-help formulas to the most thoughtful academic treatises, are *always* limited and imperfect. Such theories, mine included, are inevitably sculpted from the psychology of their authors.

And still another vantage point is my own struggle with authority, in particular my efforts to be a better father, a better husband, a better teacher and therapist, and a better man. In telling you about myself I don't mean to hold out my solutions as a beacon for you to follow. Rather I'll tell you about myself so that you can evaluate what I offer critically and objectively. And I'll tell you this right up front: Every thought that follows is shaped, in ways both obvious and not, by my own imperfect efforts to heal the fault lines and to fill the void created by my own father's death when I was five.

I'll end this opening chapter by recounting a conversation I had that involved a father and son who had come to see me after years of uneasy estrangement. The father, David, was a successful man, somewhat cautious and overly fastidious, but well meaning. His son, Zach, was seventeen, and he also did quite well—academically, athletically, and socially, but in other ways he was the opposite of his father: gregarious, charismatic, and a bit impulsive. He had gotten into some minor scrapes toward the end of his senior year in high school, and his parents were concerned that the prestigious college to which he had been admitted would rescind its acceptance.

At first Zach and I met individually. During these meetings his complaints centered on his father. "I'm about to move out for college," he said, "and after seventeen years I feel like I hardly know the guy. We never horsed around when I was a kid, he never gets mad, everything is nice, neat, and in its place. You can't accuse the guy of anything, he's done his job. But who is he? Jesus, you'd think with me getting in trouble he could at least freak out a little. My mom is all worried, but my dad, it seems like just another opportunity to 'do the right thing.'"

Zach and I decided to invite his father to our individual sessions, and in these Zach spoke, in a direct but kind way, about how distant he felt from his father. His father, in turn, tried dutifully to respond. He asked Zach what was missing, he wondered what he could do, he wasn't angry, indeed he was hardly even defensive. It was clear that he cared, and that he wanted to do right by his son. But it seemed that the harder he tried to do the "right thing" the more frustrated Zach became, and the more frustrated Zach became the more guilty the boy felt about being upset at this man, his father, who was obviously trying so very hard.

Eventually, however, David spoke of having been aware of the distance for some time. He recalled that when Zach was fourteen he had talked with a local expert in the field of parenting, a man who had prescribed a series of exercises for him to do with his son. Father and son were supposed to share their feelings with each other, to write down what each thought of the other, to communicate what each liked about the other, what each disliked, and so on. "When that didn't work," David said, "I think I sort of gave up. I didn't know how to reach you."

Zach, finally exasperated, now shook free of his guilt and inhibition with full-throated anger: "Christ, Dad, I didn't give a shit about that stuff. You just hid behind it. Don't you know what I want?"

"What?" his father asked.

"You. I want a relationship with you. I want a father."

2

The Great Masculinity Debate

O N A BEAUTIFUL spring day a number of years ago, Miles, then three years old, wandered about the yard. I followed. In my hands, unused and encumbering, were the bat and ball with which I had intended us to play. That idea hadn't flown. Maybe the bat and ball would have been useful had I been able to understand better the ideas he had for them: something about a rocket, a launching pad, and the need to transport grass to a faraway planet. But I hadn't been able to move my own conception of bat and ball that far. So he wandered and I followed.

He stopped to examine a hose. He was distracted by a bee. He pointed. He moved in the direction he'd pointed, briefly, but a flower caught his eye, and he was quickly off to that. I followed. When he returned to the hose I thought, "Maybe I can show him the pleasure of aiming and squirting," but he saw not a tool but a snake. Then he spied the bee again. "Maybe," I thought, "the bee will be common ground. There's lots for a father to say to his son about bees, about stings, about collaboration, about industry." But before my thoughts could catch and hold even the tiniest thread of his thinking, he was off again. I followed.

Then my wife joined us, and she too began to follow our son

around the yard. I was stunned by how different things were for her. She moved quickly but easily, attuned to our son's rhythm. She folded herself seamlessly into his tempo. Where I had seen only random and ceaseless redirections of attention, she found never-ending stories that seemed to tell themselves. When she stopped with him at the same hose, a game broke out. There was a snake in the grass, it was chasing a mouse, it caught the mouse. Would that mean old snake let him go? Would he eat that little mouse, or would it get away?

Where was that game when my son and I had found the hose? My wife seemed to me a paragon of parenting, towering, in her natural ease, above my journeyman talents. I watched mystified, as her thoughts and movements all seemed to dance in timed response to our son's shifting attention. And then my mind wandered. At first I daydreamed myself to another place. Then, brought back to the moment by the troubled awareness that I could not find my way into the intimate circle that my wife and child had made, I wondered what was wrong with me that I was bored, here with my first son, on this beautiful spring day.

"Why Can't a Man Be More Like a Woman?"

So what was my problem? For one thing, I was, without knowing it at the time, trying to follow the prescriptions and proscriptions of a popular new movement.

Here's what I mean.

As most people know, Freud established the very first psychoanalytic commandments, models of mental health for both men and women, largely based on what was known, or, to put it more accurately, hypothesized, about male development. The Oedipus complex, for example, initially described boys' development, and it was subsequently retrofitted in a cumbersome attempt to explain the minds of girls and women. The results of this male-oriented model are now well recognized, and well criticized. Penis envy, misguided notions about women's sexuality, inaccurate views on women's aggression and competition—women were time and again found to be lacking because they were seen through the lens of the existing "phallocentric" theory. For a long time psychology's view of women could be captured by Professor Higgins's lament in *My Fair Lady*: "Why can't a woman be more like a man?"

Then Carol Gilligan and a number of other influential women theorists—Nancy Chodorow, Judith Jordan, Irene Stiver, Janet Surrey, to name a few—corrected this problem by developing a psychology of women based on observations of how women *actually* are. Their contributions, which have been exceedingly valuable, clinically, theoretically, and politically, point out that such traits as connection, attunement, mutuality, empathy, and so on are normative for women. Stop judging women as deficient simply because they are not blessed with a surfeit of qualities like competitiveness, aggression, and separateness, they argue, for those are the ways of men. Women do it differently: by cooperating, by communicating, and by joining.

This correction was all good, a sorely needed reworking of a narrow-minded, phallocentric way of looking at women. But then a funny (though probably not surprising) thing happened on the way to the quorum. By the 1990s the tables had turned yet again. Gilligan and her followers applied their findings regarding women and girls to men and boys. A shiny new theory was formed, and now men had to negotiate views of "healthy" masculinity and fatherhood from within the confines of the new theory's persuasive arguments.

This movement (the "sensitive man" movement, as I will call it from here on) is organized around the notion that men need to become more like women (or, one might argue, like a caricature of a woman): empathic, connected, caretaking, and understanding.

The aforementioned Carol Gilligan is probably the intellectual mainstay of the sensitive man movement. Gilligan tells us that boys suffer from a host of psychological liabilities, primary among them an intolerance of feelings and vulnerability, along with an incapacity to form meaningful relationships. She writes: "If boys in early childhood resist the break between the inner and outer worlds, they are resisting an initiation into masculinity or manhood as it is defined and established in cultures that value or valorize heroism, honor, war, competition—the culture of the warrior, the economy of capitalism. . . . To be a real man or boy in such a culture means to be able to hurt without feeling hurt, to separate without feeling sadness or loss, and then to inflict hurt or separation on others." In essence, according to Gilligan, boys are traumatized by a culture that is intolerant of their inherent vulnerability. Then, like pledges in a fraternity, they go on to inflict the pain of their initiation on the next generation.

Others trumpet the same call.

The psychiatrist Eli Newberger, author of *The Men They Will Become: The Nature and Nurture of Male Character,* seconds Gilligan, positing that male aggression is but a thin facade, an armor against vulnerability. Newberger asks, "Could boys be raised to become more caring and connected men?" Not easily, he answers, at least not when they grow up in a culture that so values toughness, stoicism, and competition, and that discourages them from feeling, crying, and connecting.

Terrence Real, author of *I Don't Want to Talk About It: Overcoming the Secret Legacy of Male Depression,* joins the chorus, writing: "Boys don't hunger for fathers who will model traditional mores of masculinity. They hunger for fathers who will rescue them from it."

Olga Silverstein and Beth Rashbaum, in their book, *The Courage to Raise Good Men: You Don't Have to Sever the Bond with Your Son to Help Him Become a Man,* speak out against the age-old search for male role models. Silverstein and Rashbaum posit that traditional fathers, in their wish to make their sons "strong and brave," produce boys who are "emotionally cut off and remote."

And William Pollack, one of Gilligan's chief spokesmen in the sensitive man movement, expands on her theory of male pathogenesis in his best-selling book *Real Boys: Rescuing Our Sons from the Myths of Boyhood.* Pollack argues that culture, via its rigid and insensitive application of what he calls the "boy code," shames boys into denying and suppressing their "authentic inner voices." One of the most egregious examples of this, he believes, can be found in the way that boys are pressured into separating "prematurely" from their mothers. If only a boy were allowed to remain longer in the safety of his mother's love and understanding, Pollack declaims, he would be more likely to share his feelings (good), he would be less likely to compete aggressively (bad), and he would be more likely to connect emotionally (good). And because such a boy would not be frustrated in his desire for openness, love, and connection, he would shed that nasty, anachronistic anger—apparently the one feeling that should not be shared with others.

These authors and many others, such as Ron Levant (*Masculinity Reconstructed: Changing the Rules of Manhood*) and Dan Kindlon and Michael Thompson (*Raising Cain: Protecting the Emotional Life of Boys*), tell us that the strong, stoic man is a thing of the past. Vulnerability, openness, and connection are the new path that men must travel. As Susan Faludi writes in *Stiffed*: "The male paradigm of confrontation has proved worthless to men." Dedication, service, and caretaking, she continues, must be the wave of the future. The solution will lie in men's capacity to "husband," to make themselves useful to society.

It goes without saying that this movement has made a great contribution by focusing our attention on serious problems: the absence of emotionally involved fathers, and the painfully alienated experience of many young boys. It identifies a villain—the traditional male values of stoicism and disconnection. And it offers a prescription: We men need more exposure to the feminine, either through longer and more accepted relationships with our mothers, or through relationships with fathers whose outdated masculinity has been properly "retooled." As Michael Kimmel, author of *Manhood in America: A Cultural History,* writes: "Frankly, I'd prefer more ironing Johns and fewer Iron Johns."

Perhaps because there is seductive appeal in its warm and fuzzy vision of empathy and caring, perhaps because these ideas appeal to women (and far more women buy books on parenting and relationships than do men), or perhaps simply because of natural pendulum shifts and timing, the sensitive man theory has become enormously influential. From *Cosmopolitan* magazine advice columns to Harvard Medical School teaching conferences, the new psychology of women serves as a yardstick by which men's psychological health is measured. In an ironic twist of probably well-deserved payback the lament has become: "Why can't a man be more like a woman?"

In 1991 I knew the sensitive man mind-set well. This wasn't because I had read the literature and was converted to its gospel—indeed much of it had yet to be published. I knew it because I, like most fathers of my generation, had grown up in the 1960s, 1970s, and 1980s, immersed in the era's burgeoning feminism, terror about the destructive power of male aggression, disillusionment with the masculine way of doing things, and mistrust of authority. These forces (which on a cultural level gave birth to the sensitive man movement) molded my and my fellow men's beliefs regarding what it meant to be a good man, and a good father.

So without really knowing that I was doing it, I had set out to be a good sensitive man. I had unwittingly begun to file down the vestigial protuberances of my masculinity, to check my self-centered masculine agenda at the door in the hopes of becoming a more "nurturing" and "attuned" parent. There was just one catch. The harder I tried to be attuned and understanding, the more it seemed that I could not find my footing as a father. Skittering on thin ice, trying desperately not to break through to the place where memories of my own father, mostly absent, lay, I had begun to worry that I wouldn't be able to do the very thing I wanted more than anything else in my life—to be a good father.

Bill and Mary Jenson

When you are stuck in something you need the help of other minds. I got such help. I learned from many places that I was hardly anomalous in my dissatisfaction with my mode of fathering. Some of the most effective help came from my patients.

Bill Jenson was about forty years old when I first met him. He was a tall, slightly graying man, attired preppy-hip in khakis and a denim shirt. A slight midriff bulge had not yet camouflaged his athletic build. His wife, Mary, also about forty, was blond, thin, and carefully dressed. Visually they seemed a good fit; indeed they appeared lucky to have found each other.

The Jensons first came to see me in 1994. The parents of two children, they considered their marriage of fourteen years to be a "good" one. Like so many couples, however, they had stayed away from a few painful places over the years, and as a result their relationship had become more distant. Things had evolved into a reasonably effective "partnership," which is what they meant by a "good marriage," but they both felt disappointed in the loss of intimacy, authenticity, sexuality, and tenderness that had resulted.

The couple got straight to the point. Bill's anger, said Mary, was frightening to her. It seemed to come out of nowhere, and it felt "volcanic."

Bill felt misunderstood and responded with clear annoyance: "I don't have any more of a temper than most other guys I know. You exaggerate it—it's not so bad." Bill turned to me, his irritation now softening: "I think sometimes she can't tell the difference between me and her father, who really was an abusive son of a bitch. She thinks whenever I get angry it's traumatizing. I can't even discipline the kids without her getting scared I'm scarring them for life."

"The fact that my father was out of control," Mary countered, still holding firm, "doesn't take away my right to feel that you get too angry. I think sometimes you just act without thinking about how it affects the rest of us."

She thought he was too angry; he felt she was too touchy. She felt scared of him; he felt that she put him in a straitjacket. She felt he was selfish; he felt that he was just being himself. It was a familiar disagreement, one utterly emblematic of how men and women struggle to find a mutually compatible vision of a man's, and a father's, anger, aggression, and, importantly, authority. And I, interestingly, found

myself leaning toward familiar remedies. Let's work on understanding the differences, let's work on communicating better, men are from
Mars . . .

But then something very interesting happened, something that
made me stop and think.

Bill and Mary began to tell me about their work with a previous
therapist (I'll call him Dr. Johnson). Dr. Johnson had been very "nice."
He had seemed to understand (Mary particularly thought so), but
somehow he hadn't helped them. He had begun by pushing Bill to be
respectful of Mary's fearfulness; this was how she felt, he noted, and
it was important that Bill take it seriously. He also thought it important that Mary speak directly to Bill about how his anger made her
feel.

Not much to quibble about yet. But it was Dr. Johnson's next
intervention that really got my attention. He took Mary's fear at face
value, but he was relatively more insistent that Bill needed to probe
the roots of his anger. Most likely, he told Bill, the anger was a reflection of underlying feelings of hurt and vulnerability. Or perhaps it
was that he was depressed.

"Men," he told Bill, "tend to turn all kinds of feelings into a common pathway: anger." Bill wasn't so sure. "I think sometimes when I
get mad it's because I'm actually mad," he had said.

But Dr. Johnson persisted. He encouraged Bill to be more open
with his feelings of hurt, sadness, need, and so on. He also talked
about the effect of Bill's anger on the children, saying, "I think you
don't recognize how big, and scary, you are to them." Again Bill was
dubious. "I'm sure I'm a bit scary to them," he said. "Is that always so
bad? Is it really a bad thing if they have a little bit of fear of their
father? I don't want to just be their best buddy. I want them to respect
me too!"

"Fear," Dr. Johnson responded, "has nothing to do with respect."

A few months previously I might well have taken a similar
approach to Dr. Johnson's. But I met Bill and Mary at a time when I
was reevaluating many of my assumptions about family and father-

hood. For three years I had been involved in those aimless wanderings about the yard, and I had struggled with the surprising sense that being a father felt oddly abstract and unfamiliar. What was more, things weren't getting any better. Now, as I listened to Bill's deep sense of feeling misunderstood by Dr. Johnson, something became clear to me. Bill's reaction illuminated a hugely important bias. Certainly Dr. Johnson might be right—Bill's anger might well be too mercurial. But the doctor appeared to have made three arguable assumptions. First, he assumed that Mary's fear was to be expected. He didn't seriously consider Bill's suggestion that she might be oversensitive, that what Mary called Bill's "volcanic tendencies" might appear less frightening to someone else. Second, he diagnosed Bill's anger as being a typical male reaction in the face of his inability to feel other feelings, like depression or vulnerability. And third, he believed that Bill's anger, in conjunction with his size, was probably harmful to the children.

Over the next several months I learned that Bill sometimes did get too angry. At times he scared the children, and at times he scared his wife. He needed to learn more about the effects of his strength and size. He needed to be less authoritarian and more comfortably authoritative.

But I also learned that the problems Bill and Mary struggled with were far more complex than Dr. Johnson (and I myself, initially) had recognized. For one thing, Mary did tend to be phobic about all manner of aggression. She worried overly that her children would be injured while playing sports, she was frightened of her own anger, and she did at times stifle aspects of Bill's aggression and sexuality as a way of managing her own anxiety. For another, Bill didn't always use his anger to mask other feelings; indeed he was capable of feeling sad, warm, loving, and even, at times, depressed. His anger could be an honest expression of how he was feeling, not just an armoring self-protection.

And while the kids were sometimes scared of Bill, even this wasn't so simple. Each child responded to him differently. Ralph, age eight, seemed much more comfortable with his father's forcefulness. He loved to wrestle with his dad, and he seemed interested in Bill's hardness and bite. He responded well to his father's discipline. Oliver, age twelve, was far more skittish.

Embedded in these complexities, I submit, lies the core dilemma of being an authoritative father within our current culture. The fact is, Bill could be heard pleading against an encompassing mentality, one that at times seemed to oppose his very nature. He often felt that critical elements of his masculinity, many of which he needed in order to be truly authoritative (and, truth be told, competent and effective), made him act like an overly aggressive, insensitive lout.

"I remember when you fell in love with me," he reminded Mary. "Do you remember how you used to love watching me play football? It scared you a bit, but you liked it too. And after the games, we'd lie in bed, and you'd ask me about the cuts and bruises, and you'd ask me what I did to the guys who gave them to me. Whatever happened to that? That was an important part of me. That still is an important part of me. I know I've got to work on my anger, but I don't believe that I have to castrate myself to do it."

I knew what Bill meant. I too felt as though I lived in a world that valued my sensitivity and my caretaking, but was often unwelcoming of my aggression. Why was it that he, I, and so many other men of our generation felt like such apes? Why did we feel we had to zip ourselves up tight before going out in proper society? Were we all just too angry?

Bill was perhaps the first man I could hear clearly, but there were many others. Through the 1990s I heard the same complaints over and over. There was the father who said to me, "I go to work, I come home, I listen to the kids, I take them where they want to go, I never get mad, I love them, I think I'm a good man. So why do I feel like a zombie?"

And the complaints came not only from men but from wives and children as well. There was the fifteen-year-old boy who couldn't study in his home because his younger brother was wildly out of control, and his parents were unable to stop him. "They never get mad at him," the older boy said to me. "All they do is try to understand, and to make agreements with him. My father has never, ever in his life said, 'No matter what!' Like, 'You're going to do it, NO MATTER WHAT!'" And there was the woman who poked and prodded her husband, trying to anger him, only to have him say to her, repetitively, "I know you're not really angry with me. You're hurt and sad. I love you, and I want to understand." Finally she said to him, "Will you cut the hurt and sad crap and just get angry?" And then she turned to me and said, "*Will you do something!* I'm sick of him trying to *understand,* I just want to feel that there's actually a man in there."

These men, these families (and many more men and families too) were wrestling with the same dilemma that I was. We, like Bill, were searching for an authoritative masculine voice. And what we found within ourselves seemed completely at odds with the popular pre-scriptions of the sensitive man movement. This new way wasn't working for quite a few of us. But in the mid-1990s, it seemed like the only game in town.

The "Real Man" Movement

Now, in retrospect, it's clear that many men have been unable to find themselves within the politically correct margins of the sensitive man movement. But in fairness, many new paradigms seem promising early on, and it's only when the long-term data come in that we find out which are truly helpful, and which belong in the scrap pile of once promising, and now useless, ideas. Probably the "new man" theory is a bit of both. Sure, men need some liberation from confining gender stereotypes, some encouragement to feel and communicate more, to be more vulnerable. Yet at the same time, the new view of masculinity has big problems.

Here's what may be the biggest.

Constructs such as masculinity derive their meaning from, among other influences, the dialectical relationship that exists between culture and biology. The former, culture, shifts rapidly: Culture-based fluctuations in our sense of who we are occur in the space of ten-year intervals, sometimes even more frequently. The latter, biology, shifts more glacially: Changes in the biological underpinnings of selfhood become evident only over the course of many generations. While the pace of each of these effects are different, both, simultaneously, exert a powerful influence on our sense of identity.

The sensitive man movement errs by overvaluing the influence of culture while failing to recognize the powerful, unremitting impact of biology. The result? It offers a naively prescriptive view of what it believes men *should be,* while failing to alloy that view with a realistic appreciation of what men *are*. As a result, as Bill and so many others have discovered, its exhortations subtly and insidiously alienate men from crucial aspects of their essential natures—particularly, as you will see, those that are necessary for the construction of a solid, viable sense of authority.

So is this flawed approach to masculinity really the only game in town? Not surprisingly, there is another option. The sensitive man movement's denigration of men's traditional gendered identities has in part stimulated, and in part simply been paralleled by, another, perhaps equally flawed, approach—the retro-embrace of traditional masculinity.

We find evidence of this movement, which Michael Kimmel dubs the "men's rights backlash" (and which I will simply call the "real man" movement), on many fronts. In 1980s Hollywood, Dustin Hoffman's *Tootsie* (praised in the foreword to later editions of Betty Friedan's *The Feminine Mystique* as a paragon of the "new man") was countered by Sylvester Stallone's *Rambo,* Arnold Schwarzenegger's *Terminator,* and Bruce Willis's *Die Hard* character. Over the most recent decade, these larger-than-life hypermasculine action figures have gotten even larger, as Vin Diesel, *The Incredible Hulk,* The Rock, and yet another version of Schwarzenegger's *Terminator* have dominated the box offices. Meanwhile, on television, *The Man Show,* the World Wrestling Federation, Spike TV, and a number of television sitcoms featuring neo–macho men appeal to men's hunger for a more virile reflection. Similarly the newsstands are filled with "Lad" magazines like *Maxim,* and a plethora of publications that promise bigger muscles, bigger penises, and ever more masculinity-inflating sexual conquests. All around us (and, of course, all around our children) there are images of a pumped-up alternative to the sensitive man, though in these aforementioned pop-cultural manifestations manliness is less defined by stoicism, competition, and aggression than by beer-swilling, backslapping, and obsessions with large breasts (both men's and women's).

Moving slightly up the intellectual ladder, somewhat reactionary pro-discipline books like John Rosemond's *Parent Power! A Common-Sense Approach to Parenting in the '90s and Beyond* have, over the past twenty years, preached about the importance of traditional masculine roles within the family. Meanwhile the rigidly conservative ideologues of the Christian right claim that feminism is the enemy, and they self-righteously protest the loss of uncontested male dominance. Many contemporary Christians even use Christ himself as an image of phallic masculinity. "Christ wasn't effeminate," says televangelist Jerry Falwell. "The man who lived on this earth was a man with muscles . . . Christ was a he-man."

Yet another segment of the real man movement has, over the past twenty years, aimed to counter the cultural prominence of feminist ideology (perhaps the reader recalls the term "Feminazi"), while reacting against the idealized image of a more sensitive, Alan Alda–like man. The late Asa Baber, who wrote the "Men" column in *Playboy,* spoke out against the feeling that men had to become "male apologists." Richard Doyle (*The Rape of the Male*) wrote that feminist women are "would-be castrators with a knee-jerk, obsessive aversion to anything male." And journalist Nicholas Davidson (*The Failure of Feminism*) argued that feminists demand unnatural contortions from men, such as "trying not to feel aggressiveness or dominance toward a woman when making love to her."

Meanwhile, for those who are put off by steroidal puffing, religious dogma, and strident ideology, there is the "mythopoetic" approach. Probably the best-known author within this genre is Robert Bly, who writes about men's deep, unfulfilled hunger for some kind of male identity, and who reminds us that boys do learn valuable lessons in masculinity from their fathers. Bly's work offers a thoughtful and useful counterpoint, though for some the mystical language of "psychic twins," "inner kings," and "mythic wild men" can feel a bit contrived.

And finally, there are those who take a more academic and quite sober approach to the state of men. Lionel Tiger, originator of the term "male bonding" and long a credible observer of the complex interrelationship between masculinity and culture, writes in *The Decline of Males: The First Look at an Unexpected New World for Men and Women* of an "emerging pattern" characterized by "growth in the power and confidence of women, and . . . erosion in the confidence of men." Tiger is concerned that attitudes made popular by the sensitive man movement will undermine men's sense of value and belonging, and he fervently defends men's masculinity as something worth preserving.

This admittedly brief review highlights thirty years of the real man movement. Some of the voices heard from these quarters are tinged with polemic, some are softened by humor, some rely on stereotype, and some try to persuade with intellectual argument. But nearly all speak to men's yearning for a valid counterpoint to the materno-centric views of Pollack, Real, Gilligan, and others. Simply put, men want to have their differences from women recognized and valued.

And what about now?

While it is easy to view the real man movement as a reaction against the sensitive man movement, this isn't quite accurate. For one, the real man movement and the sensitive man movement have taken place side by side. Moreover, the offerings of the real man movement are in many ways nothing new, as is true of the entire masculinity debate. As Kimmel astutely points out in *Manhood in America,* American culture has forever bounced back and forth. At the turn of the century, for example, manuals and guidebooks such as William Blaikie's *How to Get Strong and How to Stay So* (1879) and Macfadden's *The Virile Powers of Superb Manhood* (1900) were enormously popular. At that time, a hypermasculine image quite like our modern-day Rambo was personified by popular figures like Edgar Rice Burroughs's Tarzan, Teddy Roosevelt, Jack London, Frederic Remington, and Billy Sunday and the "Muscular Christians." The same controversies and divisions regarding the hypermasculinization and the feminization of men persisted through much of the twentieth century, and similar controversy is certain to follow us into the twenty-first century.

Perhaps, however, there is one aspect of the current debate that is not old news. At times men's complaints seem louder, their grievances sharper. Men's anger tends to be defensive and retaliatory, even, at times, paranoid. Much like terrified, cornered animals, they spray furious polemical venom in all directions, attacking not only women but also, by way of demeaning caricature, their own kind, men, as well. A telling metaphor for the current mind-set can be found in the 2003 film *Terminator 3: Rise of the Machines,* in which an outdated male cyborg somehow perseveres, against insurmountable odds, to destroy his technologically superior, far more invulnerable, female counterpart. Alas, he too "dies" in the process.

Whether men's "crisis" (as many call it) is new, or whether it is little more than the revisitation of a familiar cycle, there is no doubt that men *do* feel threatened these days. We feel threatened in the marketplace, where our identity as primary breadwinner is disappearing, and where jobs that once were ours for the asking are now up for grabs. We feel threatened in the bedroom, where women are now seen to expect sexual power and equality, and where profound changes have occurred in the matter of who controls child-rearing and fertility. We feel threatened in our basic identity, sensing that what was once solid and unique about our masculinity has become fluid and negotiable. And we may even feel threatened by new research showing that the Y chromosome, that which makes us male, is unable to sustain itself in the way that the X chromosome does, a finding that leads Steve Jones to write, in *Y: The Descent of Men*: "From sperm count to social status and from fertilization to death, as civilization advances, those who bear the Y chromosome are in relative decline." Things have gone so far that a *New York Times* article entitled "Are Men Necessary?" notes, "advances in cryogenics and turkey basting have rendered human males largely superfluous."

And so, fifteen-year-old boys endanger their lives by taking steroids, there seems to be no limit as to what is a large enough penis and a long and good enough screw, and no amount of money seems to give a man the right to say that he has made it. The signifiers of masculinity have become so extreme and caricatured (thanks to computer graphics, the most recent Hulk is ten times bigger than Lou Ferrigno, the old Hulk, ever was) that they have become detached from that which they are meant to signify—the essence of being a male human being.

So there you have—at least in broad strokes—the great debate on masculinity.

On the "sensitive man" side, differences between the sexes are de-emphasized, and we find a man who is connected, mutual, and nurturing. On the "real man" side, differences between the sexes are amplified, and we find a man who is self-sufficient, unafraid of dominating, competitive, and proud of it.

The "sensitive man" is soft; the "real man" is hard.

The "sensitive man" believes that masculinity is but a social construct. Men can and must change their stripes with the times.

"No!" the "real man" argues back emphatically. "We are products of our biologies. We are what we are. Men *are* more aggressive. Men are fundamentally different from women, and no newfangled theory is going to change that."

Both men are sexual, though they might be very different on a date, or in bed. The "sensitive man" makes love. His sexuality is intended for connection and joining, and he views the seduction of a woman as manipulative and overly aggressive. The "real man," on the other hand, still fucks.

Only the "real man" values his aggression. He competes, he fights, he even revels in the surge of his testosterone. For the "sensitive man" this surge is a blast from an abandoned past, an unwanted holdover from his days as a predator.

While both paradigms of masculinity offer useful truths, each tends to be exaggerated, making the differences appear, at times, all but irreconcilable. If a thoughtful person were to try to be the kind of man envisioned by both of these camps he would end up in traction.

So where does this leave us?

Many of us feel the way Bill did about both sides of the argument: "You know," he said, "I read a lot of those books. It's like the old joke about Chinese food. It seems good at the time, but a few hours later I'm hungry again."

Bill wasn't going to learn much about being a man by reading polemics or ingesting copious amounts of popular culture. Neither are we. He needed to construct his relationship with masculinity (and, not coincidentally, authority) from the stuff of his own authentic self.

And so do we. For the fact is, fatherhood and authority are based upon core elements of men's masculinity—the very elements devalued by the sensitive man movement and caricatured by the real man movement. If we are to be better men, and better fathers, we'll have to own these elements, value them, and yet keep them in scale. Because one thing is certain. A father needs to feel solid in his own sense of masculinity if he is to help his children.

Montana

Often, as I listened to Bill talk about what it meant to him to be a man and a father, I thought about my own imperfect and unfinished journey.

When I was a child, and then an adolescent, I was shy and fear-ful. I envied my friends who had fathers (it seemed to me that I was the only one without). I imagined that all the boys I knew were best buddies with their dads, and I assumed that the size, smarts, and con-fidence that they had (and that I believed I lacked) grew directly from the daily doses of paternity that I was certain they got. When I was fif-teen I felt so unsure of myself that I asked my doctor for a shot of testosterone. I wanted to be bigger, stronger, and hairier.

The doctor was unimpressed, and I didn't get that shot. I suspect his seeming disinterest in my obvious unhappiness was tutored by clinical dispassion, but had he seen through me he would have under-stood that I really needed something that I couldn't have, and that I felt I had never had—a shot of a father.

I eventually crawled out of my hole of timid self-pity, though not without causing myself, and those who cared about me, no small amount of pain. When I was seventeen my life was a mess, even by the lenient standards that should always be applied when judging the life of an adolescent. Failing and flailing, both academically and socially, I dropped out of high school, and traveled to Irvine Flats, Montana, where I found work on a cattle ranch. The hard, physical labor—building fences, riding, branding, learning to operate heavy machinery—was good for me.

In the place in my mind where my father seems like he should be, but isn't, I hold tight to a series of memories. One is from that time in Montana. I was just eighteen. It was a late summer evening, and I was standing, clad in cowboy boots and jeans, on top of a haystack that I had built. Soft wind cool-dried the sweat on my sun-burned back, while the new muscles I had been making that day wrapped me in their welcome ache. I gazed out over the fields, past Flathead Lake some twenty miles away, to the Mission Mountains, rose-colored in the late evening light. Even in early August their peaks were touched with snow. I felt, maybe for the first time, that the world that opened under that big Montana sky might just hold a place for me.

In Montana I found what seemed to be an answer to the dilemma that had once seemed unsolvable. Toughness, hard work, physicality, independence, an unwillingness to submit, and the embrace of pain; these, I thought, were what manliness was all about.

Like most of us, I am partial to my own solutions. I believe in the value of stoicism and hard work, and tend to be critical of the de-gendered vision of a new, softened masculinity. But I know now that my solution also cost me.

The fact is, my ethos was founded as much on deficit as strength—I was drawn to what was hard and tough because I lacked a father's roughhousing and a father's discipline. This meant that my hardness has always had about it a certain rigidity and brittleness. When, as an adolescent I angrily rejected everything that was expected of me, when in college I pushed the envelope with drugs and alcohol, when as a young man I fought, and invariably lost, on city basketball courts, when, as a graduate student, my abrasive, competitive edge alienated my peers, and when, in my training to become a psychoanalyst, I had to reject my teachers before I could even consider listening, I wasn't necessarily being "manly." Sometimes I was just being defensive and fearful—a jerk, really.

By the time I had become a husband and a father, my wife could see what I could not: the limitations of my rather single-minded approach. She tried to talk to me about it. She asked me, again and again, if I might consider being a bit different. Might I try to soften around the edges, allow a little more vulnerability, admit on occasion that I was wrong. Maybe it wouldn't be so bad to surrender, even if only a little, and even if only on occasion. Maybe there were people I could actually learn from. I fought her, of course. My way had been my good friend, and it had gotten me further than I had ever expected I would get. But one day, after we had gone over it maybe a hundred times, she said to me, "I know you've come a long way, but I just don't think it would kill you to change a little. To give in sometimes. To recognize that you lose sometimes. I think you're big enough that you can afford to relax a little."

And for whatever reason—whether those were the right words, or whether I finally gave way to her persistence—I could hear that she was probably right: Maybe there was more than one way. A man doesn't have to be only hard. Nor does he have to be only soft.

He has to be a bit of both. And, while he's at it, he has to be himself.

3

Harnessing a Father's Aggression

BILL AND MARY, as I mentioned, had two children, both sons. They thought a great deal about what their kids needed: going to their events, scheduling lessons, finding camps, attending school conferences, arranging for whatever extra help was required, and so on. The children were very different. Oliver, the oldest, was about twelve when I began working with his parents. He was off-the-charts smart in math and science, but he had trouble with reading. He was a bit of a loner, shy, polite, and somewhat skittish about anything physical. Ralph was eight. He seemed, in contrast to Oliver, to be a rough-and-tumble boy's boy. He was physical, often loud, seemingly fearless, and he already had been more vocal in his displeasure and opposition to things he didn't like than Oliver had ever been.

One of the first disagreements that Bill and Mary brought to me concerned Oliver, who had a reading-based learning disability. Through fifth grade he had relied on his innate intelligence to do well in school, but as he approached high school, and the work got more challenging, his learning difficulties began to get in his way. Bill and Mary recognized that this problem needed to be addressed.

They decided to take Oliver to a specialist for testing. To Bill and Mary's surprise, Oliver adamantly refused to go. Indeed, he threw a tantrum, uncharacteristically screaming: "I don't want to go. I won't, and you can't make me."

Bill and Mary agreed that Oliver ought to have the testing, but they differed on how to go about it. Mary was in favor of letting Oliver take the lead. "He must have his reasons for being so upset," she said. "I don't want to force him on this. I think testing is such a big thing—like someone's getting inside your head. We should talk to him about it, try to find out what he's feeling. He'll do it when he's ready."

Bill, clearly irritated, disagreed: "He needs to get tested," he said. "He's two years away from high school, and if he's got a problem, which it looks like he does, we've got to get on it." And then, his voice softening, he said, now in a tone that was almost pleading: "We're his parents, and we should decide what's best for him on this. It's fine if he has feelings about it—I'm sure he does—but we can't let his feelings get in the way of doing what needs to be done. I say let's make the appointment, tell him when it is, and when the time comes we'll take him—no ifs, ands, or buts."

Old Models and New Models,
Male Models and Female Models

With her groundbreaking 1976 work *Toward a New Psychology of Women,* Jean Baker Miller dragged the matter of women's power and authority out of the closet. Miller argues that power, for women, is not based on strength and hierarchy. Instead, she tells us, "women try to use their powers . . . to empower others, to build other people's strength, resources, effectiveness, and well being."

Over the past twenty years a significant body of writing and thinking has proceeded from Miller's work. Some of this thinking grows from feminist writing regarding women, their relationships to men, and their relationship to culture. Some has evolved from ongoing contributions to the psychology of women. And quite a bit has been spawned by efforts to understand, and improve, women's roles in traditionally male-dominated organizations, particularly businesses. All of it—the work of Nancer Ballard, Joyce Fletcher, Carol Gilligan, Sally Helgeson, Judith Rosener, Jan Surrey, and many more—argues that women possess modes of authority that are as effective as those of men. What's more, these authors view a *woman's* authority as originating in qualities that are the cornerstones of a *woman's* psychology: connection, empowerment, and mutuality.

This view expands our appreciation of authority's complexity, and allows for flexibility in the face of changing cultural contexts. It also serves as an important reminder; women act authoritatively, both in the ways described by Miller, as well as in ways traditionally ascribed to men. My exploration of fatherhood is, therefore, in no way intended to argue that authority resides, or that it should reside, solely in the domain of men and fathers. But before we decide that this woman-oriented version is what authority is now really all about, let's check the bathwater for babies. Just as male psychology in general ought not to be reshaped into some idealized version of the way that women are thought to be, the entire concept of authority, particularly the way that men and fathers are authoritative, ought not to be reinvented entirely along the lines of women's psychology.

When Bill said, "We are the parents, we need to make him go," he too was speaking about the importance of being authoritative from a scaffolding of traits that are relatively gendered. But, in distinction to those feminist voices, Bill, a man, wasn't talking connection, empowerment, and mutuality; he was talking about using his masculine self—namely his power and position—to help his son. What was more, he was asking that a place be made for a critical element of his masculinity: his aggression.

Power, Anger, and Aggression

The matter of Bill's masculine aggression occupied an old and complicated place in his marriage to Mary.

On the one hand, Mary had indeed fallen in love with Bill's football-playing self. She found his competitiveness exciting, and she was even attracted to his physical fierceness. She also appreciated the way that these qualities had benefited their adult, married life: Bill, a partner in his law firm, was a highly successful trial lawyer—a profession that required him to constructively and creatively use his aggression.

At the same time, Mary sometimes thought that Bill was too "volcanic," particularly when it came to Oliver, the more sensitive of the two children. "Maybe the way you are when you're mad is okay for Ralph," she said. "He can take it. Maybe I could even agree that sometimes he needs it—you've got to go pretty hard sometimes just to get through to him. But it just doesn't work the same way with Oliver. When you come at him all big and loud, when you yell, or grab his shoulders hard and tell him to look you in the eyes, I think you just scare him."

Early in our work Bill's responses to these criticisms tended to be defensive and retaliatory. "Sure Oliver's different," he would say with some irritation, "but maybe it's because you pampered him. You nursed him longer, you were always more worried about him, more protective of him. I think he's pretty tied into you. How do you know he doesn't just have a harder time with me because he picks up on your fear of me?"

And Mary would then push back: "I was just being his mother. I didn't pamper him, I gave him what he needed. You're just jealous of the attention I gave him. And you just don't see how scary you can be to such a little kid."

"So sometimes he's a little scared," Bill might answer. "Is that so bad? The world can be a scary place, and parenting is not a popularity contest. Do you really have to protect the kids from me as soon as I raise my voice? How do we have any power with them if we don't sometimes get angry?"

One can hear, in Bill and Mary's disagreement, core questions with which men and women struggle, both individually and in marriage. What should be negotiated with children, and what demanded? Where do discipline and legitimate authority end, and where do tyranny and authoritarianism begin? At what point does a mother move from monitoring and regulating a father's anger to undermining his authority? What is the role of a father's anger? Of his power? Of his aggression?

Anger, power, and aggression: These are, sometimes for worse, but, as the reader will see, often for better, critical components of a father's authority. But do we have a consensual sense of what these words mean?

Well, most of us probably have a natural, intuitive sense of what anger is, even if we may differ as to its meaning and its origins. And probably most of us feel comfortable with our understanding of the word "power," at least as it is defined in the abstract. When we think of power, we think along the lines of the dictionary definition of the word ("the possession of control or command over others; authority; ascendancy; the capability of doing or accomplishing something"), or perhaps the one proposed by the American psychoanalyst Otto Kernberg ("the capacity to carry out a task, and in the social realm, the capacity to influence or control others").

Aggression, however, can be another matter entirely. These days having a conversation about aggression feels like working on the Tower of Babel—everybody talks a different language, and everybody thinks that their tongue is the right one. But we need to understand this concept, because trying to explain the concepts of power, and authority, without talking about aggression is like trying to explain the concept of a car without understanding the role and function of its engine.

The Biological Basis of Aggression

Let's take a few moment to look at what we do know about aggression.

Empirical research has found it surprisingly difficult to identify clear-cut behavioral differences between men and women. Aggression, however, proves to be an exception. In study after study, researchers such as Eleanor Maccoby and Carol Jacklin, Deborah Niehoff, Janet Hyde, Alice Eagly and Valerie Steffen, and many others arrive at a seemingly basic truth: Whatever your yardstick—fighting, violent crime, murder, dominance, rage, competitiveness, predatory sexuality, even successful suicide attempts—men are more aggressive than women.

Clearly one of the major reasons for this is biology. A number of biological systems are involved in both the expression and the regulation of aggression. Some of these are found in the brain, and have daunting names, at least for lay readers—such as Broca's gyrus or the amygdala. What is found in the brain, however, does not by itself account for the powerful relationship between aggression and gender. For a more encompassing understanding, we also have to look to the endocrine system, specifically to the hormone testosterone.

Testosterone may not be the all-powerful god that some popular theorists proclaim it to be, but it clearly is one very influential piece of biology. To begin with, testosterone is a decisive catalyst when it comes to deciding gender. It is the androgenization of the fetus (its exposure to male hormones) that causes it to declare itself male. When you inject newborn female rats with testosterone they grow penises from their clitorises, and subsequently they appear to know how to use them. When you block the testosterone of male rats they develop female characteristics, both physiologically and psychologically.

And we're not just talking about straight anatomy here. As it is with penises, so also is it with brain centers. There is a great deal more to learn, but it seems at this point a safe research bet that areas like the hypothalamus and the corpus callosum develop somewhat differently depending on how much testosterone the growing brain is exposed to. The same goes for brain-based cognitive abilities: superior language and verbal skills in females, superior visual spatial skills in males. The hormone has now been shown to influence a remarkable array of "male" traits and behaviors: physical strength, promiscuity, boldness, violence, temper, sexual excitation, and dominance, to name a few.

Perhaps the reader notices something interesting about the preceding list: Quite a few of these traits are themselves associated with aggression. Here too the direct and persuasive influence of testosterone is inescapably evident. As James Dabbs tells us in his book *Heroes, Rogues and Lovers: Testosterone and Behavior,* trial lawyers (like Bill) have been shown to have higher testosterone levels than nontrial lawyers. High-testosterone soldiers have been shown to be better in combat. Blue-collar workers have been shown to have higher testosterone levels than white-collar workers. Members of more rambunctious fraternities tend to have higher testosterone levels than members of sedate and studious ones. The findings, pretty consistently, support the stereotype: more testosterone, more aggression.

These data seem to support a long-standing view of man, one Freud spoke to when he wrote, "men are not gentle creatures who want to be loved, and who at the most can defend themselves if they are attacked; they are, on the contrary, creatures among whose instinctual endowments is to be reckoned a powerful share of aggressiveness." It's truly an age-old belief. Aggression is an irreducible human instinct, a kind of internal, biologically based power source that constantly seeks discharge. Changing conditions may alter whether, how, and in what way that drive will be expressed, but they won't diminish the relentless pressure to seek that expression.

At first glance, the relationship between testosterone, aggression, and gender seems like a neat package. Testosterone causes maleness. Testosterone causes aggression. Men are more aggressive than women. But alas, as any good biologist knows, the relationship between biology and behavior is never so simple.

Even within the biological sphere, it's not exactly the case that testosterone simply and directly *causes* aggression. Both animal and human studies show that when it comes to testosterone and aggression, the cause-and-effect relationship is bidirectional. Just about everyone knows that increases in testosterone lead to increases in aggressive behavior. Not so widely recognized is the fact that successfully aggressive behavior increases testosterone. To again draw on

James Dabbs, when monkeys fight, the winner's testosterone level rises, while the loser's falls. Among tennis-playing and chess-playing humans the same patterns have been noted.

And the biology gets more complicated yet. It is not simply the case that the higher the level of testosterone, the higher the level of aggression. Instead, the testosterone-aggression relationship is governed by what Robert Sapolsky refers to as a "permissive" effect, which refers to the fact that changes in behavior occur only when testosterone levels are either decreased below 20 percent of normal, or raised to twice those of normal. Anywhere in between and the brain "can't seem to tell the difference."

The closer we look at the data, the clearer it is that the biology of aggression is elegant and subtle in its complexity, and hence highly resistant to reduction and simplification. Nevertheless, it's hard to refute the notion that aggression, masculine biology, and masculine psychology are inextricably linked.

Bill was a trial lawyer, not a sociologist or a biologist, but he intuitively recognized this linkage. He argued that his anger, his competitiveness, his professional forcefulness, and his version of fatherly authority were distinctly male parts of him. "I'm a guy," he would say. "I do what guys do—I get mad, I push, I'm a pain in the ass. It's in my blood. And you," he would say to his wife, only half jokingly, "are a gal. You protect the kids, and you tell me when I go too far."

The Role of Social Conditions in the Genesis of Aggression

In linking his aggression with his maleness and his biology, Bill spoke to a fundamental truth. But this truth is not the only one that needs to be considered when it comes to the complex set of relationships that exists between aggression, masculinity, fathers, and their authority.

Mary, in addition to being a "gal," was a physician. While her specialty was not psychiatry, she, like Bill, had a clearly articulated theory regarding masculine anger and aggression. She expressed her view, which was quite different from her husband's, in response to his statements about his male nature. She would say: "I think you use that 'it's in my blood' stuff as an excuse. Lots of times, when you get angry, I think it's because you feel helpless, or hurt."

With these words, Mary was speaking to an entirely different, and equally important, side of the equation, the side on which Dr. Johnson, Bill and Mary's previous therapist, had positioned himself.

Nearly 100 years ago, Freud posited that human aggression was a drive, and he viewed human destructiveness as originating from this endogenous, biologically based source of pressure and motivation. From this angle, man, as Stephen Mitchell aptly puts it, could be viewed as "guilty man," "driven by [his] instincts toward hatred and cruelty."

Over the past hundred years, however, our perception of man's aggression has changed dramatically. Erich Fromm, in his 1973 book *The Anatomy of Human Destructiveness,* the American psychiatrist Harry Stack Sullivan, the American psychoanalyst Heinz Kohut, and many others have argued that aggression is less a "drive" than an inevitable, even perhaps adaptive, response to environmental, biological, social, and psychological influences. Aggressive behaviors and feelings such as rage, sadism, violence, and so on are, therefore, reactions to alienation, pain, deprivation, and fear. No longer do we see ourselves as "guilty man," Mitchell tells us; rather we consider ourselves "tragic man," man who is "made hateful through the deprivation and cruelty perpetuated upon [him]."

Kimmel, Newberger, Pollack, Real, and the other proponents of the sensitive man movement lean hard on this "tragic man" view (one that can also be understood as the nurture side of the age-old nature-nurture argument) to explain masculine aggression. Often using the recent rash of school shootings to illustrate their ideas, they argue that boys' violence is symptomatic of social conditions such as Pollack's "boy code" and Gilligan's warrior culture, not an unmodulated expression of their basic instincts. As Bill Pollack said to Maria

Shriver on the *Today* show: "The boys who pick up guns, the boys who are suicidal and homicidal, the boys next door or the boy living in the room next door is also, I have found in my research, isolated, feeling lonely, can't express his feelings. And that happens because of the way we bring boys up."

Aspects of this view are clearly inarguable. When it comes to school violence, one hears the same story again and again. Boys who rampage and kill feel ostracized and alienated. When they don't direct their aggression at themselves in the form of depression, self-hate, and suicide, they sometimes direct it at those they feel have victimized them. Reflected here is a general truth about human, and even animal, nature: Social deprivation, injurious life experiences, and hurtful relational interactions generate aggression. If you harass a rodent—by shocking it, or by denying it food—it becomes more aggressive. If you deprive a baby monkey of expectable maternal nurturance, it will become an aggressively out-of-control adult, one who is far more likely to kill in a dominance fight (monkeys raised in non-depriving environments tend to back off the fight once they have established their superiority). And when you assault, deprive, oppress, or otherwise injure a person or group of persons, there will eventually be aggressive payback, even if it comes a long way down the road.

When it comes to aggression, it takes more than nature and biology to tell the whole story. Nurture and social context inarguably play a major role as well.

Bill and His Father

As is true for all men and women, Bill's and Mary's relationships with aggression had been shaped both by their biologies and by the lives that each had experienced long before their marriage began.

Bill frequently thought about his father during our sessions. He had been a banker, successful up to a point, but he had never fully invested himself in either his family or his career. For years Bill's father would arrive home every night after eight, having taken the two-martini train from New York City to their Westchester home. He would walk in the door, grumble about the lack of an immediate dinner, and sit down with a third martini in front of the television. On weekends he played golf, and didn't come home from the club until he'd had another few drinks. Over the years the heavy drinking took its toll, and Bill's father began to fail in his work. The more he failed the more he drank, and the more he drank, the more irascible he became. Often he yelled at Bill, criticizing him brutally for minor faults and transgressions.

Bill often returned to a memory from when he was ten. One Saturday his father had come home from playing golf at his club, his face red and his speech slurred. Bill, taking a risk, had asked him to take him golfing the next day. His father had exploded, saying: "I work my ass off all week—the one time I get any time for myself is at the club. And you want to spoil that now too? Don't you have any friends your own age to play with?" Bill never again asked his father to do anything with him. He wasn't the only one who gave up on his father. When his father died, shortly after Bill's graduation from college, it seemed to Bill that he died a lonely man. He had few friends during his final days, and not many came to pay their respects at his funeral.

This memory brought home to Bill how much he had lacked a father, and how badly he wanted to be something different for his own children. It also helped him to see something about his own anger. He realized that sometimes, when he got angry, he felt as though he was being the father he remembered—irascible, short-tempered, and dismissive. It may strike the reader as odd, but this was the first time he had made this connection.

In one sense, Bill was right: He was a high-test, high-testosterone guy, a successful trial lawyer with an ample aggressive endowment. But Mary was right too: Bill's aggressive endowment had been shaped by his own personal history. Like so many men these days, he sometimes felt like a fatherless boy himself, not a grown and successful man and father. At times he felt brittle and insecure about his own authority, and his ability to father. And, when he felt this way, his aggression did not come from a position of paternal (and authoritative) strength; rather it expressed his unacknowledged hurt and insecurity.

But We Need Our Aggression!

To this point, we can safely say that aggression is *both* an omnipresent human response to injury, oppression, and deprivation, *and* a "prewired potential"—an enduring, instinctual aspect of human nature. We can also say that this prewired potential is not distributed equally; men are demonstrably more aggressive than women.

Okay. But if we were to stop here we might well arrive, as do many members of the sensitive man movement, at a fallacious conclusion. Aware that aggression has driven, and will continue to drive, many of mankind's most egregious actions, we might conclude that all manner of aggression, from competitiveness on the playing field, to anger, to hazing, to school shootings, is pathological. And, given that men are more aggressive than women, we might further conclude that it behooves men in particular to single-mindedly renounce their aggressive inclinations for more civilized attitudes like husbanding, connecting, nurturance, and so on.

And we would be missing something profoundly important. I'll illustrate by telling you the story of a provocative boy, and of the efforts of his school to deal with that provocation.

Robert, a fourth grader, was being repeatedly teased by his classmates. Certainly it was wrong for the other boys to tease him, but it was also understandable: Robert was an easy target. He flaunted the fact that he had more money than the other boys, he ridiculed their intelligence, and generally, for complex and painful reasons within him, he set out—unconsciously of course—to make himself a scapegoat.

On the advice of a consulting psychologist who believed that the boys would all love and accept Robert once they understood him, the school organized an encounter group. The group leader instructed Robert to taunt each of the boys who had been teasing him while the teasing boys were made to keep silent. Then he asked all the boys to share their feelings. The theory was that this exercise would teach the teasing boys what it felt like to be teased. Meanwhile, the school principal met weekly with Robert, and Robert was also given a "protected" seat near the teacher's desk.

Not surprisingly, these interventions failed. Indeed they backfired, because they further aroused the sadism of Robert's classmates, who felt he was being made even more special. The teasing escalated, and it was at this point that Robert's parents asked me to get involved.

The first thing that jumped out was that the teachers and the administration were responding to Robert's provocation with an unwitting sadism of their own. Though they were loath to admit it, Robert had angered them as well, and they had retaliated. Inadvertently, by making Robert appear to be even more special, they set him up for more abuse.

A different tack was needed. I suggested that the school stop treating Robert in a special way and that they stop the encounter sessions. Discipline and safety were needed, not group therapy. The teachers were helped to recognize that they too were responding to Robert's provocation. The teachers then told the teasing boys, in no uncertain terms, that their sadistic behavior would not be tolerated. They also showed Robert, firmly but respectfully, how he was provoking the teasing. Robert then began therapy. He needed a place where he could sort out why he was scapegoating himself, and he needed help learning how to use his aggression to fight back. Finally, Robert also began karate lessons. Obviously it was preferable that he fight back with words, but I thought it important that he know how to protect himself in other ways. Sometimes, particularly among boys, words are not enough.

Gradually the teasing stopped.

The point, to which I will return repeatedly in the pages that follow, is this: Authority involves harnessing and channeling aggression for a positive, constructive purpose.

In Robert's case, the school needed to use its collective force on two fronts. First, the school authorities needed to stop hiding behind a touchy-feely perversion of empathy: They needed to use their aggression to appropriately police the bullies. At the same time, it was equally important that they approach Robert not as a helpless victim but as an aggressor in his own right. Their job was to encourage him to express his aggression not as provocation but as self-assertion. Once Robert had a better relationship with his own aggression, he, in turn, became more confident, and so became less angry and provocative.

Robert's story adds a critical element to our understanding of aggression. Aggression is not, as some would have it, a monolithic, immutable beast. While aggression can most assuredly be a profoundly destructive force, it can also be an enormously constructive force. Aggression is, in other words, neither "good" nor "bad" in and of itself; "goodness" and "badness" derive from what we *do* with our aggression. To quote the primatologist Frans de Waal: "To present all aggression as undesirable, even evil, is like calling all wild plants weeds: it is the perspective of the gardener, not the botanist or ecologist."

Men (and, as you will read in a later chapter, women as well) sorely need their aggression for the "goodness" that it can foster. As Robert's story illustrates, aggression helps us fight back and protect ourselves and our children. It enables us to assert, to succeed, and to prove ourselves. Like Bill Jenson, we use it to provide for our families (aggression, in other words, is even an essential component of good "husbanding"). Aggression is our ally when we do our duty and fulfill our responsibilities. It is a critical component of healthy sexuality. Without aggression there would be no real creativity, which, after all, involves rearranging, and sometimes even destroying, the status quo.

And, of course, as the faculty at Robert's school learned, properly channeled and regulated aggression imbues authority with necessary focus, backbone, and weight.

Unlearning an Old Lesson

Bill and Mary spoke with me for over three years. Early on, their conversations tended to end in acrimonious stalemate. Bill insisted that he was no more angry than other guys, and he felt that he couldn't discipline when Mary undermined him with her overprotectiveness. Mary, meanwhile, held firm to her concerns about the effects of Bill's size, forcefulness, and anger on her and on the children. Each member of the couple was reluctant to give up fervently held beliefs and wishes, and so it was hard for each to hear the other's point of view.

Over time, however, Bill and Mary grew more able to listen to each other. Mary began to sort out her own reasons for being uncomfortable with Bill's anger, and this helped her to be more specific about what she saw as the problem. "I realize that sometimes I overreact," she said, "but I don't think that my reaction is only to the level of your anger. I feel like, when you're mad, you disconnect. I can't feel that you care about me. I can't find you. That, as much as the anger, is what scares me."

While Mary wrestled with her reflexive criticism of Bill's aggression, learning to better discern whether she was reacting from a place of old fear or legitimate, maternal protectiveness, Bill took a hard look at himself. "I think it's true," he said. "Sometimes when I get mad I'm not really thinking about how the other person is feeling. When that happens I feel I'm just like my father, and it horrifies me to think that I could ever be as ugly and hurtful as he was." At the same time, Bill also talked with Mary about how important his anger and aggression were to him as a man and as a father. He didn't want to be like his father, but he also didn't want to resolve things by settling for some bloodless and impotent version of "assertiveness"; he wanted to make a legitimate place for the visceral experience of aggression. "I don't think these parts of me are always all bad," he said. "And I don't mind if the boys grow up to have a little of my hard side. Sometimes you need some of that out there in the world."

Mary, in turn, could hear and respect this.

There were no quick-fix recipes. Bill didn't need cookbook advice; basically, his solution was one of hard-earned self-knowledge. With work, and by becoming more tuned in to his wife's and children's reactions, Bill learned to discriminate between different qualities of anger and aggression. He became able to identify and control aspects of himself that were harsh rather than firm, irascible rather than disciplining, and authoritarian rather than authoritative. His words, I believe, speak for themselves:

"There are times when I feel this ball of hurt in me. Like I have to get rid of some feeling I can't stand, or like I have to prove something. I can feel my face harden. It's like I have too much at stake. In that state, I try to control people. That may work for me in court, but I don't think that's what being a father, or a man, is really all about. And then there are times when I feel just as strongly, but it's different. Like I say, firmly, even sometimes angrily, 'Pick up your socks,' or whatever, but it's like I have a little more distance. It's because *they* need it, not because *I* need it. That's when I really feel like a father."

This approach worked with Oliver. Bill changed his tone, and his words, ever so slightly. Speaking firmly but supportively, he told his son, "We are your parents, and we want you to have the testing—we really think that this is important. But what's going on? We know you're really upset. Can you tell us what's up? I don't think I've ever seen you so worried—it must be pretty important."

Oliver didn't run to his room. He stayed put, and eventually began an important conversation with his parents. Over the course of several discussions—not so much sitting down and talking, but, in the way that things happen best with kids, spontaneously, driving to school, going to bed, and so on—he let them know that he had long felt that he was different from other children. He knew that he was smart, but at the same time, he'd been worrying that there was something wrong with his brain. If he was so good at math, then why was reading so hard? And why, sometimes in class, would he be thinking about other things, not even hearing the teacher until she had raised her voice to get his attention? What would happen when people found out that he was different?

Oliver went on to get the testing, and he got some focused help with his learning disabilities. Over time, his self-esteem came to be less based on being smart, and more based on a sense that he could persist, work hard, and contend with adversity.

Real-life solutions are, as you will see repeatedly in the pages and stories that follow, rarely "cures." Oliver's learning difficulties, while not paralyzing, remained an ongoing issue for him and for the family. Bill and Mary continued to struggle with questions of when to push, when to support, how to negotiate the relative "softness" and "hardness" of their respective stances. Importantly, however, they had made a place for an ongoing familial conversation. Bill could talk with Mary about his sense of urgency, his need to *do* something. Mary could talk with Bill about her concern that he was sometimes "too much" and the fact that he sometimes seemed frightening. Beyond arriving at an answer to the relatively narrow question of whether or not to get the testing, Bill and Mary made a place in their relationship that could value, and yet when necessary regulate, Bill's aggressive nature. And, perhaps surprisingly to some, making such a place not only made Bill a more effectively authoritative father, it also helped him to become a more related, more connected, and better-listening husband.

Like it or not, relationships between the sexes are shaped by the fact that men are, by and large, more aggressive than women. As Bill and Mary prove, this in-the-marrow difference does not have to make things divisive—in fact, it can make them strong and robust, though in order for this to be so both men and women often have some work to do. It falls to men to learn about how their aggression feels to women, and so to shape their responsiveness respectfully, without becoming inauthentic or passive. Similarly, women need to learn more about the language of masculine anger, aggression, and force-fulness. This does not mean that either men or women should give up on their own distinct perspectives, it means that each of us ought to expand his or her consciousness in those places where overly reflexive assumptions and judgments are likely to occur.

Most things, fatherhood included, go better when they grow from our own genuine, and gendered, human natures.

Anxiety

Bill had made his way in a world very different from mine—the milieu of law and the courtroom, of jostling and fighting for an advantage. He lived, interestingly enough, in a world that was much like my father's.

My father had been an investor, a "wheeler-dealer," whose compatriots and antagonists had been Boston politicians and businessmen during the 1930s, 1940s, and 1950s. I had veered away from that world, partly because I was more interested in the mind, partly as a way of rejecting my father, and, truth be told, partly because the world of successful men intimidated me. I was interested in Bill's world, and at times I envied his ease in it.

Because Bill and I seemed so different on the surface, I frequently had to remind myself that Bill faced a task that I, myself, knew very, very well. Probably it's a task that every boy faces if he is to form a working relationship with his own aggression and, not coincidentally, if he is to become a man: that of confronting the ghosts of his father.

After my stint on the cattle ranch I had begun to turn my life around. I had, however, built up a great deal of momentum going the wrong way, and the turn was a long and slow one. I didn't really have a realistic vision of a future until I was twenty-four, when I decided I wanted to be a psychologist. To do this required quite a bit of work: I had to go back to school, take courses, work for a few years in the field of mental health.

But the real work I had to do was internal. In the years after I began to take my ambitions seriously I tried on virtually every anxiety-related symptom known to man. I had panic attacks—the real deal:

heart fluttering like a canary, a band of steel tightening around my forehead, and a sense of drowning in an invisible, unidentifiable fear. I became hypochondriacal, and I spent two years convinced that I was dying of a brain tumor. I felt "derealized," like everything around me was one of those strange and surreal movies that seem so meaningful when one is an adolescent. (I can confidently say that I now have a thoroughgoing, in vivo, understanding of most of the anxiety disorders listed in the American Psychiatric Association's *Diagnostic and Statistical Manual of Mental Disorders IV*.)

At that time, however, I didn't really have much of a clue as to what was going on with me psychologically. I figured that I really was dying, or going crazy, or something else from which I would never recover. In the absence of sorting things out, I mostly just plowed through. Probably my most effective mental health intervention involved playing basketball until I was exhausted, and afterward drinking a lot of beer. Only then it seemed could I get some sleep.

Understanding came later.

When my father died, just short of my sixth birthday, he was sixty-nine. He had been sick since I was born, and mostly sick is how I remember him. Sick and old. Probably I loved him, probably I still do, but mostly I remember resenting him for his absence from my life, and, in my little-boy mind, for the claims he made on my mother. His sickness made it hard for me to understand the legitimacy of those claims. It seemed to me that she mostly had to worry about him, and take care of him.

I was already in a huge battle with my father by the time I was five, but, like so many fathers, mine hardly seemed to know that we were fighting. Maybe if he had lived to deal with me during my adolescence we would have had the chance to struggle things out between us. But he didn't, and so we didn't. I now know that when my life was careening wildly out of control ten and twenty years after my father died I was still looking for the fight I had never had. And, because I hadn't had it, I was anxious about what was pushing its way forward from inside of me. I was frightened of my aggression—its edges, its possibilities, and its limits. I hadn't had, with my father, the survivable collisions through which a boy comes to learn about the nascent power of this core and necessary side of himself.

The opportunity to have such an organizing and formative struggle is, I can tell you, one of the greatest gifts a father can give his children.

4

Fatherhood and the Music of Masculinity

JEFFREY STANTON, a forty-five-year-old business consultant (and the previously mentioned father who worried about being a "tough love tyrant"), came to talk with me about his relationship with his two children—Phil, sixteen, and Lora, fourteen. "I feel like I'm losing them," he said, palpably distressed. "They're having trouble in school, they're hanging out with bad kids, they stay out late, I think they're getting into drugs. I try to talk with them, to understand what's going on, but they won't talk with me. When they were younger it was like we were best buddies. Now we're a million miles apart, and it's killing me."

Jeffrey calmed a bit as he told me about his work and marriage. He had combined a business degree with an aptitude for numbers and computers, and he worked for a high-tech consulting firm. Though he had often been told that he had the skills to go out on his own, he had preferred the security of his firm. He felt appreciated, and he was comfortable with his boss, a charismatic and well-known man who attracted a great deal of business. "Probably I could make more money, have more freedom on my own, but there's a lot of security in being part of a big, successful company."

Though Jeffrey seemed comfortable with his work situation, I sensed in him a certain resignation and lack of vitality when he spoke of it. The same seemed true of his marriage. His wife, Denise, had left her job as an advertising executive when the children were little, and she had only recently returned to work. Their relationship, he told me, had grown sexless and emotionless. He seemed accepting of this. "I have fantasies about something more exciting," he later told me, "but that's not the way it is in the real world. You get a few years that are fun, and then you try to keep it together. We'll never get divorced—it's good enough."

I wondered about the resigned, narrow view that seemed to pervade every nook and cranny of Jeffrey's life. One could even sense it in his physical presence. He bent his tall, thin frame into a slouch, clasped his hands in front of him, and generally spoke in a tired, cautious voice.

The only change in Jeffrey's subdued demeanor came when he spoke about his children. He told me, once again quite distressed, that he had finally decided to talk with a therapist after knocking on Lora's door one night, only to hear her say to a friend on the phone, "Hold on—it's my dad. He probably wants to try to have one of those stupid talks with me. God—he can be such a dufus." Jeffrey was crushed. Neither he nor his wife knew what to do—about school, about the drugs, about the friends, and about the burgeoning lack of respect. "You're being really reasonable with them," Denise said. "It's not like we can *make* them behave. I expect it's just a phase, and we just need to ride it out."

It didn't sound like "just a phase" to me, it sounded more like a trajectory. The drug use appeared to be regular, grades had slipped dramatically, the crowd that both children had joined was a bad one, and both kids appeared to be depressed and uninterested. The family was spinning and sputtering, and Jeffrey seemed to have no idea what, if anything, he could do to change things.

One reason for this was that his fatherliness lacked critical capacities that his family desperately needed: Not only was Jeffrey unable to use his aggression in the service of being authoritative, he also had not managed to assume a position of leadership and responsibility vis-à-vis his children.

Fish Out of Water?

Certainly those who speak of the value of a woman's way—mutuality, joining, connection, and sharing—make an important contribution. We men have much to learn.

The symphony of life, however, is not played in one repeating note. Rams butt heads. Fish, birds, and all manner of creatures evolve elaborate rituals that determine their places in the pecking order. Male primates develop complex hierarchical social structures in which each position on the ladder of power and centrality has specific meaning and purpose. These hierarchies not only reflect competitive success and failure, they bind and channel all manner of aggression so that social order, rather than blood and mayhem, are the rule.

The same is true for humans, at least for human males. We men have not yet "evolved" beyond checking out the wealth, attractiveness, intellectual prowess, and physical strength of our potential competition the moment we walk into a room. Experts in organization and leadership have, over the past several years, learned that the "level," nonhierarchical management style, first developed by the Japanese and later idealized by the business press in this country, has severe shortcomings: Workers become unmotivated when there is no hierarchy to climb, and they become disoriented when there is no predictable order within which to locate themselves. Moreover, we follow, at times passionately (and, admittedly, at times idiotically), our favored sports teams, and we derive some sense of our worth from their relative place in the standings.

Both for better and for worse, competing, jostling, and jockeying for a better place in life's many and varied pecking orders are the ways of men. This hierarchical orientation is by no means our only way, but it is to some degree defining of who we are, and how we do it. Those who place men in an unrealistic, idealized world in which the life-realities that require competition are ignored, who seem to imply that their "pathological" aggression is cause for including "male" as a diagnostic category in the next edition of the American Psychiatric Association's *Diagnostic and Statistical Manual of Mental Disorders,* are partially deaf to the age-old music of masculinity. They might as well take a fish out of the water, and then argue that its gills and fins are maladaptive.

The fact is, along with their innate aggression, men often feature an edgy inclination to seek a better place in the hierarchical order of things. This way has its problems, to be sure, but it can also prove a valuable quality in a variety of real-world endeavors—work, sports, even relationships. And, as you will learn, this hierarchical mode of relating is a critically important part of being a father.

Bees

One summer my daughter, Chloe, then three years old, stepped on a bees' nest and was stung many, many times. I didn't know exactly what these stings meant to her, but she was very hurt, very frightened, and generally very stirred up. Her mother and I went about helping her in fundamentally different ways, not by design but, as you will hear, by our essential differing natures. For several nights, while the pain and distress kept her awake, my wife stayed up with Chloe, talking with her about her experience of bees, pain, surprise, fear, itching, and every other experience imaginably related to bee stings.

I, on the other hand, was not content with soothing and understanding. I needed to do something. While her mother sat with her by night, I plotted with her by day. We scouted out the bees' nest and made careful, elaborate arrangements to kill the bees. Importantly, the complexity of our military operation paled in comparison to what was going on emotionally. Chloe was certainly angry at the bees, and the prospect of taking out the hive was an exciting one, but she worried about all this killing. As she once put it, "I feel angry, I feel sad, I feel scared, and I feel all of them A LOT!" Eventually, however, she resolved her concerns with the realization that, if we didn't get the bees, someone else was likely to get stung. Thus decided, we carried out our mission and had a great time. Many months later Chloe still talked about bees and bee stings with a bit of fear. But she also talked about killing bees with a fair bit of excitement, and a great deal of pride.

This episode is like thousands of others that take place in the course of growing up. Sometimes these events are well negotiated, other times not, but in their entirety these experiences weave a tapestry of inner meaning. Moments like these shape how we see ourselves, how we see the world, how we feel, what we want to do, and what we feel we are able to do. I offer this interaction not because I think it remarkable. Nor do I mean to offer myself as a paragon of normality. I offer it because I believe that it illuminates the fundamental interplay of two gendered ways of relating that, when they work together, contribute to a child's developing relationship with his or her self, and with what at the time seems like such a great big world out there.

A Mother's Way

I'll begin by talking about my wife's way.

Our daughter was hurting and more than a little shaken. My wife responded, intuitively and spontaneously, by being flexible, receptive, and attuned. It seemed to me that she didn't think very much about herself, about her own needs, or about the fact that she would have liked to take off from our summer cabin for a hike. Nor did she seem particularly aware of how exhausted she was from staying up three nights running while the stings hurt, and then itched. What she did do was to join Chloe on her level, focusing almost exclusively on the nuances of our daughter's reality and experience, instinctively matching her own agenda, rate, and rhythm to that of our child. She was careful to reflect that experience, rather than to add to it or adjust it in feeling, tone, or content. She was, to put it another way, utterly non-hierarchical.

This attuned way of being with a child has been identified by those who study parent-child interaction as deeply emblematic of a "mother's way." The British psychoanalyst Donald Winnicott, one of the first to describe this mode, wrote about how a mother's facial expressiveness accurately reflects the experience that she sees, and senses, in her child. The infant, in turn, sees his experience reflected in his mother's reaction and, through repeated interactions like this, learns about his own experience, his own state—in short, his own self.

Unlike much psychoanalytic theorizing, the largely clinical observations of Winnicott have been confirmed by systematic, nonpsychoanalytic mother-infant research. The noted pediatrician T. Berry Brazelton, child psychoanalyst Jim Herzog, and others have also observed that mothers, in a way quite different from that of fathers, track, mirror, and echo their children. In this mode of "homeostatic attunement," as Herzog calls it, they closely and accurately follow the experience of their children, and then return that experience to the child in a way that allows him or her to accurately see, feel, and know his or her self on many levels. When this fails to occur, children tend to become upset and disorganized.

Attuning, mirroring, echoing, and reproducing—these are the ways of mothers. And it is worth noting that these articulations of how mothers mother have great resonance with the current view of women's psychology. As psychologist Judith Jordan notes: "Women typically demonstrate more emotional/physical resonance with others' affective arousal than do men."

Is a Mother's Way the Only Way?

As I've mentioned, the sensitive man movement implores men to eschew their emotional Neanderthalism for a move in the direction of this maternal way. Obviously one problem with this prescription is that it resorts to stereotype. Men are certainly more capable of empathy, attunement, and reciprocity than this line of thinking acknowledges, while the construction of women as a living "breast-mirrors" fails to capture the range and complexity of women's capacities and vulnerabilities.

There is also a more subtle, but no less important, problem with the idea that we'd all be better off if men were more like women. What if mothers and fathers always and only did it this way? How would development work if we all single-mindedly devoted ourselves to reflecting our children's experience?

Consider an everyday example. A friend comes to us upset that his boss has been unjustly critical. We sympathize. But, knowing that our friend can at times be quite difficult, we also surmise that his boss probably had good reason to tell him off. What do we do? Do we support our friend's version of reality, even though we suspect that it's not the whole story? Do we confront him, and tell him what we think the real truth is? Most of us probably decide to wait. If we do choose to suggest that he may be partly to blame for his troubles it will likely be at a later time, when our friend has regrouped a bit, and his feelings of hurt and injury are not quite so raw.

By choosing not to confront in this moment, we essentially configure our response along the lines of that aforementioned maternal way of relating. We are highly attentive to our friend's subjective reality. In essence, we "mirror" his experience.

But in this example there is an interesting twist. Our response does more than "mirror" our friend's subjective reality. It "privileges" it. By this I mean that we have to set aside one truth—the notion that our friend probably contributed to the situation by being a pain in the ass—in order to mirror another truth, his pain.

Here's the point.

Mirroring the subjective reality of another is an important aspect of relatedness, but there is more to real relatedness than this kind of mirroring. Let's shift back from the role of friend to that of parent. As mothers and fathers we perform a complicated balancing act. We help our children find and feel themselves by reproducing and mirroring their experience, to be sure. But we also help them learn about how to be themselves in a world that is not perfectly tailored to reflect them. As parents we walk a fine line: We are in the business of understanding and empathizing, but, because we are not in favor of sustaining the illusion of omnipotence, we are also in the business of communicating to our children realities that they need to hear, even when those realities conflict with their subjective experience.

Sometimes a parent's task is not to accompany but lead the way. Not echo, but speak from another vantage point. Sometimes a parent has to be the boss.

A "Tough Love" Tyrant?

This whole business of communicating unwanted realities was exactly what Jeffrey was having trouble with. He didn't feel that he could forcefully confront his children with the truths they needed to face—that a life of drugs would lead to their downfall, that they had to work hard, that school was important, that which friends they chose mattered. He was all reason and understanding, but he offered no counterforce, no opportunity for meaningful collision. And as a result, he had no authority, no weight.

And so Jeffrey's children continued to struggle. During the first three months that he spoke with me, Lora was suspended from school for suspicion of drugs, Phil was brought home by the police at three in the morning, having been found intoxicated outside a 7-Eleven store, and both kids turned in terrible report cards. Meanwhile, through it all, Jeffrey did little more than ask them to talk with him about what was bothering them. He hoped that things would change for the better if everyone could reach an understanding. After each incident, and each discussion, there would indeed be a few days in which the kids would behave better, but soon the staying out late, the suspicious smells on the breath, and the phone calls from seedy characters would resume.

I talked with Jeffrey about trying a different approach. Why, I wondered, did he model his fatherhood along the lines of friend and therapist? Why did he believe that everything had to be the product of a negotiation? What about being the boss, and demanding that their behavior change? I suggested that the children might feel frightened by their own out-of-control behavior, and that their upping the ante might represent a cry for limits and authority. "Your children are by no means terrorists," I said. "They sound like decent kids underneath. But the rule about terrorists may apply. They're out of control, and I don't think that you can negotiate things, talk about feelings and motives and all that, until you establish ground rules and safety. And that you may have to do unilaterally."

Jeffrey listened with some interest, but he was reluctant to take my advice. Once again he uttered his familiar refrain: "I'm a father, not some kind of 'tough love' tyrant." And then he added, "It just doesn't feel to me like that's what loving your children is all about."

A Father's Way

I wasn't proposing tough love tyranny, I was trying to talk with Jeffrey about a real and valuable way that parents can be and, significantly, that men and fathers are naturally inclined to be. Here's what I mean.

As I've mentioned, I felt a bit better as a father by the time Chloe and I killed the bees. In contrast to those moments of frictionless nonengagement, those times of alienated wanderings around the yard, and those countless other instances of looking for, and not finding, a solid place within my family, I had begun to find a fragile but hopeful sense that I could be a good father. The first step to an apparent solution was a surprisingly obvious one: I realized that it just didn't work when I tried to do it like my wife.

While she seemed able to single-mindedly shape her responses to our children's needs and still feel authentic, even if she was at times thoroughly depleted and frustrated by her self-sacrifice, I just couldn't do it that way. At least I couldn't do it that way for very long, not without becoming, as one father I know put it, a "dead man walking." I found that it was better for me to do it differently. Actually, this is putting it too mildly: I found that I *had* to do it differently. I felt more engaged and more myself when I didn't worry so much about being perfectly responsive and attuned. It worked better when I held on to my own interests and agenda. To put it bluntly, it worked better when I didn't try to be such a good mother.

So when it came to the bees, my daughter had a lot of help from her mother, but she also had to deal with me, and with my ways.

I can't say that I was highly attuned to the nuances of my daughter's temperament and psychology during our bee killing. I didn't begin by finding out, with great sensitivity and care, what she was feeling. There was work to do. We had to get ourselves some bee poison, a plastic tarp to cover the nest when the angry bees flew out, and a funnel with which to pour the poison into the nest. Our assault would come in the early morning, when the bees were slowed by the still cold mountain air. Basically I set our agenda, and then I asked my daughter to join me. Actually, I kind of insisted, and, with relish, she went along as we set about not only to kill bees, but also to teach her about agency, self-protectiveness, aggression, planning, and much more.

Now I suppose that you might call this way self-centered and narcissistic (as well as, you might argue, environmentally destructive). In a sense it was. But I submit that my approach to the bee problem is representative of a nonpathological and generative way in which men relate. Fathers have done this for ages, and perhaps we men did it more freely before we were made to feel so self-conscious and defensive about some of our natural inclinations.

There are data to support this.

We now recognize, from intensive study of mothers, fathers, and infants, that fathers are more likely than mothers to play physical, arousing games with infants and toddlers. Fathers' play is more "unpredictable," and it tends to be more stimulating, vigorous, and arousing. Fathers, to put it bluntly, intrude, disrupt, stir up, demand, and insist. This mode, which Jim Herzog refers to as one of "disruptive attunement," is natural for fathers. In it a father will shift his child's state to fit his own. He will lead the way and ask his child to follow. He will even, at times, see his children not only as they are, but as he wishes them to be.

This paternal mode of relatedness is uniquely suited for a number of essential parental tasks. In it a father might stop unfocused, or unacceptable, behavior with a sharp word. He might tell a dawdling child to hurry up. He might, on seeing a daydreaming child poking around an electrical socket, act in a way that startles him or her to attention. In this paternal mode of "benevolent disruption," to borrow a phrase from Steven Cooper, fathers teach children to focus, to become alert, to change their mental state—for example, from passive to active—and so to respond to a world that is not always so perfectly attuned, or so perfectly empathic. And, in seeing his children as he wishes them to be he might not be acting like a narcissistic son of a bitch. He might, in fact, be holding out a vision of hope, of growth, of possibility—indeed of the future.

As Shakespeare noted, "Sweet are the uses of adversity."

Things are, of course, rarely as straightforward as I have just made them out to be. It is certainly the case that mothers, and women, often relate in a "paternal" mode, and fathers, and men, relate in a "maternal" mode. The point is *not* that things are always and only one way. The point is if we men and fathers don't value our masculine selves, if we don't recognize the validity of such "benevolent disruptions," we will likely find ourselves echoing these words, taken from J. M. Coetzee's novel *Disgrace*: "I can't help but feel that, by comparison with being a mother, being a father is rather an abstract business."

Changes

One morning, I awoke to a message from an obviously shaken Jeffrey. I returned his call. His son, Phil, had been driving with a bunch of friends, and the driver, drunk and probably stoned, hit a tree. The worst injury was Phil's broken collarbone and mild concussion—but Jeffrey was desperately upset.

We met later that day. "All night at the hospital I was thinking that maybe I should try what you're saying," he said. "And then, at breakfast, Lora said to me, 'Christ, Dad, what do you expect? We do whatever we want, and nobody ever says no.' So look, I hear you. I'm willing to try. But I've got to tell you, I'm still not sure. Like I say, it still sounds like some crazy tough love thing. And even if it is right, I don't know if I can do it. It's just not my way—it never has been. But who knows, maybe the change will do me good. You know, on my way over here, I realized that I've never been able to straight-out tell anybody in my life what I want them to do."

Jeffrey and I started to dig deeper. First we sketched out a striking pattern in his life: It had always been very hard for him to take charge, to be authoritative.

We began with his current job, where he submerged himself self-lessly in his boss's agenda. He was content to be productive, never rocking the boat, never setting his own course. He was valuable to all and threatening to none.

We moved on to what had been, until now, the one great regret in Jeffrey's life. On graduation from college he had been offered a prestigious scholarship. Had he accepted it he would have spent a year abroad studying mathematics. An academic career (his great but secret wish) would likely have been launched. Jeffrey turned down the opportunity, telling me that it had seemed, at the time, arrogant to think that he could "fly so high." Instead he took a secure job and went to school part-time for an MBA. He had stayed on the same safe track ever since.

Then Jeffrey's mind took him even further back, to his career as a high school basketball player. Jeffrey was tall (as I mentioned, one didn't notice this because he slumped and carried himself small), and he had been a pretty good athlete, one of the better players on his high school team. Now he told me that when the coach had diagrammed plays, he would move to the back of the huddle, in the hope that the coach wouldn't call his number. On a few occasions he had given up the ball in key situations. He had justified passing up the shot by thinking of himself as a team player, but now he could see that he'd been too frightened to take the lead.

A man's relationship with his aggression, leadership, and authority is shaped, in large part, by his relationship with his own father. This was certainly true with Jeffrey. His mother had often been angry, depressed, unpredictable. But she had her reasons. The most striking aspect of Jeffrey's childhood was that his father had been diagnosed with severe multiple sclerosis when Jeffrey was four and had died of its complications when Jeffrey was in college.

Jeffrey recalled how, when he would "horse around," his mother would tell him to be quiet. "You're disturbing your father," she would say. He told me that during these moments he would look over at his father, who was invariably sitting in the same living room chair that he always sat in, a blanket over his legs and a pained, faraway look in his eyes.

"I think I got quieter and quieter as he got sicker. I always thought of myself as a 'bad' kid, like I was too loud, a bull-in-a-chinashop. So I just kept ratcheting myself down. But actually, it wasn't that *I* was too loud, it was that I was too loud *for him*."

You can hear Jeffrey coming to the realization that he had stifled his forcefulness and aggression so as not to upset his father. This was important to know, but it was only part of the story.

One day, almost a year into our work, Jeffrey said, "You know, I think that the pained look on my father's face when I was rambunctious wasn't so much because my noise was bad for him. It was complicated. For one thing, I think maybe he wanted to play with me. I have these vague memories of when I was a very little boy, before he

73

got sick, and we would wrestle, horse around. I think he liked that, and he missed that he couldn't do it anymore. And I also wonder—maybe this is a little weird—if he envied me. It must have killed him to see me using my body, given that he couldn't use his."

Jeffrey could now see how he had held himself back so as to spare his father pain. He had let his father be stronger, even though it meant stifling his own interests and agenda. He had never had the experience of going hard and knowing that his father would not let things get out of hand. The cost of this deprivation was high. Now he related to all the world—to his wife, his children, his boss, and his co-workers—in the same way. He was tentative, afraid of butting heads. He leveled himself off, and he organized himself around the rhythms, and the agendas, of others.

These understandings fortified Jeffrey's resolve to change. Obviously, things didn't proceed smoothly and without interruption toward a happy ending. As is the case with all of us, moments of resolve were followed by reversions to old ways. But over time, Jeffrey worked on being more in charge with his children. He relied less on understanding and negotiation, and he communicated expectations. He made his children do their homework. When the kids came home with alcohol on their breath he grounded them. He forbade them to see the most troublesome of their peers. These authoritative stances were uncomfortable for him—he hemmed and hawed, and his children relentlessly tested his resolve. He worried and questioned himself, he suffered from the foreignness of the position he was taking, but he stayed with it, and he began to turn things around.

"Sometimes I Have to Fire the Guy"

When we talk about fatherhood, we are, of course, talking about men raising children. But in fact, all of us, if we are fortunate, have relationships with many "fathers" over the course of our lives. These men—coaches or teachers when we are young, bosses and mentors when we get older—serve the important role of father figures, and from them we learn a great deal about being a man and a father. This should come as no surprise. The principles of fatherhood are, in many ways, the principles of masculine mastery.

Consider the case of Jorge Rivas.

In the early 1980s, Jorge began a computer company in his garage. He built hardware that proved to be essential to networking, and he built it well. Like many young entrepreneurs, he went public and made a great deal of money. Unlike many entrepreneurs, however, he held on to his company, and stewarded it all the way from successful start-up to established company. This meant that he had to shift his management style from one that worked for thirty employees, to one that worked for three hundred, and eventually, to one that worked for three thousand.

A colleague and I called Jorge and asked if he would be willing to talk with us about what had made him so successful. He graciously agreed.

Jorge focused on his interest in management theory. He had consulted with experts in both the United States and Japan, learning about various approaches to organizational development. He told us that he had settled on a "level" style of organizational management. His organization was divided into small groups, each having a fair amount of control over itself. Though upper-level management decided on overall goals, and delegated tasks to each group, hierarchy was explicitly deemphasized. Decisions were reached, whenever possible, by consensus.

The approach appeared to have been successful. The company was expanding in leaps and bounds, and employees seemed satisfied. But we had a question.

"What happens when you get someone who just won't get with the program?" we asked. "Every company has people who are really difficult."

"His group talks to him," Jorge answered.

"What if that isn't enough?" we pressed.

"They keep at it," Jorge responded.

"But haven't you had situations that just can't be handled within the group?" we countered.

"Yeah, it happens," Jorge told us.

"What do you do then?"

"Well, we keep trying to work within the system."

"But if that doesn't seem to work?"

"Sometimes I have to fire the guy."

This conversation afforded my colleague and me a simple and clear insight into masculine, and paternal, authority. Jorge really did believe in a "level," nonhierarchical style of management—his democratic philosophy was not, as it sometimes is, cover for a more authoritative, or even authoritarian, style of leadership. Furthermore, this democratic approach was clearly valuable to his company. Nevertheless, more than Jorge was aware of, he and his company also relied on the backbone of his masculine authority. Indeed, as we learned more about how his company worked, it became clear that negotiation and egalitarianism worked *because* the employees always knew that, if things got tough, Jorge would come through. "This is a great place to work," one woman said to us. "People get along, the environment is relaxed, and people get treated fairly. Besides, we always know that the man is there when we need him."

Jorge's authority was imbued with two now familiar qualities.

First, Jorge was willing to act decisively, firmly; even, when needed, punitively. He was willing to be aggressive.

Second, Jorge was the man in charge. Everyone knew that, in the end, he was responsible for what happened. "Sometimes I have to fire the guy" is hardly a comment reflective of consensual negotiation.

Jeffrey One More Time

Jeffrey began to "feel his oats." At work and with his wife, he noticed, with a mixture of anxiety and pleasure, that he was finding it easier to push, argue, and fight. A little sex had even returned to their marriage. With Phil and Lora he began to be more comfortable with the belief that it was his job, as father, to shape their behavior.

Of course, the kids struggled and tested. One school night, Jeffrey found Phil heading out the door at eleven. This got his attention, as there was now a midnight curfew.

Jeffrey asked Phil where he was going.

"None of your business."

"It *is* my business. Where are you going?"

"Out of my way, Dad," Phil answered. Then he stared at Jeffrey defiantly, as if to say, "And what are you going to do about it?"

Jeffrey felt a flash of rage. He grabbed Phil by the shoulders and pushed him onto the couch. Then, standing over him, still holding his shoulders, Jeffrey looked Phil in the eyes and said, "I am your father. Don't you ever, ever talk to me like that again."

Phil was speechless. Man and boy stared at each other for a moment, and then Phil looked away. Saying nothing, he walked to his room. Jeffrey himself was shocked at his response, and he worried: "I thought maybe it was way too much, that I'd gone over the edge. I went down to apologize. But Phil seemed okay somehow. He didn't say much, but there was something softer about him. He was upset, but not too upset. Still, all night I felt tortured. I figured maybe I'd really lost it, been abusive."

"What did you imagine the abuse was?" I asked.

"I keep thinking of what it felt like to stand over him. I felt big. I never feel big. You know, I'm ashamed to admit it, but part of it felt good. I think that's what I feel so bad about. It seems like it shouldn't have felt good."

Jeffrey had found his way back to a critical moment of derailment. Since the early years of his father's illness he had learned to shrink himself, to steer clear of being on top and in charge. The image of his ill father, slumping ever lower in that same living room chair, had sat squarely in his mind all these years. Jeffrey, it turned out, had spent his life hunching over, both physically and figuratively, so as not to feel the pain, the risk, and the excitement of standing tall over his father. The cost of this solution was that he had cut himself off from his aggression, his competitiveness, and from other robust, healthy elements of his masculine endowment that were essential to his assuming an authoritative paternal position. And now he worried that his pleasure in his strength meant that he had gone too far.

I began by supporting his concerns about safety, saying, "Obviously you have to keep things safe. That's part of any parent's job." But I also trusted Jeffrey. He was thoughtful and caring, and he stayed connected. I did not believe that he would become sadistic or abusive, and so it felt reasonable to add, "But of course it feels good. It feels good to be able to act without worrying that you're standing taller than your father. It feels good to unshackle yourself. More than anything, it feels good to use your forcefulness, and your position as a father, to help your son, and your family. Phil has been in trouble. You've needed to help him, and you're doing that."

Jeffrey and I talked about this moment over many weeks, and, as we did, he drifted repeatedly back to that time when he had watched his father slumping ever deeper, ever more disabled, into his chair. The process of remembering was a painful one, but it enabled him to free himself from the sense of guilt and fear that had imbued that earlier memory, and that had accompanied the experience of "standing tall." And with this he began to grow more fully into himself as a man, and as a father.

Violin

It's time for my children to do their violin practice.

Which sometimes means that it's time for a struggle.

I most appreciate the power of genes when I watch someone with real talent do one of the many things that don't come naturally to me. So it is with my children and music. When their mother hears music the notes make sense. She sees the patterns, and she can feel what is happening. It's true for all her relatives. It's true for my children.

I, on the other hand, am completely musically challenged. So when my children began to learn the violin I was wary. Music wasn't going to be my turf—I had envisioned baseball games, not recitals.

I feel differently now. I've watched them learn about how much hard work goes into getting good at something. I've seen them experience the thrill of performing, along with the pleasure of the music itself. Now I support the effort.

But oh, the practices.

My younger son, Dylan, is seven. At his age the deal is one half-hour a day, five days a week. This morning he is doing his best to put off his practice.

"Dylan," I say, "start now." He smiles his bright smile. "I'm tired." "Now, Dylan. That's our deal." "What are you writing?" he asks, looking over my shoulder. This is a particularly effective diversion; Dylan knows I'd love to talk to him about it. Even though I know it's a ploy, I start to answer, for it's not easy to resist his twinkling eyes, his playful awareness that he is seducing me. Then I feel my wife's unspoken presence; she's wondering how I'll handle this. I get back on track. I say, "No more discussion, my friend, do it." "Could I pleeeease do it this afternoon, Dad?" he says. "I'll be able to do it better then."

Would it be so bad to compromise? Isn't it important to learn negotiation? Doesn't he need to know that people will be flexible when he is reasonable with them? That he can ask for what he wants?

These are sane ideas. But they are misguided. At least they are this morning, when it comes to Dylan, me, and violin practice. We have a deal. Thirty minutes of violin, then it's time for fun. And the deal includes no arguing, so he's already reneging on our bargain.

But my feelings are complicated. These negotiations pressure one of my greatest fault lines. I need my son to be happy with me. I need it too much. My need comes from my vulnerability, my uncertainty that I can be a good father after not having had one. And sometimes these feelings lead me to borrow on my paternal capital, at loan shark rates. At these times I'm likely to offer my children that unreliable sugar high of unnecessary gifts, and of saccharine appeasements.

This morning I fight the undertow, and I hold my line. But I feel a familiar twinge. Even though I know that my son's displeasure is not evidence that I have failed as his father, there is a place deep within where I am not so sure.

And I also feel a little lonely in my authority. I'll have to do without my son's sweet smile, his confirmatory "Thanks, Dad." At least for the moment.

5

"So Who Put You in Charge?"

THE CAPACITY TO OWN and use one's power and aggression, and the willingness to assume a position of parental responsibility: These are the cornerstones of a father's authority. But does my paternity, in and of itself, mean that I am being authoritative whenever I insist that my children obey me? When both Bill and Jeffrey said to their children "I'm your father," were they claiming the right to express their anger, and their aggression, in whatever way they saw fit?

Of course not. There's more to fathering and authority than expressing one's power from a hierarchically one-up position—a great deal more. For one thing, to be a good father requires legitimacy.

When it comes to fathering, however, what is meant by "legitimacy" is not so clear. There is no training, other than on the job. There are no elections to determine the best man for the position. There is little or no supervision. Only in the most extreme circumstances can a father "get fired" (as occurs when children are taken into the state's care and protection, or when one parent is granted sole custody during a divorce). Indeed, the standards for fatherhood are so uncertain, it seems that children would be well within their rights to ask of their parents, "So who put you in charge?"

Of course, many fathers can answer this question by way of biology. "I made you," they might say, "that's why I'm in charge." But, as we all know, there is also one hell of a lot more to being a father than making a baby.

Peter and Jennifer Jackson

Peter and Jennifer walked into my office as if they had arrived together by coincidence. Peter looked me over, sizing me up. Jennifer looked around the room for a seat. Neither looked at the other.

On first impression, Peter seemed a man accustomed to having the world in his hands. Thirty-four years old, tall and handsome in a very presentable sort of way, he had gone straight from an Ivy League college to a prestigious law school, and from there to the partnership track of an established Boston law firm. I'll admit that when he first walked into my office, shook my hand firmly, sat down, and looked me square in the eye, he put me off balance. Usually even the most accomplished and confident people have a shyness, an embarrassment, about them during their first visit. They have, after all, come to talk about things that they can't manage themselves, often things that they feel reticent to discuss. But not Peter.

Jennifer, in contrast, seemed far more uncomfortable than her husband. She was easily as attractive a woman as Peter was a man, but where Peter looked to be someone who took great care with his appearance, Jennifer seemed unaware of hers. They had met me in the middle of the day, and while Peter had come from work in an expensive suit, Jennifer had arrived in jeans and a sweatshirt. While Peter was impeccably groomed, Jennifer had, at most, run a comb through her hair at some point that morning. And while Peter made a point of his presence with his handshake and gaze, Jennifer receded, seeming distracted and wary.

Peter began. "I want to talk about my marriage," he said. "Specifically"—and with this he gave a slightly forced laugh, his first hint of discomfort—"I want to talk about sex."

Directing his remarks toward me as his wife looked on, Peter told me that Jennifer had been uninterested in making love with him since the birth of their daughter, Leah, now two. "Maybe every couple of weeks, maybe once a month. That's it. We had a good time before Leah was born, but now Jennifer's just not interested. These days the marriage is basically a practical arrangement. I work, she takes care of Leah, we confer in the evening, that's about it. I get tempted. I assume she knows that, I assume she worries about it, but it doesn't seem to matter. And it's not only the sex, it's everything. I can't remember the last time we had fun together. I wanted Jennifer to talk with someone about what's going on with her, but she insisted we both come. So that's what I have to say, at least for starters."

Now it was Jennifer's turn, and when she began to speak my impression of her changed dramatically. She exuded a quiet strength and presence. "I know Peter thinks that I need to see someone, that I have a problem with sex, or, if he's being insecure, that I don't love him anymore. Probably it surprises you that he's sensitive, the way he comes across when he first meets you, but he is." With these words Jennifer looked at Peter and smiled—the first glimmer of warmth I had seen between the two. Peter smiled shyly back, the first hint of softness I had seen from him. "But I don't think it's *my* problem," she continued. "I think it's *our* problem. I hope you can understand this. I wanted to see a woman because I think there are things going on that men just don't get, but Peter really wasn't comfortable with that. He felt that a woman just wouldn't understand what he was feeling about sex."

I asked Jennifer to tell me more.

"Our little girl, Leah, she's two. She is a delight. She's still breast-feeding. I know I probably need to wean her, but it's hard. When I nurse her I feel more at home in myself than maybe anything I've ever done. But it's not all fun. My breasts hurt, my body feels scuzzy, I don't get any exercise. When Peter gets home from work I just want him to take Leah so I can take a shower, get into some clean clothes, and the last thing I want is for him to touch my body. I want it to be mine, which it just isn't all day long. This will probably change if we get through this, but I just don't feel like sex right now. I understand that he's frustrated, and sometimes I give it to him just to take care of him, but he wants me to want it, like I used to, and I just can't right now." And, again turning to Peter, she said, "I can give you my body, sometimes, but I can't give you my mind."

"I hear you," answered Peter, "but it drives me nuts. I feel like our entire relationship is about Leah—Leah this, Leah that. I love her, don't get me wrong, but"—and now for the first time Peter turned to Jennifer—"I need something from you too."

"I know you do," Jennifer answered. "But you know what? I need something from you, and you just don't get that. This is why the problem is not just me, and not just sex. You want to make love, but you don't have the faintest idea what my life is like these days. You feel like a stranger to me. I know you make a good living for us—I stopped working when the baby was born," Jennifer said, turning back to me, "but, and I'm sorry if this hurts your feelings, I feel like you're just a big kid sometimes. You say you want more of a relationship, but I feel like you want things for you, not for us. You say you want to make love because you love me, but it feels to me you're just frustrated, you just want sex. I understand, but I need to feel like we're not so far apart. I don't think you've adjusted to the fact that we're in a different place than we were when we got married, and it asks different things of us."

As we moved forward, I learned that Peter and Jennifer had been married a little less than four years. They had met at the law firm where both had begun working after graduating from law school. "It was love at first sight," Peter told me. "She was smart, beautiful, sexy. I'd been with a lot of women before, but no one I ever wanted to marry. I knew right away, and she did too."

"I knew I wanted to marry him pretty quickly," Jennifer acknowledged. "But I am a more cautious person than he is. I'm never totally sure about anything."

A little over one year after the wedding, Jennifer became pregnant with Leah. Peter had at first suggested an abortion, for he didn't feel ready to move from being a twosome to a threesome. Jennifer, however, was adamant. "We can't have things just the way we want them," she had said. "The baby's here, and there's something wrong with feeling like we control our lives so completely. We can't say exactly when a baby is going to come, when it's just the right time *for us*. Life happens on its own terms sometimes."

Peter had agreed without much of a fight, but Leah's arrival changed their relationship dramatically. While Peter had been, as Jennifer had noted, a "terrific boyfriend and fiancé," he was, she felt, "not as good at being a husband and a father." And, her reticent greeting notwithstanding, Jennifer was well prepared to tell Peter what she meant by this. The three of us were off and running.

"I'm not sure that there's anything that could make me want sex right now," she said in one of our first sessions. "But I'll tell you what doesn't help. I don't think you have the first idea of what is involved in taking care of a baby. When was the last time you changed her diaper? When did you last get up with her in the middle of the night? When she cries, you give her to me to hold."

"But you soothe her better than I do," Peter had answered.

"Sure, but why is that? Because I'm some super earth mother whose mission in life is to take care of your children? That's bullshit, Peter. I know how to soothe her because I've taken the time to learn about her. *It's work*. You have this idea that it all comes to me so easy. I think you hide behind this stuff. If it's all so natural for me then there's no point in your trying to do what I do. And besides, when you don't realize what hard work it is, I feel like you don't really appreciate me, or what is involved in what I do day in and day out."

To his credit, Peter listened. As time went on, and as he grew more comfortable in our discussions, he came to recognize that he had some growing up to do. "I guess part of it is everything has always come so quickly to me—school, sports, work, relationships. I was my parents' favorite, and I feel like the world is easy for me. But this stuff about being a father is different. I don't really know how to do it."

From Biological Inheritance to
Earned Legitimacy

Often, when I talked with Peter, I thought about the night that I awaited my first son's birth. While my wife worked at the hard business of labor, I, feeling useless and peripheral, thought about the person-to-be we had made. Certainly I understood less about what we were embarking upon than did my wife. She had already carried, and cared for, our son for nine months, and from this body-based experience (and more) she had a much deeper awareness than I did of what is involved in being responsible for another life. I seemed to rely more on my naive optimism. Sometimes, when I look back on that time, I liken myself to a drunken fool who fancies himself a bullfighter simply because he steps out onto a street in Pamplona.

My experience, which I liken to Peter's, is common among first-time fathers. Many of us men embark upon the business of fathering rather ill-prepared—particularly in comparison to the way in which many women embark upon the business of being mothers.

This disparity in parental preparedness begins early on, with the body. When boys begin to masturbate, they see the semen come out of them, but they have no idea of its meaning, of its transformative and procreative power. For an adolescent boy the fact that an ejaculation can lead to children is little more than an abstraction. Through adolescence and young adulthood, boys may learn about how to make a baby in a cognitive way, but this is not the same as real knowing. We know we can get a girl pregnant, but the reality of carrying and giving birth to a child is not deeply in us. We have control, to some degree, over our bodies—when and where we masturbate, the way we can see our genitals on the outside, the sense of control the world feeds back to us as men and boys. We may try to learn. We may get help with this learning. One man told me, "My father gave me two directives: 'Don't drive drunk, and don't get a girl pregnant.'" It's an important message of responsibility. But probably even good help like this doesn't impart the true creative, and potentially destructive, power of male sexuality.

It's not the same for girls. While boys masturbate largely when and where they choose, and while the masturbatory activity of adolescent boys can be ritualized, entertaining, and even the source of a certain degree of camaraderie ("Where ya been, jerking off?"), girls meet the reality of their reproductive potential in a very different way. Periods don't happen when a girl decides; they arrive with a rhythm and timing of their own. A girl's physical sexuality is located inside her body, not appended to the outside. For a woman, the physical experience of sex is more connected to the mental and emotional than it is for men. For women the experience of sexual arousal is a whole-body experience (in comparison to men's relatively part-body experience of sexual pleasure). Girls and boys alike know, from an early age, that the nearly unfathomable reality of germinating a new life occurs within a woman's body, not within a man's. In these ways and more, women live in their sexual and procreative bodies earlier and more fully than men, they live in real time more than men, and they feel, in a palpable way, the impending future of motherhood much more profoundly, and much earlier, than men and boys do fatherhood.

In order to earn legitimacy as a father, a man must overcome this initial disparity in parental preparedness. And to do so, he must, among other things, develop a real sense of his sexuality and his aggression. He must learn to live out of his authentic male self. One of the reasons I have been critical of the sensitive man movement in the early pages of this book is that its naive vision of a de-gendered, nonaggressive masculinity works at cross-purposes to such self-knowledge; no man can be a good man, and a good father, if he does not come to know, respect, and harness his drives and instincts.

When Leah was two, Peter had not yet taken this maturational step, and as a result his fatherhood was little more than a biological fact. It was still, in effect, little more than an unearned endowment. He could say, "I made this baby," but he did not really know what it meant to be her father. He had not taken on the basic responsibilities of husbandhood and fatherhood—from simple things like changing diapers, getting up in the middle of the night, and making the effort to get to know the ways of his daughter, to more sweeping commitments like wrestling with his own narcissism and entitlement such that he did not act like Jennifer's second child.

From the moment when Jennifer and Peter had learned about the pregnancy, and Jennifer had opposed Peter on the matter of an abortion, Jennifer had been the "legitimate" parent. Now she wanted a partner. And she didn't much feel like making love with a man who, in many ways, had yet to grow up.

Earning Legitimacy

To his credit, Peter accepted the idea that he didn't really know how to be a husband or a father, and he set about trying to learn. At first he looked for pragmatic guidance, from Jennifer, from me, from his friends. Some aspects of what he needed to learn were relatively straightforward. "Like stopping at the bar for a drink with your buddies after work most nights," Jennifer mentioned. "What's that about? I'm home with Leah, I'm exhausted, my nipples are raw, I haven't had a moment to have a thought of my own all day, and you're at the bar with your buddies. Sure, I understand you're tired, and I do appreciate how hard you work. But do you realize, when you step out of your office to go to the bathroom, what a luxury it is to be able to pee without someone crying that they need you?"

Jennifer was talking to Peter about something beyond the pragmatics of changing diapers, strapping a child in a car seat, and getting up on occasion in the middle of the night. Peter could learn the specific tasks of fathering, but Jennifer wanted something more from him. She wanted to be able to *feel* him as a father. She wanted a partner not only in deed but in spirit.

Peter and I met alone many times during the first three years we worked together, and much of this effort was spent talking about his own father. He had grown up in a wealthy family, and his parents were primarily organized around work and social activities, not children.

His main caretaker had been a live-in nanny who had stayed with the family until he was twelve, when he had gone off to boarding school. "I was talking with my father about this stuff the other day," he said. "I told him that I was trying to be a better father, and I asked him how he thought he had done. You know what he said? 'Benign neglect. I practiced benign neglect. I figured as long as I didn't screw you up you'd turn out okay, and I look at you, I figure I was right.' Well, you know what? I want to do more than that for my kids."

Over the several years that I knew him, Peter worked hard to make this happen.

He worked on what he came to see as an underlying sense of entitlement. He was not an overwhelmingly arrogant guy; indeed, despite his early self-assuredness, Jennifer's description of him as "sensitive" was closer to the truth. He was successful at work because he was smart, competent, and ambitious, to be sure, but he was also well liked. However, when it came to being a father and husband some of the little-boy entitlement of his upbringing emerged. He had a sense that Jennifer would take care of things; in fact, he had a sense that she *should* take care of a disproportionate amount of the family work. This was particularly problematic when Jennifer returned to work full-time, and Peter still expected her to do most of the household work. For Peter, part of being a good father meant recognizing, and subduing, his embedded sense of feeling that his life ought to be an easy ride.

Peter also had to work on letting go of his wish to not grow up. While he had succeeded thus far, he had done so in part by being a golden boy, well liked and often mentored. He had not fully stepped into the notion of succeeding by dint of his own ambition and ability. This boyishness had initially appealed to Jennifer, but she wanted and needed something different now.

As you can hear, Jennifer was a strong, thoughtful woman, and she pulled Peter forward into being a better father and husband. But she too had work to do. Like Peter, she had been on the partner track at the law firm, and had taken an extended leave of absence when

Leah was born. While she was largely comfortable with this decision, she nevertheless envied Peter. "You get to sit in a meeting cutting deals, being a big shot, having the secretary bring you coffee and smile at you like she'd give you a blow job if you needed one, while I'm sitting here cleaning up your daughter's poop," she would note, in her acerbic but still playful way. If things were going well Peter might answer in kind: "If you were there, I'm not sure what you'd do with the blow job," and the couple would begin a useful talk.

Jennifer, it emerged, had turned off many aspects of her own sexuality and ambition in order to take care of the baby. As she put it, "If I was aware of *me* while I'm doing what I do all day I'd probably be so pissed I'd leave the kid on the changing table and run out into the street screaming." She came to see that she envied Peter his freedom, and the time and space he had in which to care for himself. She dealt with these feelings in a fairly common way. In addition to suppressing them, she, without meaning to, tried to control and subdue her husband, turning him into something of a castrated Mister Rogers. She stopped seeing him as a sexual man, and she sometimes treated him as another mother who might help her with her mothering. Peter didn't much like this, and it also wasn't so good for Jennifer. She needed Peter's help with Leah, but she also needed something less obvious. She needed Peter to hold on to the fact that she was more than a mother, that she was a woman with desires and ambitions of her own. She needed Peter to keep this knowledge for her through the time when she did not have enough space to hold it herself.

For Peter, therefore, growing up to a position of "legitimacy" meant not only being a good father but also being a good husband, a man who could know, and hold, his wife in the aforementioned way. This surely didn't happen when Peter approached Jennifer, sexually and otherwise, like an adolescent who acted as if he were owed sex simply because he was horny. Neither did it happen when he imagined that Jennifer should want their lives to be the way they were before Leah. These attitudes made it easy for Jennifer to not take Peter seriously, which was too bad, because then she didn't get the help that she needed from Peter to hold on to those parts of her that had been suppressed to facilitate her mothering.

As Peter's story illustrates, paternal legitimacy (and, it follows, paternal authority) requires that a man mature into his role as both a husband and a father. It means being responsible. It involves knowing oneself, one's wife, and one's children. It means channeling one's masculine endowment, including one's aggression and inclination to relate competitively and hierarchically, in the service of authority. It means using one's sexuality, aggression, kindness, experience, and other potential tools of husbandhood and fatherhood wisely and well.

Peter worked on all these things, and in doing so he moved from an essentially adolescent position to a mature one. Thus he transformed the biologically based legitimacy of his early fatherhood into an earned legitimacy. He described it well several years after we had begun, when Leah was about ten: "I've had a lot of success in my life, and most of it has come surprisingly easily. But the things I'm most proud of are the things that have been harder for me. My father showed me how to be successful, how to get along with people, but he never showed me a thing about being a father. Everything I know about being a father I've had to learn myself. I've had help, but at the end of the day it feels like mine."

Eric Robeson

We can deepen this discussion of paternal legitimacy by thinking about fathers who have only the role, and none of the biology: adoptive fathers and stepfathers.

Eric Robeson came to see me because he felt depressed. At first I wondered whether this round-faced, dark-haired, soft-spoken man's depression might have more of a chemical than a psychological origin: Eric had been feeling increasingly dispirited and withdrawn for over a year, and more recently he had been anxious, overly sensitive, and irritable. He could see no apparent cause for his unhappiness, telling me right away: "There's no good reason for this. I'm married to a wonderful woman, she has a daughter who is a great kid, and they have a great relationship. Work is okay My life is going as well as it ever has."

Over our first couple of sessions I couldn't find any better angle into the causes of Eric's unhappiness. I didn't think that things were so great—he seemed distant from his wife and twelve-year-old step-daughter, and his job, managing a chain of retail stores, seemed dry, but, apart from his recent marriage, which he claimed was a happy one, there had been no major changes in his life, and nothing seemed to account for the dive in his mood. I referred Eric to a psychophar-macologist, who found him to be depressed, and who started him on a course of antidepressants.

Interestingly, though Eric claimed to have no complaints beyond his mood, he wanted to continue our conversations, even after his depression lessened upon taking the medication (although he did not improve as fully as I imagined he might). Gradually a theme emerged, one that the discerning reader may already have noted: Eric continuously referred to the relationship between Donna, his wife, and Devon, his twelve-year-old stepdaughter, as "their" relationship. He never spoke of "our" or "my" relationship.

So I inquired: "You know, you speak of your wife and daughter as if they're a team, and you're somewhere on the outside, not really a part of it."

"What would you expect?" Eric answered. "Devon's grown up with her mother, her father was, and is, an asshole, and she hardly knows me. I'm not her real father. I wish it were a different, but it is what it is."

"Doesn't that feel lousy?"

"What can I say? I learned a long time ago not to have feelings about things I can't change."

I began to wonder whether Eric's depression might emanate from feeling left out of the seemingly sealed twosome that his wife and daughter had formed. I considered saying this out loud but didn't think Eric would find it very helpful at this point, so instead I inquired further.

"How do you think Devon feels about you?"

"I think she likes me, but I don't imagine I'm that important to her. She has her mother, and, even if he is an asshole who only sees her every month or so, she has her own father. Donna and I are going to have a baby of our own, and that will be our child. I'll do my best with Devon."

Through exchanges like this, the reason for Eric's resigned unhappiness and festering irritation revealed itself. He *was* upset by how excluded he felt as a husband and a father, and, for reasons not yet clear, he had no idea how to approach this.

Eric and I worked our way into his unhappiness by talking about fights that he and Donna had over seemingly mundane matters. Often these occurred in the evening, when the three of them were home together.

"I'm doing the dishes after dinner," Eric told me, "and I'm just standing at the sink getting furious at her for no reason. She cooked, so I should do the dishes. What's the big deal? Why am I getting so pissed off about it?"

"What's the situation?"

"What do you mean?"

"What are Donna and Devon doing?"

"They're in the living room reading together."

"Well, how does that feel to you?"

"The truth?"

"Of course."

"I feel like their maid. How's that for being a big baby?"

It didn't take many discussions like this for Eric to realize that his anger and frustration could be located, at least as a first layer, in the complicated configurations of his family life. And, as he became more aware, feelings that he had suppressed came more forcefully to the surface. One day, perhaps two months after we began talking, Donna informed Eric that she planned to take Devon to visit her parents.

Before Eric could check himself he found himself yelling, "What the hell is this? Does it even occur to you to run this by me first? The two of you are like a little unit. How am I supposed to fit in here?"

Both Donna and Devon were shocked by the force of Eric's feelings, but, to their credit, both recognized the seriousness of what Eric had said, and they began a discussion. Donna told Eric that she assumed he didn't care that deeply for Devon, and that Devon felt overlooked. Eric, surprised, answered that he imagined that Devon was the one who was uninterested. "Oh no," Donna had answered. "She needs you. She needs a father. It hurts her to feel like you don't care about her."

In a neat and tidy world, this would have been the breakthrough that cleared the air. Eric would have felt more confident and welcomed, and Devon and Donna would have been more inviting. Alas, in the real world this conversation did not bring on such a breakthrough. It did, however, create an opening for the kind of change that occurs through commitment and hard work.

Like all families, Donna, Devon, and Eric lived within an intricately woven fabric of individual fault lines and vulnerabilities. For example, while Donna welcomed the *idea* of Devon and Eric having a closer relationship, she was also protective of her daughter. As I learned, both through Eric and through conversations with Donna's therapist (having, of course, first gotten permission from both Eric and Donna), Donna's father had been a hurtful and critical man, as had been her previous husband, Devon's biological father. Donna had been drawn to Eric for his gentleness and kindness, but she mistrusted him more than she knew, and she had subtle ways of minimizing her sense of danger by shutting him out, and diminishing his presence.

Devon, in turn, hungered for a kind and interested father, but she also had reason to fear the potential hurtfulness of men and fathers, and, as much as she was angry at her biological father, she was also loyal to him.

And Eric brought his own conflicts about being the father of a twelve-year-old girl to the situation.

Eric's father had been a successful academic, far more devoted to his career than to his family. When he was a little boy Eric often ran to his father in the hopes of playing, but his father frequently responded by mocking his need. Eric had felt humiliated and demeaned, and, by the time he was twelve, he had withdrawn into the relative safety of his relationship with his mother, who cared for him, but who also turned to him for what she didn't get from her husband.

Eric, you can imagine, brought to his interactions with Devon and Donna the feeling that fathers were, by nature, distant and unimportant members of the family. He also had a strong belief that he could not fight for what he wanted and needed—he imagined that to do so meant inviting humiliation. Both at home and at work he had assumed a place on the outside looking in. And, because he was sensitive to ridicule, he could be overly touchy and reactive. This was particularly so with Devon, who frequently related to him through what was, at least to my ear, gentle and playful teasing.

Eric needed to become a more involved father and husband. But to do this he needed to struggle with issues that predated his relationship with Donna and Devon, that is, he needed to come to terms with the long-standing fault lines and proclivities that made him overly passive, inhibited, and withdrawn.

We got into these issues primarily through his relationship with his stepdaughter.

Devon was, in many ways, a rather remarkable girl. She was spunky and lively; as I mentioned, one of her primary modes of relating to Eric was to tease him. Eric had often felt this teasing to be ridicule, responding to it with the same hurt he had felt at the hands of his father. The teasing, however, was far more layered. When Devon would say, for example, "Late from work again, huh, Dad? Mom's going to be mad at you. You were a bad boy again," I could hear her taunt, and I could understand why Eric had felt so upset. Devon might well need to be helped to put a lid on the put-down quality of her joking. But I also thought I could hear another note, one that did not feel critical and demeaning. Often during these exchanges Devon would playfully chuck Eric on the shoulder, or she might give him a wink, or she might follow up her ribbing by asking Eric how his day had been. She had a quality of playful relatedness that was rather precocious for a twelve-year-old girl.

I suggested to Eric that he might be underestimating Devon in seeing her as strictly dismissive. I pointed out that the taunts sounded like probes designed to find him, to call him forward. Even if this were not the case, I noted, Devon's teasing warranted a response. If she was simply demeaning him, as he seemed to feel, he probably should call her on it.

Eric and I worked on his passivity. We came to understand that he worried about being an "asshole," like Devon's biological father and like his own father. Better, he thought, to "do no harm" than to be too harsh. As we dug deeper, we also found that Eric feared that Devon's biological father would be angry with him if he assumed a paternal role. He was daunted by the notion of competing with this man. And as we dug even deeper still, we found that Eric had complicated ideas about being the stepfather of a girl. Once he could see that Devon was indeed being playful with him, he feared his wish to play back. "It's almost like something incestuous," he said. "I don't think I'd feel that if she were my own daughter, but it's like there's some barricade that's not there. I know this sounds nuts, I'd never do anything to hurt her, but I feel like I have to be extra careful."

As Eric gradually became more mindful of these underlying anxieties, he began to relax and feel the hunger behind Devon's teasing. With this he became somewhat less rigid. Still, he held back a great deal.

It was Devon, once again, who helped Eric take the next step.

The young girl had been visiting her biological father for the weekend, and she returned home distraught. She first spoke with her mother alone, but then Donna, visibly upset, came out of the girl's bedroom to tell Eric: "She wants to talk to us together." The story unfolded. Devon's father had been his usual critical, cutting self, finding fault with everything from Devon's complexion to her grades. Eventually he had gotten around to Eric, calling him "that wimp stepfather of yours." Devon, perhaps more secure in her relationship with Eric, had leapt to his defense, saying, "He's a good guy, Dad. He's not a bastard like you are." With that her father had slapped her face, and not spoken to her for the rest of the weekend.

Eric was furious at Devon's father, and moved to hear that Devon had defended him as she had. Without thinking he sat down next to the sobbing girl and put his arm around her. She laid her head on his shoulder, and with the feel of her hair against his cheek, he began to cry.

These feelings of compassion and fury galvanized Eric. Over the next week he called Devon's father, warning him that he and Donna would seek a shift in custody if he ever hit Devon again. He became concerned about Devon around these visits, and his concern carried over into their overall relationship. He found himself, somewhat to his surprise, becoming interested in Devon, in her grades, in her friends. One day a few months after the slapping incident he told me that Devon had said of his increased interest: "God, you're being such a dad." But, as Eric noted warmly, "I think she said it with a smile on her face."

After about a year of our talking together Donna became pregnant, and Eric, who by now felt a great deal better, stopped meeting with me. I suspect he still struggles with the same challenges, but I also suspect that he has found a great deal more room to be a father. In one of our final sessions he noted, "Devon gave me a gift. It's one I should have taken for myself, but frankly, I have a hard time taking what I need for myself."

"If you hadn't stepped forward some yourself, she couldn't have given it to you," I answered.

"Yeah, but you know as well as I do that I couldn't have done it without her. I hope I can keep doing better with her, and I hope I can do better with my own child. It's not like a guy should need an engraved invitation just to be a kid's father."

Adoptive Fathers, Stepfathers, and
Paternal Legitimacy

In this story, Eric found his way to a sense of paternal legitimacy with Devon, both against the backdrop of his own individual conflicts and uncertainties (a task that every father faces), as well as within the special circumstances of fathering a child not born of his own genes.

The matter of fathering children who are not biologically one's own is a huge (and growing) issue these days. With one third of all children born out of wedlock and half of all marriages ending in divorce, with rearranged family structures as much the norm as not, with adoption an increasingly important aspect of family life, and with amazing advances in fertility technology, there is a rapidly shifting mind-set around our assumptions about origin. Where once the only real question about paternity had to do with another kind of "legitimacy," now fatherhood (and for that matter parenthood in general) is a fluid and negotiable concept. Certainly these issues of non-biological parenting and fathering are worth exploring in and of themselves. However, my focus will be on the subject of how these issues shed light on the overarching notion of paternal legitimacy.

To begin with, stepfathers and adoptive fathers have to deal with the disconnect that exists between their genes and their children. They must somehow foster the growth of the psychic connective tissue that biology naturally breeds. Eric can be heard struggling with this dilemma when he said: "Donna and I are going to have a baby of our own, and that will be our child. I'll do my best with Devon." As I came to learn, it wasn't that Eric didn't care about Devon. It wasn't that he didn't want to be a good father to her. He feared that he wouldn't succeed, and he retreated from the task before even starting.

Certainly the trauma of loss and disconnection for children who do not know their biological fathers, or whose biological fathers have been displaced, is a weighty matter, and it can affect capacities to trust and to connect. Likewise the task of feeling fatherly toward a child born of different genes is a complicated business. As one woman, the mother of both a biological and an adopted child, said to me, "Gerry [their adopted child] doesn't have that quirky obsessive gene that Regina [their biological child] does. It's kind of weird, because she is somehow so familiar. But we don't love him any less, we don't feel any less attached, it's just different."

"We don't feel any less attached." These are important words. The business of fostering attachment is, in certain ways, not as daunting a task as some imagine. For one thing, mothers and fathers bring their own urge and will to connect. As one adoptive mother, a woman who thought deeply, and cared passionately, said to me, "I never felt worried about being able to love my daughter, to connect with her. I know people assume that this is an issue for adoptive parents, but I never did, and frankly, most of the adoptive parents I talk to never have either." Add to this the fact that mothers have preexisting notions, templates as it were, for how they want their husbands to father (as both Jennifer and Donna demonstrate), that fathers likewise have templates for how they want, and expect, mothers to mother, and that both urge and encourage each other to engage, and it becomes clear that familial and parental relationships occur in highly interactive, highly connecting systems that facilitate and encourage attachment.

What's more, stepfathers and adoptive fathers get help from an unexpected place. Consider Devon's relationship with Eric. The young girl worked very hard, and very creatively, to recruit Eric to be a good father. In her teasing she was trying to get him emotionally and viscerally aroused, to elicit some aggression, to wake him up from his passivity and withdrawal. Sure, her biological father's cruelty was part of her history, and sure, like most of us, she sought out what was familiar, which meant that her teasing could easily have elicited sadism from Eric. But mostly she wanted Eric's caring and interest, not his cruelty, and when Eric gave this to her he passed her test, and he and Devon were able to form the bond of a father-daughter relationship. Things even got to the point where Eric felt a degree of paternal proprietorship, so much so that Devon could say, "God, you're being such a dad."

It is true, as Eric noted, that a father shouldn't need an engraved invitation to be a father. But, in a sense, he gets one anyway.

Such paternal connection is obviously crucial to all father-child relationships—it serves as the underlying glue that makes all else possible and meaningful. Indeed, such connections need to be strong, even, to use the word of a few lines previous, to the point of "proprietorship." This may sound jarring—to most of us the idea of "owning" one's children has a pejorative connotation. Indeed, there is truth to the notion that kids should be free, that we parents need to let them be themselves. But this truth, like so many, is a partial one. Children are not simply granted their independence by us; they must also earn it. They form a sense of their own selfhood by breaking free of parental connection, even, as I say, from underlying assumptions of proprietorship. Through such relatively forceful, even in some ways unilateral, declarations of individuality they gain more access to, and comfort with, their aggression, and hence more strength and solidity, thus coming to own themselves in a way that they never could were the freedom granted without the struggle.

So connection matters. It matters to kids, and likewise, being "in it," being attached, is also essential to being a good father. But is such connection, however necessary, sufficient? Does a father assume a position of "legitimacy" simply because he is loving and involved? No. More is required. In all parent-child relationships, both biological and nonbiological, if a father is to feel a sense of paternal place, of legitimacy, he must be present, palpable, and immediate, and he must relate in a way that is mature, responsible, and paternal. And to do this a man must be willing to come to terms with himself, including his history, his conflicts, his sexuality, his aggression, and more.

In this regard, the landscape of adoptive fathering and stepfathering can, at times, present some specific obstacles. Here are a few admittedly selective examples.

There are, invariably, certain powers and advantages that accrue to parents as a result of biological relatedness. It is, therefore, no easy matter for stepfathers to contend with the presence of displaced, and often angry, biological fathers for the privileges, rights, and responsibilities of fathering. Similarly, adoptive fathers must come to terms with the ever-present specter of an absent and often unknown father. Of course all men confront the long shadow thrown by another man—their own father—in becoming men and fathers in their own right. Stepfathers and adoptive fathers, however, have the added complication of having such a presence, or absence, standing nearby at all times as they discipline, organize, love, and otherwise shape their stepchildren's or adoptive children's experience.

Eric's struggle with rivalry and competitiveness is a case in point. Eric was painfully jealous of Devon's biological father. Indeed, in the early years of our work he spoke of how every time he saw Devon he pictured Donna and her former husband having sex. Plagued by these images, he would reflexively retreat from his stepdaughter in order to get the lovemaking out of his head. He would feel like a small boy when he imagined himself in relation to Devon's biological father, much as he had felt with his own father. He found his way to feeling more like a father only when he was able to confront this father figure, to fight for Devon, to use his anger and aggression in the service of being paternal. The ruminative jealousy, incidentally, ended with the confrontation.

And then, to continue this admittedly cursory review, there is the omnipresent matter of guilt and pain.

A child who has suffered through a divorce, or an adoption, is often burdened with more than his or her share of pain. Sensitive parents are, of course, aware of this pain. It can be hard not to feel a sense of overprotectiveness, of overresponsibility, when a child is hurting. Such concern is, of course, a lovely paternal impulse, but it can also be a complicated one when it comes to those aspects of using one's aggression in the service of fathering—to discipline, to insist on better performance, and the like. As one adoptive father said to me, "I can't raise my voice toward him [his adopted twelve-year-old]. He's already been through enough. I'm like putty in his hands." Our work involved his coming to terms with his own guilt such that he could emerge not only as a loving father, which he was, but also as a structuring, organizing, and disciplining father, which he also needed to be.

These complex configurations regarding guilt, rivalry, protection, and aggression will, of course, play out in different ways for each man, depending on his biology, his psychology, and his history. Again, there are no universal prescriptions; each man must negotiate his own individual circumstances in his own way if he is to become a good father. But there is a deeper and more important principle at play here. As the struggles of adoptive fathers and stepfathers show, legitimacy is not a biologically based right; it is, for all fathers, a privilege earned by the hard work of learning about oneself and about those one loves.

Tools of the Trade

Fathers start off with a free pass; children don't tend to ask "so who put you in charge?" (at least not until adolescence). Initially our children's recognition and respect grow from an unearned endowment. But in the long run, if a father is to maintain his legitimacy, he must solidify the mantle that biology first bestows. How does a father do this?

Just as a surgeon will hold the respect of his or her operating room staff only if he or she possesses real medical skills, as will an athlete on the playing field, and a pilot in the cockpit, so also must a father garner and care for the tools of his trade.

But what are those tools?

One can attempt to list what makes a good father. Included in the mix would be love, industry, self-sacrifice, stability, generosity, creativity, protectiveness, trustworthiness, and concern. So also would be a capacity for purposeful forcefulness, the kind that comes from being able to harness one's masculine aggression and competitiveness. Vision and a sense of the future would be important. The capacity to live in real time, as you will later see, is a huge yet quiet piece of the paternal puzzle. But these and still many more attributes, while hard to argue with, are not the whole answer. The truth is, the job description "father" (like the job descriptions "mother" and "parent") calls for such a remarkably wide-ranging set of abilities that there's no point in trying to make a list; it would be too long, varied, and fluid.

Perhaps the best way to bring this exploration of paternal "legitimacy" to a close is not to attempt to answer what may be ultimately an unanswerable question, but to relate a story told me by the father of three young children, whose oldest son, Eddie, suffered from asthma.

"I was dropping Eddie, he's twelve now, off at summer camp. It's his first time at this camp. We got there, everybody's milling around, I put his stuff in the bunk, and we walked down to the lake. There was a swim test going on. Eddie starts to swim laps, but he's laboring, and I can tell he's having an asthma attack, maybe because of anxiety or the really cold water. We walk back to the cabin, get him a shot of albuterol, which usually helps, but he's shaken by what happened, and I'm thinking, 'How do I put this kid back together because I'm leaving in an hour, and it's a 250-mile drive home?' I see the basketball court. He's good at basketball—and he knows it. We go over to play some one-on-one. We're doing okay, but even though he's breathing fine now he still seems a bit shaky, so I decide to bump him. He bumps back. Soon we're bumping each other, having a great time. I can tell he's fine, I'm reassured, but I don't say anything. That might be counterproductive, actually. The game ends, and Eddie says 'Okay, Dad, you can go now.' I walked to the car, looked back, and he gave me this confident wave. I feel confident he's okay, I convey it to him, he feels confident too."

Good mothers, without a doubt, know their children very well. In fact there is a standing joke about how we men and fathers come in a distant second when it comes to such knowledge. But, as the preceding story illustrates, there are ways that good fathers also know their children, ways that by virtue of our being men are different from those of mothers. This knowledge, which also involves self-knowledge, and knowledge of the comfort zones and precipices of the father-child relationship, is the means by which we fathers help and shape our children. It is our most important paternal tool, and, I daresay, the bedrock basis of our paternal legitimacy.

6

Keeping Things Safe

———

PATERNAL AUTHORITY is among the easiest forms of authority to abuse. The danger is one that most well-meaning parents are well aware of; indeed, I have found the major reason many fathers shy away from using their authority is that they fear being hurtful to their children. "Do no harm" is their motto, and it's a reasonable one.

Yet such reticence can be a mistake, a means of achieving safety at too great a cost. Because the fact is that by using our strength and our paternal position, we fathers give our children a weight with which they can collide. Our authority anchors them while they learn how to set their own course. It prepares them to contend, on their own terms, with life's all too often intractable realities.

But if we are to give our children this gift of authority, we must be willing to repeatedly and unflinchingly take on a critical and as yet unmentioned responsibility, one I'll introduce by asking a question that flows from the story of Jeffrey Stanton: When a father angrily pushes his son onto a couch, looks him in the eye, and says, "I am your father. Don't you ever, ever talk to me like that again," is he being abusive? While each reader might well answer this question differently, depending on his or her beliefs and biases, one thing is clear: If a man is to be an authoritative father, he must make absolutely certain that he is also a safe father.

Baseball

On the day that my older son and I first played baseball, the early spring sun warmed the still cool air. As we walked to the field I was eager—too eager, it turned out. He was five, two years older than he was on that spring day when I had wandered aimlessly after him, and he was unsuspecting. How could he know that the weight of his father's fatherlessness was about to come crashing down on him yet again?

My son Miles is very creative. He wasn't exactly opposed to the idea that a baseball bat was meant to hit a baseball. He had, however, a highly developed appreciation of the many possible ways in which it could be used. So we had to get through a series of ideas—a gun, a plane, and a few others that I couldn't even begin to fathom in my pathologically hyperfocused state—before we had ourselves precariously arranged: he standing next to a makeshift plate, bat in hand, me some thirty feet away, ball in hand.

I lobbed the ball underhand (a real baseball, if you can believe it), trying with all my might to will it to hit his bat. Miles tried, as he tries very hard at everything he does, but his hands and eyes were still a few years away from working well together. He wasn't ready for what I had in mind. Of course that shouldn't have mattered. We could have had a great time, if I had been free to play.

But I wasn't free to play. What we were doing mattered too much to me, and for the wrong reasons. Instead of letting my son's mind go where it wanted to go, I insisted that he shut out the wonder that was around him. I told him to focus on the ball. He tried—he wanted to do it for me—but his mind was somewhere else.

Anyone walking by at this moment of our first baseball game would have seen an irritated asshole father, pushing his not-so-ready son to do something that he was not so interested in doing. Actually, "pushing" is too generous. I was guilty of saying such things as "Miles, look at the goddam ball," "Where exactly is your mind today?" and, "It's really not that hard." And this doesn't even begin to convey my tone—critical, impatient, dismissive. I had entered a paternal danger zone.

Of course, beneath this surface there was much more. What was there doesn't excuse how I was, but it does, to some degree, explain my intolerance and impatience. I had, back from the time when my son was only an idea, painted a picture in my mind of how this moment would go. It was, however, a moment of my own pure construction, unshaped by the tempering reality of another being, and, having germinated for so long in my private mind, my fantasy was basically not malleable. There was no room in my script for my son's actual self, and so I was, amazingly enough, intolerant of the very person whom I had so long, and so eagerly, awaited.

I am enormously fortunate in the son that I have. From an early age Miles has had a good sense of who he is. He knows when things are working for him, and he knows when they are not. I have wondered whether he has had to develop this strong sense of himself precisely because he has had to resist being conscripted into the pictures I have constructed for him. Whatever the reason, he knows how to say no, and he said no here. After only a few minutes of baseball he asked me if we could go home. I wanted to keep at it, but I could see what I was doing to him. Unchecked by my wife's thoughtful governance, and having momentarily lost my sense of him as his own person, I had oppressed him with the weight of my own unfulfilled need.

And so we went home. It would be six years before we got back to baseball.

Larry Miller

A father, even a well-meaning father, can do a great deal of damage in the name of authority and discipline. The story of Larry Miller shows just how easy it can be to step over the line that demarcates paternal authority and paternalistic authoritarianism.

Larry, a wiry, middle-aged man with dark, piercing eyes, came to see me with Jessica, his wife, on her insistence. She thought that Larry was too harsh with their only child, a nine-year-old boy named Charlie. Larry disagreed. Staring intently at me, seemingly from a self located well behind those eyes, he told me that his responses were "nothing to worry about." His opinion was that Jessica was overprotective. "Charlie needs limits," he said. "I think the problem is that you're too soft."

At first, it seemed to me that Larry and Jessica Miller's concerns might mirror those of Bill and Mary Jenson. After a few sessions, however, it became clear that any resemblance between Bill and Larry was but a superficial one. Bill's anger could, at times, get out of hand. But he was curious about how he responded, and, while he could be defensive, he also worried about whether he could be "too much." He tried hard to stay in contact with his children. I didn't always agree with Bill, but I trusted him. Larry, on the other hand, threatened and bullied Charlie. His anger seemed cutting and belittling, and he was not in touch with the effect it had on his son. Neither did he seem to be curious about himself, or interested in changing. I confess that early on Larry scared *me*.

Jessica took the lead during our first few meetings. This was hard for her—she clearly did not feel comfortable criticizing her husband—but she had grown worried about Charlie, who was developing the reputation of being something of a bully himself. "I respect your right to discipline him," she said. "And Lord knows he needs it. But when you say stuff like 'Pick that up right now or you'll be sorry,' and you say it in that angry tone, I think it scares him more than it helps him. And I don't feel comfortable with the way you spank him. I don't think I'm necessarily against spanking—my father spanked me—but he always seemed in control when he did it. When you spank Charlie I don't think that you're totally in control of yourself."

I expected Larry to respond angrily and defensively, but his reaction made me even more uncomfortable. "You have a right to your opinion," he said, coldly and contemptuously, "but I disagree."

Jessica looked as uneasy as I felt. "What are you thinking?" I asked her.

"Worried," she said. "I know he's mad at me. But he won't tell me until we leave here."

It crossed my mind that Jessica might be in danger. "Do you feel safe with him?" I asked.

"He's never hit me, if that's what you mean," she answered. "I trust him about that. It's how cold and angry he can get that scares me."

Over these first few sessions, meeting with both Larry and Jessica, I came to believe that Larry did indeed have a serious problem with his fathering. He seemed to use his aggression defensively, as if it were covering fire for his insecurities. When he spoke of saying to Charlie "I'm your father," I had the sense that he felt deeply unsure of himself, and that he needed to dominate the boy in order to puff himself up. And when Jessica described how Larry would say "What's the matter with you?" and "Are you a complete idiot?" I didn't feel he was just "getting Charlie's attention," as he put it. He was contemptuous and scathing, and he seemed to be buoyed, even excited, by the power he held over his son.

As I saw it, the problem in the family lay asymmetrically with Larry. What was more, I couldn't seem to help him open up with me. I proposed that he and I meet alone for a while to talk about his fathering.

To my surprise, he readily agreed. Even more to my surprise, he showed, in these subsequent individual meetings, a more accessible side. While Larry was not yet prepared to agree that he had a problem with his anger, and with the way that he disciplined, he had a genuine concern for his son that had not come through in the presence of his wife. "I feel like I *have* to come down hard on him," he said. "It worries me that he is becoming such an angry guy. I know where that can lead."

"What do you know about angry guys?" I asked.

"My father," Larry answered. "Today people would probably call him abusive, though people didn't talk that way back then. He whipped me and my sisters pretty regularly with his belt, and there were a bunch of times when I saw him slap my mother. When he died, I don't think there was a single person at his funeral who didn't hate him—myself included. Jessica thinks that I'm too hard on the boy. I don't think she understands—I'll do whatever it takes to make sure that Charlie doesn't end up like my father."

I sensed that this was not the time to tell Larry that he was, without consciously intending to, doing everything he could to make sure that Charlie *did* end up like his father. I also thought it unwise to point out that he was using methods much more like those of his own abusive father than he realized. I didn't think that he would be able to hear me. But learning about Larry's father helped me feel more kindly toward him; he had grown up in a tough situation, and I could better understand how he had come to cover up his insecurities with swagger and bluster. I was also pleased to learn that Larry cared about Charlie, and that we had the common goal of helping him to better help his son.

Safety

"All over the world and throughout history, by far the vast majority of violent acts have been committed by young males." So writes social psychologist Roy Baumeister in his book *Evil: Inside Human Violence and Cruelty*. In other words, the same robust gender-based differences that characterize studies of aggression are also found in studies of violence. We men are not only the more aggressive sex; we are also—no surprise—the far more violent sex.

Interestingly, many authors have noted an intriguing anomaly when it comes to child abuse. "Boys are more likely to be physically abused by a parent," family therapist and author Michael Gurian writes in *The Wonder of Boys: What Parents, Mentors, and Educators Can Do to Shape Boys into Exceptional Men*. And, he continues, "the parent most likely to physically abuse a boy is a mother." But as

Gurian and others recognize, the statistics supporting this latter statement may mislead. As historian Robert Griswold notes, and as feminists also point out, the findings are probably the result of fathers
spending fewer hours with their offspring than mothers.

The question of whether mothers, or fathers, are more inclined to
act abusively toward their children is an important and interesting
one, and that the data are somewhat less straightforward than one
might expect is worth observing here. Certainly (as will be noted in
chapter 9) women are capable of aggression and violence. But for now,
keeping the focus on fathers and authority, let me underline a single,
salient, and unassailable fact. Men, and fathers, are quite capable of
violence, and some would argue, inclined toward it. Furthermore, I
am contending that a father's authority relies on aspects of masculine,
human nature that are intimately connected with violence: aggression, power, and hierarchy. Indeed, I am adopting a normative stance
on these issues, in that I am not only saying that this is how it is, I am
saying that this is how it should be. Accordingly, I am led to an
inescapable caveat: Any model of fatherhood, and of a father's authority, *must safeguard* against destructive expressions of masculine power
and aggression—not only physical and sexual abuse, but also hitting,
bullying, belittling, scaring, controlling, and so on.

As the father of the bride puts it in Mira Nair's film *Monsoon Wedding,* "It is a father's job to protect his children, even from himself."

Authority and Authoritarianism

Perhaps the most revealing illustration of the core difference between
destructive and constructive expressions of paternal aggression can be
seen in the distinction between authority and authoritarianism.

When Larry said to his son, Charlie, "Pick that up right now or
you'll be sorry," his stance was an aggressive and powerful one. When
he said, "I'm your father," he was calling on the leverage accorded to
him by his hierarchical position as father. Aggression and a position

of hierarchical power—it would appear that Larry's responses, like Bill Jenson's and Jeffrey Stanton's, met the two conditions set forth thus far as essential to authority. But should we consider Larry's position a genuinely authoritative one, as we did the other two men?

No. Parents possess hierarchically endowed power over their children, governmental leaders are accorded power over their citizenry, bosses over their employees, and so on. But power is not synonymous with authority. Abusive parents, despotic leaders, and thoughtless, incompetent bosses all exert power and position (as do baseball-obsessed fathers who conscript their sons into their own narcissistic fantasies). But none of these people are being authoritative. They are being authoritarian.

What's the difference?

Psychoanalyst Otto Kernberg answers this question clearly and succinctly: "Authority," he writes, "refers to the adequate application of power to the task, and in the social realm, to the adequate and legitimate exercise of power in order to carry out a socially desirable task. Authoritarianism, in contrast, refers to the exercise of power beyond that required to carry out the task, and, in the social realm, the illegitimate use of power beyond what is justified by the socially sanctioned task."

Simply put, when a father uses the right amount of power for the right reasons, he is being authoritative. When a father uses too much power for the wrong reasons, he is being authoritarian. It's a critical distinction for fathers, one worth keeping in mind throughout this exploration. As Stanford psychologist William Damon observes, authoritative parents have been shown to "lead the child towards genuine competence and responsibility," whereas the children of authoritarian and permissive parents alike tend to "behave well only as long as the adult is looking."

This leads us to the next question: What ensures that a father will use the right amount of power, and that he will use it for the right reasons? That he will act from a legitimate, rather than an arbitrary, position of authority?

"Not Bad, Doc"

Larry was surprisingly willing to talk with me about his fathering. He never missed his appointments, and he talked honestly and openly about what he did and said. He told me about spanking Charlie angrily a couple of times soon after we began, and he seemed to listen when I told him that I was concerned about the degree to which the anger he expressed during these spankings was not modulated. He talked to me about the harsh and hurtful things he said to his son, and again he seemed interested when I told him that I thought he was too cutting. Ultimately he would disagree with me, and he didn't yet seem inclined to change. Nor did he seem particularly curious about his internal landscape. Still, I thought it a positive sign that he talked to me openly and honestly.

Though I didn't really understand what was holding our relationship together, things seemed solid between us. I decided to confront Larry more aggressively.

One day, Larry told me about how Charlie had gotten in trouble at school for pushing a classmate. "I really let him have it," he said. "I yelled, 'If you don't stop being such a goddammed jerk, I'll give you a taste of your own medicine.'"

"Consequences and limits are good," I responded, my exaggerated calm covering for my rising worry and irritation. "But, as you know, I don't think calling him a jerk, or threatening him, is so helpful."

"I think that's liberal bullshit," Larry answered.

Beginning to feel that Larry was provoking me, I answered, with a noticeable edge in my voice, "I'm not so sure, when you talk to him like that, that you're necessarily coming from a position of strength. Besides, you model for him the very thing that you want to change."

"You experts all have the same ideas," Larry spat back, with a disdainful wave of his hand.

Now sure that I was being provoked, I responded with more full-throated anger: "Look. I'm not just some knee-jerk, hug-your-kids-and-everything-will-be-okay guy. You've got to hear me here. I talk all the time with kids whose fathers talk to them like you're talking to Charlie. I see what it costs those kids. You talk about your father having been abusive, but I'm telling you that there are times when *you* are abusive. You've got to learn to regulate it better."

Larry surprised me once again. A smile, more engaging than nasty, played at the corner of his lips. "Not bad, Doc," he said.

I tried to talk to Larry about the meaning of his "not bad, Doc." He didn't have much to say, but I didn't really need him to spell it out for me. It was finally dawning on me that Larry and I were finding our way into something important. By making me mad he was, in essence, provoking me into disciplining him. Would I respond critically and abusively, or would I channel the feelings he provoked into appropriately disciplinary responses? Would I act like him, and like his father before him, or would I act like a father should?

All this was, of course, my own private supposition. When I raised my ideas with Larry he would smile and say, "Ever the shrink, huh, Doc?" But by now I was less worried about his apparent lack of insight; the unusual way that he was using me seemed to be a productive one. What was more, I had begun to notice slight changes. There were occasions when his tone sounded a bit less pressured, and he seemed to have less to prove. His threats were milder ("Charlie, do as I say, or there'll be trouble"). He sometimes said things that were slightly less critical ("Jesus, Charlie, I've told you a thousand times"), and he occasionally seemed aware of Charlie's feelings.

Larry had not yet come to an earned understanding of the origins and meaning of his anger. He didn't really recognize how much he bullied to cover up his own sense of smallness and inadequacy, nor did he see how he was repeating aspects of his relationship with his own father in his relationship with his son. Nevertheless, by soliciting my responses to the way he fathered, he had started to change.

External Systems of Checks and Balances

Gary Palmer, Bill Jenson, and Jeffrey Stanton all found their way to more authoritative stances. Larry Miller, it seemed, was headed in the right direction.

Each of these men's stances was constructed, in no small part, from healthy doses of aggression and hierarchical relating. But each man's ability to use the right amount of power for the right reasons, was also constructed of much more. For one thing, each man operated within a system of external checks and balances.

Gary responded to my encouragement, as well as to that of his wife, and so brought more of himself to his relationship with Jason.

Bill and Mary parented within the family structure that they had created. Time and time again, Mary found a way to say to Bill, "You're being too harsh. You've got to soften it, to modulate it, or he won't hear you."

When Jeffrey, in a flash of anger, pushed his son onto the couch, and then spoke so sharply, he immediately turned to me for my reaction. Had he gone too far?

And when Larry responded, albeit reluctantly, to his wife's insistence that he seek help for his fathering, he brought his anger, his aggression, and his experience of fathering and being fathered into an interactive arena with me. Seemingly without meaning to, he elicited my help in a very effective way. He provoked my aggression, and in doing so generated a badly needed counterresponse to his own abusive inclinations. When I responded in a constructive and disciplining way, rather than a destructive and critical way, I contained Larry with my authority, while simultaneously giving him a model for how to better use his paternal aggression.

Given how destructive things can, and do, become in families, Larry and I were working in a relatively mild danger zone. While I worried about the effect of Larry's poorly controlled aggression on his son, I sensed that talking things through was a sufficient intervention. In the course of my work, however, I have all too often come across far more extreme examples of the need for these kinds of external checks and balances. Sam Burke's story is unfortunately a common one.

Sam had been committed against his will to the hospital in which I worked. He had crashed his car while drinking and driving, and, in addition to being in legal trouble for this, his third DUI, he had threatened to kill the policeman who arrested him. Within a few hours he sobered up, and his homicidal threats became suicidal ones. At this point he was taken first to a psychiatric emergency service, and then to my hospital.

I found Sam to be an instantly dislikable character. He met me with sneering dismissal, called me "money-grubber," and accused me of hiding my greed behind my "do-gooder profession." He denied having any problems and refused to talk with me about anything other than leaving the hospital. During our first meeting he told me repeatedly that if I didn't get my "ass in gear" and get him "unincarcerated" I'd hear from his lawyer. Barely containing my annoyance, I told Sam, "Nothing doing," that there were things that I needed to sort out before I could discharge him. (I met Sam several years ago, when it was easier to hold someone in an inpatient setting, and so I had leverage of the sort that I would not have today.)

Over the course of the next two weeks, Sam mostly threatened me, insulted me, and refused to talk with me. Fortunately I had other ways of figuring out what was going on: When it became clear that I wasn't going to get anywhere with Sam alone I began to include his wife, Jane, in our meetings. While Sam glared silently at me throughout these sessions, Jane, while largely silent herself, communicated volumes. She seemed frightened, like she wanted to say something but could not.

So I met with Jane alone. Freed from Sam's oppressive presence, she talked more openly. She and Sam had two children, sons aged thirteen and nine, and, she told me, shaking with anxiety, they were frightened of their father's drinking. I pressed. Jane didn't want to get Sam "in trouble." Now was the time to talk, I noted. With Sam in the hospital we could offer her some protection. Did he ever hit her? Sometimes, she allowed, but only when he was drunk. How often was he drunk? Well, quite a lot.

Sam was, to put it bluntly, an abusive drunk.

It was now clear that Sam's cussing and obstructing related, at least in part, to his no longer secret abuse. I suspected that beneath his sneering demeanor he felt a great deal of guilt and shame, and I hoped to appeal to his better side.

But—no surprise—when I told Sam what I had learned from Jane, he still threatened, yelled, and screamed like a cornered animal. No way was some "pussy-assed do-gooder social worker going to stick his nose in my family," he spat. For another week, still committed to the hospital, he fought my insistence that he confront his problem with alcohol and violence.

By now, however, I had another bargaining chip. I arranged for Sam's wife to get a great deal of support with an excellent social worker at the hospital, and Jane held her ground with Sam, refusing to allow him to come home unless he agreed to enter counseling, join AA, quit drinking, and participate in a program for violent husbands and fathers. I also reported Sam to the Department of Social Services, and they agreed to monitor the situation. Still Sam kicked and screamed—often I would arrive at work to find that he had left a slew of abusive and threatening messages on my voice mail—but everyone held firm, and Sam was discharged to a halfway house. After three months of his remaining sober, vowing to stop the abuse, and agreeing to continue his treatment, Jane allowed him to return home.

Truth be told, Sam's life remained quite miserable after this. He talked with me every six months or so, even though I was not officially his therapist (he had begun treatment with someone from the halfway house, and he continued that counseling off and on for many years). Occasionally Sam would meet with me in person, but more often we would talk for fifteen minutes or so on the phone. Sometimes he would ask for a referral, perhaps to a primary care physician, perhaps to a psychopharmacologist. Largely he called to complain about how miserable his life felt, often stating that he would be better off dead. But just when I would begin to wonder why in heaven's name this man was calling me, and whether I needed to act in order to ensure his safety, Sam would allow: "Well, at least I stopped drinking and beating up my family. If I did one good thing in my life, it's that."

Sam's case may seem extreme to some, but the truth is that much that is dark can happen in the absence of an empowered observer who is willing and able to bear witness and wield judgment. The very privacy that promotes the healthy intimacy of family life can also serve as a dangerous vortex: When privacy becomes secrecy, there is a temptation to regress, to replay old conflicts and feelings in ways that would never occur in public. These are the times when aggression and sexuality are most likely to be discharged into and upon vulnerable family members who may, for their own reasons, feel driven to receive and forgive.

Fathers, therefore, must *always* operate within a familial and cultural set of checks and balances. To this end, wives, friends, social norms, and even governmental agencies constitute an observing and regulating matrix within which a father evaluates, and is evaluated for, his authoritative behavior. No man is above needing these kinds of regulation and governance.

"Christ, Dad, Don't I Do Anything Right?"

So is this all there is to keeping authority safe? Just locate yourself within a reliable system of external checks and balances, and then let your power and authority rip? Obviously more than this is required. Persons in positions of authority must also be *personally* aware of and responsible for their own expressions of power. They must, in other words, govern and police themselves. Let's return for a final time to Larry's efforts to be a better father.

Larry began to acknowledge that there might be value in the new way he was doing things. "I think that Charlie's settling down some," he said. "I feel like he feels easier with me, and I feel easier with him. It's not always such a battle."

I was glad to hear that things felt better, but I was cautious in my optimism. Though Larry was *doing* things differently, he had very little understanding of where his anger and sadism came from. His improved fathering was more a product of my serving as an external, regulating influence than it was the result of change within his own paternal mind-set.

At one point, Larry suggested that we occasionally include his wife in our talks. He felt that he was behaving more in line with what she wanted, and he had some complaints of his own that he wanted to talk about. These joint meetings were themselves an interesting part of our work, but I will use the simple fact of his wish that we all meet together as a jumping-off point for what then developed.

I had, from the very beginning, wondered why it had been easier for Larry to talk with me when his wife was absent. I now raised this with him. Larry thought for a while, then said, "It's one thing when you give me a hard time when we're alone. I can take that, man to man. But when Jessica is here, I don't know, it's like I shouldn't let you be on top of me in front of her."

I wondered about Larry's interesting wording: "let you be on top of me." Larry thought for a while, and eventually said, "You know, I just realized, my father used to slap me around in front of my mother. I don't know if this has anything to do with it, but it's what I thought of."

Larry could be a thoughtful man, but he was not exactly enthralled by the process of introspection: He preferred to be pragmatic, to keep things on the surface. Now, as was typical of him, he responded to my queries about having been "slapped around" by asking, "Why do you shrinks make such a big deal out of everything?" He characteristically slammed shut the very door that he had momentarily opened. Still, I thought that something important had been said. It dawned on me that Larry had known that he needed help, that such help would require confrontation, and that he would have felt humiliated had this occurred in front of his wife. It would have reminded him of how his father had humiliated him in front of his mother.

I was certain that Larry still had deep feelings about his father's hurtfulness toward him, and that these were part of his troubles with Charlie. I pushed. Over a period of several months, we had numerous exchanges that went something like the following.

Discussing one of Larry's critical comments toward Charlie, I said, "So how do you think that felt to him?"

"It probably bothered him," Larry answered. "But it's supposed to, isn't it?" His tone had a slightly mocking quality to it, somehow off-putting and inviting at the same time.

"Do you think it bothered him a lot?"

"I doubt it."

"I wonder why you doubt it. Do you remember what it was like to be a kid with your father?"

"Look, my father was an asshole," Larry said, momentarily coming out from behind his eyes to stare at me with a burning intensity. Then, looking away again, he said, "That's all there is to it. But I was pretty tough. I could take it."

"You're not really answering me directly. Do you remember yourself as a little boy?"

"Not really."

"So how do you know you could take it?"

"I guess I'm just that kind of guy."

Larry's provocative tone had again entered the picture. My read, by now, was that he secretly hoped that I wouldn't let him avoid the question.

"Maybe you were tough," I told him, "but I think it's more complicated. I think it's hard to remember how your father went off on you like he did because you weren't always so tough. I think you eventually toughened yourself to survive, but there was a time when you felt really hurt by him."

Time and time again, Larry and I went back and forth like this. I grew to respect Larry's toughness; just as he had "taken it" from his father, now he was "taking it" from me. I only hoped that my criticism was more constructive. I also came to understand that Larry's toughness caused him real problems as a father. The main reason he couldn't empathize with Charlie's sensitivity and hurt was that he had become so hardened against *his* own boyhood vulnerability.

One day, after several months of these sparring exchanges, Larry came in uncharacteristically upset.

"When I picked Charlie up at school I overheard him putting down this other kid he knows. When he got in the car, I called him on it. I said, 'So what makes you think you're such hot shit?' He started to cry. Then he said, 'Christ, Dad, don't I ever do anything right?' I thought I'd just been kicked in the stomach. That's what I used to think with my father, though I never had the guts to say it."

This proved to be a most useful kick in the stomach. I didn't have to point out to Larry that these words showed that his father's criticism had indeed hurt: His son's words had already made him realize that. He began to acknowledge his own vulnerability, and, as he did, he could begin to see how much his anger, and criticism, hurt his son.

Larry and I worked together for many years—in fact, after nine years together, we still met perhaps once a month. I came to know his solution quite well: It was one that had been forged out of real hardship, and so was itself brittle and imperfect. Larry remained, on occasion, cutting and hurtful. He rarely spanked (by the time Charlie was thirteen he had stopped completely), but, when he did, I still worried about his self-control. His self-esteem, while improved, remained unsteady. Above all, the echoes of his father's anger and cruelty still resounded in his mind, and he all too often memorialized the man he claimed to only hate by acting quite a bit like him.

Still, Larry did change. He continued to need my real presence to help him keep an eye on his anger and his aggression, but through our relationship, and his own commitment, he developed a better understanding of the effect of his aggression—of his weight—on his son. He developed a serviceable sense of paternal authority.

Internal Safeguards

Each of the men I have described succeeded, by virtue of hard work, at becoming a better father. But, it should be noted, each man's "better" was still flawed. It's to be expected. All of us return to old and problematic solutions far more often than we'd like to admit. The bad news is that most of us, at best, change but a little. The good news, however, is that when it comes to one's character, a little change can go a long way.

When it came to the limits of Larry's capacity to change, I was, as you can probably tell, not entirely comfortable with the responsibility of continuing to police him. The best outcome would have been for him to learn to temper his aggression with other, stronger aspects of his own character.

But, as I've noted, his traumatic childhood had left him hardened both to himself and to his son. This remained a vulnerability in both Larry's overall character, as well as in his capacity for authoritative fathering.

Larry's flawed but worthwhile struggle leads us to articulate yet another essential component of paternal authority. While an *external* system of checks and balances is needed to keep authority from devolving into authoritarianism and abuse, a father's authority must also, absolutely and unequivocally, include in its bedrock composition personal capacities that modulate and channel his power and aggression.

These capacities can be seen in three dimensions.

First, those in authority must possess empathy, concern, sensitivity, and thoughtfulness. (How these qualities are developed is, of course, a hugely important matter—really a topic for another book. Here let me say again that revisiting one's own history, and understanding the vulnerabilities of the past, can help foster them.)

Second, while the aforementioned qualities keep things safe along a *psychological dimension,* integrity, trustworthiness, honesty, reliability, and the like keep things safe along a *moral dimension*. No parent can be empathic toward his or her children twenty-four hours a day, seven days a week. A good deal of the time, perhaps most of the time, a parent must act instead from a consistent sense of what is right.

And third, because authority involves actions that are for a greater good, in the case of a father's authority for the good of a child, and because most things worth achieving require a sustained process that occurs in real time, authority necessarily involves persistence, farsightedness, and fortitude. Effectively authoritative people have a sense of their relationship to time, and so they tend to be active and not reactive, consistent and not scattershot. They plan and predict.

And of course, all of the above are organized by the ability to love and care.

To summarize, all authority figures, even the best and most decent among us, must contend with the undertows of human imperfection: narcissism, self-interest, the hunger for power, deformations in our aggression, sexuality, and many more. These invariably exert pressures that can warp legitimate authority. We must all, therefore, commit ourselves to dealing with our ceaseless, natural tendency to write ourselves large on the world, and on our children, by committing ourselves to maintaining our empathy, integrity, farsightedness, and caring, and by making certain that we embed ourselves in communities, both personal and societal, that discipline and organize our relentless inclinations to narcissism and authoritarianism.

Baseball Again

Time and time again, my older son gives me a great gift. A second chance. Third and fourth chances too.

We have made our way back to baseball.

Perhaps my wife deserves the credit. She has braved my petty retaliations, and called me on the unreasonable demands of my narcissism. But I too can claim some credit: I have struggled with my beasts, and with my need to heal my own fatherlessness on the backs of my children. Or maybe it's not me at all—maybe having a brother and sister has diluted some of my older son's dosage. Certainly my son deserves the credit: He is, in his own way, already quite strong, and surprisingly able to deal with the burden that comes to him from me.

Whatever the reason, we are back at it. He's thirteen now, and he's become persistent and tenacious. I pitch to him, hit ground balls, fly balls—we work on his skills. I offer the usual instructions. "Loosen everything as you settle in—your wrists, your hips, your legs. Let your body flow through the swing, all in a piece. You don't have to stride too far. Too far and you're off balance."

In terms of coaching, I say too much. I know this at the time, and years later my son tells me. But in another sense, probably what I say doesn't matter very much; the content of my teaching is probably more for me than for him. What matters is that we are doing it together, that we are both sweating and dirty, that my old muscles and tendons, and his new ones, are sore together.

I still walk a fine line within myself. It's not so much what I say, it's how I say it. The exact same words ("C'mon, guy, keep that shoulder in when you swing") can be meant in very different ways.

When I'm at ease with myself, when I'm simply grateful that we are here, at the altar of this age-old ritual together, my words aren't much more than an expression of the joy I find in our being together. I offer a space to play, to learn, to practice. I can lighten our time with a little humor. My voice can stay firm but calm, not rising and falling with the results of my son's work-in-progress swing. This is not about preparing my son for a career in professional baseball, it is about time together, about his learning the pleasure of making his body work for him.

But at other times, when my son's hitting and fielding become a referendum on my fatherhood, when I envy his having with me what I never had with my own father, and feel he should repay me by becoming the reincarnation of Joe DiMaggio, my same words take on another meaning. My tone moves from firm and calm to shrill and urgent as the demon of my narcissism rises within me. My words begin to implode our together-space, and it becomes all about me.

Now I know enough to sense this, and sometimes I can start an inner conversation. "You fucking idiot," I say to myself. "You think it's his job to make you feel okay by hitting a baseball? Get a grip. Get a life."

Sometimes my internal belt, my rather harsh version of self-discipline, works. I can get back to a more even keel, and we keep going. Sometimes, though, the power of the old wounds just won't quit. I can't get that edge out of my voice, and I can't hate myself into a better place. My son has learned, over the years, how to manage me at these times. Sometimes he lets me know that I should cool it, and sometimes I do. Sometimes we decide it's time to quit for the day.

These days my highly imperfect ways seem to be okay. (Probably he'll let me know in ten or twenty years whether I'm right about this.) We both know we'll do it again. Maybe it will go better, maybe worse, but we'll keep doing it. We'll play, we'll go to Fenway, we'll talk statistics, and we'll introduce his younger brother to the game. I don't have to be a combination of Gandhi, Patton, and FDR to teach him. I just have to stay with it, and to hold on to the modicum of empathy, morality, and perspective that sometimes keeps me on the right side of that thin line.

7

Discipline

———

My last memory of my father dates to 1959, the year he died. I was five years old. He was meeting with several men in his study. Sick with a cancer that he had ignored, his liver ravaged by alcohol, he had lost all of his once substantial wealth and power. It's likely that the men in the study were creditors.

I opened the door and headed straight for my father's lap. At first he ignored me, but I was persistent; I wanted his attention. He told me to leave, sternly but calmly. Still I didn't go. To this day my tenacity puzzles me; nothing I remember from our relationship suggests that I had reason to hope for his attention. Still, whether because of my stubbornness, my innate optimism, or perhaps just the drive of a little boy to touch, to roughhouse, to make contact with his father, I persisted.

My father sent me away angrily and unequivocally. I didn't go politely; I slammed the door hard. From here, I remember events with unusual clarity. My father stormed out of the library—red-faced and furious. I was frightened, and I ran, though, like running in a dream, I knew I wasn't going to get away. My father caught me within a few quick steps, grabbed my wrist, turned me, and then swatted me hard on my rump. I still remember the sting of his hand, and, at least in that one moment, the force of his presence.

Discipline and Authority

Probably some would say (indeed some have said) that my father, that day, was nothing more than an injured, defeated man taking out his frustration on his helpless young son.

But it's not that simple.

Over the past twenty-five years I've spoken with countless people on both sides of the discipline issue—parents and their children, teachers and their students, leaders of organizations and their employees, ministers and their parishioners, coaches and their players, judges, and even wardens and their prisoners. Just about everyone, it seems, struggles with the same core set of questions: Does reasonableness suffice? Is there a need for force in discipline? Is there ever a place for anger? Do the more aggressive elements of a disciplinary response give it its necessary weight, or do they simply intrude into the disciplinary arena, wreaking injury and havoc, begetting trauma, needing to be neutralized and extruded?

These are questions that every father, indeed every parent, needs to ask, and answer, on his or her individual terms. Because discipline, though not synonymous with authority, is an important expression of authority, and, as is the case with authority, being an effective disciplinarian requires honest self-consultation. It demands that one own and use one's aggression, and one's position of legitimate parental power, all the while organizing and monitoring one's actions with an unwavering commitment to safety.

Bouncing

Important experiences carve indelible grooves in our developing minds. These grooves, in turn, conscript present-day experiences, forcing them into old and familiar shapes.

One late summer day, when my older son was four, he and I were sitting on our porch. My wife was there too. Miles was bouncing on me, riding me with a little boy's exuberance. At first it was fun—I enjoyed the contact, and the life and energy in his movement. But after a while the bounce began to wear on the same spot on my leg, and his up-and-down began to hurt. I tried to shift, to find a rhythm that would work for both of us. He didn't shift with me; he was bouncing to his own beat, as he is wont to do, and my discomfort was not on his radar.

I began to get irritated, but I was, as I can often be, clueless about my feelings. As my voice tightened, and my rebukes grew louder, I receded to an almost somnambulistic state of being unaware. When finally I did react it was from a place my son could not have antici- pated, and with a force that shocked us both. "Stop, damn it," I said harshly. And then I whacked him on the bottom.

I had never hit my son before. He looked at me stunned, his eyes welling with tears, and then he ran crying to his room. My wife, who is neither dogmatic nor precious about these things, looked at me with something like horror. "He never saw that com- ing," she told me rightly. I was mortified. My son had been doing the very thing that I had never been able to do with my own father, and I had responded not by welcoming him, but by yelling and swatting.

It would have been a good time to sit and reflect, but, for a man who is supposed to spend his life reflecting about what people (myself included) feel and think, I can be remarkably dense and impulsive. So now comes what I think was even worse than the swat itself. I sug- gested to my son that he even the score by hitting me. Fortunately he had more of his wits about him than I did, and he declined my offer with a confused shake of his head. I think that on some level he knew that I had already violated a trust and made things unsafe, and man- aging my guilt by making him the father, thus overturning the proper order of things, was a really bad idea. Even I knew, at this point, that I had lost my bearings, and, making my first halfway decent decision in the course of this entire event I apologized, and I went to talk things over with my wife.

The "Reasonable Negotiators"

My actions obviously did not make for effective discipline. For one thing, a son bouncing on a father's leg hardly calls for a disciplinary response. Clearly the way that I handled matters was everything that effective discipline is not. But what do we mean by the phrase "effective discipline"? While it's easy to intuit that I was way off the mark, spelling out precisely what does, and what does not, constitute legitimate and effective discipline is no easy matter.

My first focus, in thinking about my paternal ineptitude, was on the fact that I had impulsively spanked my son. This fit with how my wife and I thought about things. Like many urban, educated households, where money is made with minds and not with hands, and where ideas about fairness and equality are valued over order and hierarchy, we had begun our parenting life with a decidedly liberal and democratic mind-set. We were the leaders of our democracy, to be sure, but we aimed to be highly responsive to our citizenry—the kids. Decisions, we believed, had to be thoughtful, and they should be made with sufficient input from all concerned. Reasonableness would be the order of the day; discipline would be moderate and never corporal.

Our way of doing things was consistent with what was already a very popular approach to discipline and child-rearing, one that grew from the same context that spawned the sensitive man movement. Indeed, the main proponents of this position on discipline (called by its critics "permissive") include many of the same figures who populate the sensitive man side of the great masculinity debate: William Pollack, Eli Newberger, Dan Kindlon, Michael Thompson, and others. These largely academic psychologists and psychiatrists propose that we move away from the "spare the rod and spoil the child" culture of yesteryear. In their reworking of Benjamin Spock, whose 1950s ideas may well have influenced their own parents, they emphasize nurture and understanding. And, of course, they rely on the basic principles put forward by Carol Gilligan and other members of the sensitive man movement. Mutuality is good, hierarchy not so good. The stuff of discipline is equality, listening, mentoring, and negotiation—not power, force, and punishment.

Eli Newberger personifies this fair-minded and evenhanded approach. As Newberger sees it, optimal discipline, which he calls "inductive discipline," occurs when "[parents] establish a foundation for communication and trust. [They] guide, teach, remind, set limits for behavior—and make mistakes; every parent-child relationship is strengthened when a parent acknowledges mistakes to his child, and makes amends. . . . Eventually the boy's discipline will come as much from within as without."

Newberger offers the following example of how a parent might respond to a concrete situation: "I know it's hard to share mommy's attention with your baby brother," he writes. "I know you are angry when Ben refuses to share his toys. . . . But you may not hit the baby because it hurts him and it hurts me, too. But you can't take away his truck just because you want to play with it. Would you like to build a tower of blocks with me?"

With these words of reasonable negotiation, Newberger captures the essence of the new discipline. But to really understand its message, we must also, maybe even especially, understand what it adamantly is not. As you will see, for the majority of these "reasonable negotiators," parental and paternal power and aggression are about as welcome as the plague.

The reasonable negotiators' most obvious villain is, not surprisingly, corporal punishment. Newberger and others review the relevant data and declaim that corporal punishment is now proven to be correlated with anger, hitting back, depression, and a number of other problematic outcomes. Though the data are less straightforward than they would have us believe (as you will soon see), many writers and mental health professionals of this persuasion have become activists against all forms of corporal punishment.

For the reasonable negotiators, injurious expressions of discipline are not confined to corporal punishment. Other villains include the kinds of traditional paternal attitudes that according to Gilligan make for stoic, unfeeling men. Dan Kindlon and Michael Thompson, for example, warn against the dangers of noncorporal expressions of parental force and hierarchy. In their book *Raising Cain: Protecting the Emotional Life of Boys,* they write: "A parent has enormous power in a child's eyes. From their earliest memory, we tower over our children in size and smarts; we are giants, incredibly competent, and we rule their world. . . . Children are easily frightened by adults and for a long, long time believe what adults tell them, even when adults say irrational or destructive things in moments of anger. Your child does not necessarily know that you're on edge after a bad day."

When considered as but one part of the larger disciplinary puzzle, these words are inarguably good advice. Children are easily frightened by adults, particularly by adults who don't appreciate the awesome power that is invested in them by virtue of their parental authority. Certainly respect and moderation are an essential part of any parent's repertoire, and we should always bear in mind the importance of empathy and deep engagement.

The problem, however, is that the viewpoint espoused by members of this school can too easily become dogmatic and caricatured. All too often they arrive at positions like that of Thomas Gordon, who, in his book *Teaching Children Self-Discipline at Home and at School: New Ways for Parents and Teachers to Build Self-Control, Self-Esteem, and Self-Reliance* writes: "Discipline is hazardous to children's health and well-being." And, as Gordon adds, "we must urgently adopt the goal of finding and teaching the alternatives to authority and power."

In certain ways the reasonable negotiator position is hard to argue with. What can one say? "Actually I think children should be hit hard and often"? But there is a problem. The words are too "nice." There is often something precious and self-righteous, something muffled and pretend, in this lovely world of mutuality and negotiation—like Mister Rogers without the sincerity. What do you do with highly aggressive children—boys in particular? Deliver reasonable and kindly sermons while being run over? And what about the facts of biology, bodies, real anger, and that little Johnny not only needs to learn to share, he also needs to learn to compete and to protect himself (and others) in a world that will often resist and oppose him, at times in hard and painful ways?

The Authoritarians

After swatting, and offering to be swatted by, my son, I talked with my wife. A surprising and interesting thing emerged. She was upset with me, to be sure, though not because I had spanked him. She thought that it had been uncalled for, but, to my surprise, she wasn't opposed on absolute principle. She focused on something different. "He never saw that coming," she had said. Essentially her message was that there was a place for getting angry, maybe even expressing that anger in a physical way, but it had to be done differently. It's how you do it that matters. "And," she added, "don't let him spank you. You're supposed to be the father."

Her response got me thinking. I began with that memory of my father spanking me. One could argue that I had filled the vacuum created by my father's absence by putting an overly positive spin on every interaction that I could recall having had with him, just so that I could have something of him to hold on to. Fair enough. But even after adjusting for this bias, I believed that there was something worth holding on to in my memory of my father's anger and swat. Aren't the realities of bodies, of competitiveness, anger, and aggression, a part of what fathers and sons are all about? Isn't there more to fathering than delivering thoughtful lectures about the proper way to share with "little brother"? In my relationship with my own children I hoped there would be room for something on the other side of "nice." So as my son grew older, and my daughter and then my second son were born, I looked beyond the reasonable negotiator approach for one more attuned to the real world, where what is positive and even wonderful about life must often be sculpted from the sometimes obdurate stone of reality. I found myself briefly interested in the school of parenting that I will now call "the authoritarians."

The dictionary tells us that "to discipline" means "to educate; to develop by instruction and exercise; to teach." But *Webster's* does not stop with these thoughtful, collaborative tones so reflective of the reasonable negotiators. Discipline also involves, as a noun, "punishment by one in authority; retribution for an offense"; "control gained by enforcing obedience or order"; as a verb, "to chastise; to whip or scourge in order to mortify or subjugate will or passions." Here the dictionary begins to speak the language of the authoritarians.

Partly as a movement unto themselves, and partly in reaction against the perceived overindulgence and permissiveness of the liberals, the usually male and often Christian authoritarians—John Rosemond, Kevin Ryan, James Dobson, among others—campaign under the banner of parental authority. They emphasize morality, which they sometimes seem to claim as their own discovery. They decry individuality, which they thoughtlessly equate with pathological narcissism. They think that children have altogether too much sway and power. And they achieve quite a bit of notoriety by condoning, even promoting, corporal punishment. The family, they argue, is not a democracy. The parents are in charge, and the kids should follow the rules.

The siren song of the authoritarians can be compelling: It appeals to anyone who finds it ludicrous to negotiate with a toddler as if he is an equal, and it also resonates with those parents who feel fettered by their own inhibitions and anxieties when it comes time to use their parental force and power. It encourages the weak of heart to feel justified in restoring and maintaining orderliness and hierarchy within their families.

But there is a dark underside to this point of view. Consider these words of Rosemond, taken from a *New York Times Magazine* interview: "If you punish your child he will hate you. He won't talk to you for three days. It's a blessing. Take a vacation."

Just a throwaway line designed to get attention? I don't think so. Such sarcasm colors many of Rosemond's pronouncements. He and his colleagues, with their irony and devaluation, time and time again minimize the sensitivity and vulnerability of children, and in doing so they encourage parents to preserve their control and power without having to experience much, if any, conflict and uncertainty. In short, they encourage self-righteousness.

On closer examination, it becomes clear that the authoritarian philosophy provides cover for an overly self-serving approach to parenting. Consider again the words of Rosemond, in this case his thoughts on spanking: "Rule Number One of a Well Done Spanking: Don't wait. For me, spanking is a first resort. This is not to say that I spank for everything or spank a lot. I seldom spank, but when I decide, quite arbitrarily, that the situation warrants it, I do it and that's the end of it."

The key word here is "arbitrarily." Discipline, judgment, and punishment may at times be mistakenly meted out, but they should *never* be arbitrarily meted out. Despite their protestations to the contrary, the authoritarians *do* blur the difference between "authoritative" and "authoritarian." They undermine family safety by encouraging self-serving and cavalier expressions of aggression.

The Middle School

The liberal and conservative schools, caught up in the rhetoric of their mutual antagonism, migrate, to their detriment, to caricatured and polarized positions in the discipline debate. The liberals, with their defensive emphasis on gentleness and mutuality, stick their heads in the sand. They exile important realities of force, power, and the body to never-never land, ignoring the fact that these are important aspects of family life. Meanwhile the authoritarians tend to be impulsive and dictatorial. Each generation must gradually, if grudgingly, cede dominion to the next, but the authoritarians would have us believe that it is a fine thing to preserve our parental power selfishly, even if by force.

What about a thoughtful integration? There actually is a "middle school" on this issue. Its generally acknowledged leader is Stanford psychologist William Damon, who emphasizes discipline and moral values, believes in punishment, and warns against overnegotiating. At the same time, he also warns against spanking. Reasonable punishment, according to Damon, should be part of child-rearing. Children need to learn to take no for an answer, but parents should also engage respectfully, explain when necessary, and tailor the degree and depth of explanation to the child's developmental needs. Two-year-olds, as Damon points out, can understand that they shouldn't draw with crayons on the wall, but explanations of how this is not respectful of mommy's time are not terribly useful. The middle school position counters the ineffectiveness and abdication inherent in the liberal position by seeking to preserve discipline, and it also aims to police the underlying sadism, self-centeredness, and impulsiveness that characterize the authoritarians' stance by making a place for respectful talk and understanding.

Self-Help, and Real Life

So why don't we just adopt the middle school approach to discipline and be done with it? The problem lies not in ideology but in application. It lies in the repeating refrain of authenticity.

Thomas Lewis, the coauthor of *A General Theory of Love,* writes: "Self-help books are like car repair manuals; you can read them all day, but doing so doesn't fix a thing. Working on a car means rolling up your sleeves and getting under the hood, and you have to be willing to get dirt on your hands and grease beneath your fingernails."

Lewis is right. It's easy for experts to talk about good parenting in the warm and fuzzy, pat-on-the-back world of self-help, and in the protected and rarefied atmosphere of academic theorizing. But when real-life parents care for their own children things get a lot harder. The unexpurgated experience of life in the family involves not only love and caring; it is also filled with deeply conflicted emotions such as self-interest, envy, resentment, guilt, and, maybe especially, sexuality and aggression. Everything we do with our kids must be negotiated while we are being buffeted by our feelings and our impulses, and while our minds are screaming at us to replace our best intentions with powerful, and often problematic, scripts from the past. Within this maelstrom, even the most obvious and straightforward of the positions proposed by the experts can seem like little more than linguistic Band-Aids—eminently sensible, but very hard to implement and hold.

Haystacks

When I was fourteen I went to an all-male boarding school. It was my mother's idea: She thought I needed to get out of the house, out from under her skirt, to be in the world of men and boys.

I still believe that her idea was a good one. Nevertheless, I was miserable. I wandered the halls, lost, feeling like a ghost, among boys who seemed to taunt me with their born-on-third-base-thinking-they'd-hit-a-home-run attitudes and their expensive golf swings. Of course they didn't really taunt me—most were actually quite decent—but I felt diminished as I imagined them heading seamlessly into the future, first to Yale and Princeton, then to business school or medical school, and then to marriage and fatherhood. I simply could not see the doors that seemed to open so easily for them ever opening for me. Sometimes I silently ridiculed my classmates for their privilege, but more often I drowned in the envy from which my contempt sprang. It wasn't about their money or lineage, though I did not have these advantages. What I couldn't stand was feeling their fatherfulness next to my fatherlessness.

I was miserable at that boarding school, but there were a few bright spots. One was a man named George Stone, who kept coming after me, trying to pry me from the haze of resentment and insecurity in which I had wrapped myself, and who ultimately talked me into dropping out of school so that I could work on that Montana cattle ranch.

Which was where I began to learn about discipline, and self-discipline.

The ranch was owned by a man named Chuck—a strong, tough, competent man whose infrequent words often had quite a bite. Chuck worked hard, and he expected the same from me. He didn't know what to make of my adolescent fog, of the fact that I would again and again grind the gears on his truck, that I would get his tractor stuck in ditches, that I would build his fences crooked, and that I could cross behind his horses and cattle without realizing that they very well might kick me in the ass, or worse. But he stayed on me about these things, maybe because he cared about me in his taciturn way, and certainly because he needed to get the work out of me.

One of my most lasting and vivid memories of that time in Montana is of the day I screwed up my haystack. Haying, if you've never done it, is an experience to remember. Eighty-pound bales of hay, grasped by hay hooks held in gloved hands, lifted with the shoulders, back, and legs, pressed into the stack with the knees of one's jeans, over and over again in an eight-to-the-minute rhythm, from dawn to dusk. Backbreaking work for a seventeen-year-old city kid. But at the end of the day I could look up at a three-story stack of solid cattle feed for my efforts.

But like everything else I did when I was seventeen, I was irresponsible and undisciplined about haying. And so, on the evening of the day that I had built my first solo haystack, Chuck walked into the dining room, bullshit angry. "What the hell were you doing out there today?" he said to me, in front of his wife and a hired hand (a guy who was, unlike me, a real-deal cowboy). Chuck had inspected my work, and the last two layers I had stacked, the top layers, were out of line. There were open spaces where the bales should have been tight, places where water and ice would get in, where the stack could come apart, where the hay would molder and ruin.

After dinner Chuck drove me back to the haystack, and watched as I worked into the dark, fixing my carelessness. Though he didn't say a word to me the entire time, his message—a message of consequence that I had not learned from failed Latin tests, from blown-off homework, and from other of my screw-you-and-screw-me-too adolescent behaviors—was clear. Here, driving back to the bunkhouse that night, as I sat beside Chuck's softening anger, and as I felt the day's work in my hands and body, I understood that my carelessness had endangered this man's livelihood. I could see that the survival of this ranch, of the animals and those who lived off of them, depended on real work. Out here, his "what the hell were you doing" got through.

Developmental Psychology, Neurobiology, and Discipline

Chuck scared and intimidated me, but I respected him. It was through him that I learned to ride, to drive well, to brand, to build fences straight, and to keep a tractor out of the ditch. I began to build a sense of competence, I learned to finish what I had started, and I found out that I could work through fatigue and pain. Chuck got through my adolescent fog and passivity, and proved to be one of a long line of men who served, over the course of my life, as a kind of "father by committee."

To me, Chuck's question, "What the hell were you doing out there today?" was not injurious, even if it didn't feel so great in the moment. Indeed, I submit, it was disciplinary in a most elemental way. I'll explain why this is by way of a side journey into the fascinating realm of developmental psychology and neurobiology, one that will further illustrate why a father need look no further than his own human nature to find the real stuff of discipline, of authority, and of good parenting in general.

Let's begin with a simple, everyday example. Your child runs into the street, impulsively, thoughtlessly. Terrified, you reach out to catch his arm, and you yank him to a halt. Your fear begins to ease, but you notice another feeling: You're angry. It may seem irrational to be angry in this moment of near-catastrophe, but you are, and it shapes your next action: an urgent and sharp rebuke. You may even feel like adding a whack as an exclamatory reminder. So far your responses have all largely been reflexive, but now, as the flood of adrenaline recedes, as the natural intensity of the autonomic response cools, and the chords of anger and fear mute, another tone becomes dominant. You want your child to understand, and so you say, now somewhat more calmly, "You terrified me, what you did is *dangerous*." And then you explain firmly about cars, about attentiveness, and about danger.

What's happening? You're helping your child negotiate the dangers of the world through a kind of interaction that occurs, in myriad modes and milieus, over and over again: with a hot stove, with an electrical outlet, with driving a car, with sex, with drugs, and so on. You're not following any text; you're following your instincts. And, by doing so, here, in this moment, and then over and over again, you're doing something deeply important. You're shaping the mind of your child.

How?

Infant researchers and theorists such as Dan Stern, Beatrice Beebe, Ed Tronick, and others would say that you are helping your child create a "representation," which is their somewhat technical word for the present-day mental embodiments of the repeated past experiences we have with important people in our lives. En masse, representations evolve into a flexible fabric of mental templates that filter and translate our expectations, interpretations, and assumptions about how things were, how things are, and how things will be. If, for example, parents regularly and reliably communicate to a child the expectation that he get his work done promptly, the representations, or templates, related to self-discipline will likely be activated when he sits down at his desk. If, on the other hand, the culture of the family is procrastination, then representations related to getting "just one more cookie" are more likely to be primed for action when it comes time to take care of business. Chuck is part of such a template in my mind—a programming, organizing presence related to focus, attention, and respect for doing a job promptly, thoroughly, and well.

One could say that the sum of these representations becomes the mind's core software; a functional, reliable self-operating system.

If the mind's software is built by accumulating and cataloguing interactions with important people (like parents), what runs this software? What is the mind's hardware? Let's now turn to matters of neurology.

Every experience that befalls a person makes its mark on the mind's circuitry, the ten billion or so neural cells with which we are born. As Thomas Lewis puts it, "Experience rewires the microscopic structures of the brain—transforming us from who we were to who we are. At a Lilliputian level, the brain is an elaborate transducer that changes a stream of incoming sensation into silently evolving neural structures." Metaphorically speaking, Lewis is describing a process that is similar to the way water carves grooves in the sand, grooves that in turn cause subsequent rivulets of water to flow in the same pattern. As the mind collects a library of experience, certain of our neurons, and then certain groups of our neurons, get used to firing in response to similar and related experiences. These groupings are called "neural networks." Unless new channels are carved—unless these neural pathways are shifted by new and necessarily weighty experiences—these networks endure, organizing experience in predictable ways.

One more contribution to this admittedly oversimplified review: Every experience makes some mark on the mind simply because every experience, every perception, and every thought causes a neuron, or pattern of neurons, to fire. But importantly, some experiences are more equal than others. Repeated experiences, experiences with important and loved people like parents, and experiences that occur in an atmosphere of highly charged emotion (trauma, for example), tend to make more indelible marks on the brain. Neurologically speaking, more "weighty" experiences lead to the creation of more enduring and influential neural pathways. That the brain prioritizes in this way is of course bad news for victims of trauma—this is what can make genuine traumatic experiences so intractable. But it is good news for parents—it allows us to profoundly influence our children.

Representations, Neurobiology, and Two Kinds of Disciplinary Responses

Let's proceed just a bit further with this side journey. Let's add to our understanding of representations a consideration of how memory works. Then we'll use our combined understanding of representations, memory, and neurobiology to construct a nuts-and-bolts model of effective discipline.

There appear to be, as neurobiologist Joseph LeDoux has noted, two essentially distinct forms of memory. One involves more rational, nonemotional experience, the other more emotionally intense experience.

Memories of relatively rational, nonemotional experience tend to be governed by processes that occur primarily in what is called the neocortical brain (which, as Richard Brockman points out in *A Map of the Mind,* is the most recently evolved part of the brain). The neocortex is the site of free will, abstract reasoning, and our most complex thought processes. These higher level brain structures are the domain of thoughtful, reflective evaluation, of what we think of as our conscious will. When memories that are not so highly charged with emotion come into play, they are, as Brockman says, "evaluated and compared with prior experience before a response is initiated." In other words, memories of relatively nonemotional events (LeDoux calls these "declarative memories") tend to produce relatively thoughtful and deliberate responses.

In contrast, memories of more emotionally intense experiences appear to be governed by structures within what is called the limbic brain, or what LeDoux calls the "emotional brain." In contrast to the neocortex, the limbic brain is home to such capacities as emotional and instinctual reactivity, nurturance, and social communication. Relative to memories of emotionally neutral events, emotionally charged memories tend to prompt reflexive and immediate action, often via relatively direct pathways to the autonomic nervous system and to muscle tissue. This is why (again to quote Brockman) "[Emotional memory] is crucial for survival in a Darwinian sense. . . . When faced with an emotionally arousing, potentially life-threatening situation, one does not have to think through each step of one's response."

The summary I've just put forward is rudimentary. But if we use the preceding as an explanatory metaphor, and not as inarguable hard science, we may well have found a valuable way of constructing an integrative model of effective discipline.

Let's return, for a moment, to the example of your child running into a busy street. Let's imagine that, when the dust settles, you take your child by the hand, and, in the spirit of Newberger's inductive discipline, you speak calmly—about cars, balls, watchfulness, and danger. You do this because you want him to think things through, to be careful. You rationally hope that maybe next time he'll stop and think, that he won't play on a busy street. Maybe he'll make a point of remembering not to run after the ball without first looking.

This rational, inductive language (which, by the way, was the language Chuck used with me a few days after that night on the haystack, when he talked to me about what happens to hay when the stack is not properly built) is, as we have seen, the language of the neocortex. It speaks to those parts of the brain that are involved in thoughtful, reflective consideration. Truly important, to be sure. But will this language suffice? What if, despite your child's thoughtful planning, he still, on an impulse, dashes into the street? Do you want him, in that moment of danger, to engage in the kind of thoughtful internal dialogue that Newberger calls inductive discipline? "There's a car—if I keep running it might hit me—that would be a bad thing—I should stop." No. *Something else is needed.* Here is where your initial response proves valuable. When you first respond from that adrenaline surge of anger and fear by speaking sharply and angrily, and maybe even by conveying your feelings through something physical, like a hard grab of the shoulder, or even a whack to the rear end, you want him to call on something more immediate and jolting. You want his mind to remember your voice, urgent and intense. (Mine still vividly remembers, even I would say "feels," Chuck's "What the hell were you doing out there today?") You want him to respond accordingly. You can't, as with a hot stove, depend on him to learn from the pain of his mistakes—it's a mistake he may make only once. Now you are speaking the language of your child's limbic brain.

In the academic debate on discipline, these two modes of discipline—measured versus emotional, reasoned versus forceful—are often seen as at odds. But when we consider discipline in a common-sense way, and when we add to this common sense our developing understanding of how our brains work, these modes can, in fact, be seen as working together, strengthening and reinforcing each other. The reasonable, thoughtful tone of the liberals speaks to the logical, sensible, cortical experience of "declarative memory," of thinking things through with a kind and understanding companion. Meanwhile the louder, sharper, and more penetrating chords of a parent's authentic emotional response speak to "emotional memory," to those parts of a child's brain that work immediately and directly, getting his attention, helping him to be self-protectively alert, to shift to a more proactive, energized state, to focus, to get out of a daydreamy head and into the world. When both modes of responsiveness are available to a parent, a child will, over time, build inside himself memories and representations that are simultaneously forceful and reasoned. A child will develop a solid sense of self-discipline.

So—Should You Spank?

No discussion of discipline would be complete without a consideration of spanking. Easier said than done, however, as this subject is an extraordinarily hard one to engage productively. As with abortion, capital punishment, gun control, gender, and a number of other topics, the major discussants at either end of the argument tend to have highly conflicted, hugely pressured, and largely unacknowledged aspects of their own psychologies at stake, and, as a result, projection and polarization rather than reason and thoughtfulness tend to dominate the controversy. In this environment of blame and name-calling (if you spank you're an abusive reactionary, if you don't you're a liberal wimp), it is hard to get beyond the narrow question of whether or not to spank to the more important issues that lie beneath.

I'll begin with the debate itself.

In the 1990s two popular books stimulated and personified the outcry against spanking: *Beating the Devil Out of Them: Corporal Punishment in American Families,* by New Hampshire sociologist Murray Straus, and *Reading, Writing, and the Hickory Stick: The Appalling Story of Physical and Psychological Abuse in American Schools,* by Temple University psychologist Irwin Hyman. These and other authors (Eli Newberger chief among them) claim that reliable data demonstrate that spanking is associated with numerous problematic outcomes in children, most of them involving displays of excessive aggression. This leads them to issue a blanket injunction against spanking. Straus writes: "I am convinced that if parents knew the benefits of not hitting their children and the risk they were exposing them to when they spank, millions would stop."

On the other side of the coin, pro-spanking conservatives draw up a predictable position: Spanking is a justifiable, even necessary, means of enforcing discipline. Here arguments tend to veer toward the self-serving and irresponsible. As leading spokesman Rosemond writes, "I spanked my children . . . not because I had given it a lot of thought or believed that children needed to be spanked or I had reached the end of my rope, but simply because I felt like it."

As is so often the case, the truth does not belong to either of the extremes.

To begin with, the anti-spanking contingent appears to have overstated its claim. A number of researchers have now reviewed the data that Straus, Hyman, Newberger, and others use to support their position, and their conclusion is that these data are both inconclusive and methodologically flawed. After careful review of the anti-spanking data, for example, Diana Baumrind, a research psychologist at the University of California, Berkeley, finds that there is little evidence that spanking is associated with the harmful outcomes enumerated by Straus. She writes, "Biased reporting or 'spin,' or ignoring findings that contradict a theory one 'knows is right,' are practices inconsistent with the scientific method. Straus's polemical claims concerning the potential effects of physical punishment go well beyond his data."

More recently a number of studies have synthesized data from methodologically acceptable studies of corporal punishment. The results further undermine the position of the anti-spankers, suggesting that there is little evidence that spanking is detrimental to a child when it occurs in the context of a relatively healthy family life.

I suspect that the equivocal nature of the spanking research reveals the deeper truth in all of this. Spanking, like most matters human and psychological, is an individual matter; there are no "one size fits all" descriptions, or prescriptions, to be had. As a result, available data cannot give us a completely clear picture regarding whether spanking is abusive, if it is then what makes it so, and if it is not then what makes it a legitimate disciplinary response. The one thing we can say with a good bit of certainty: The anti-spankers overstate their claim.

So how is a father, or a parent, to find his or her position in all of this? Should one spank? I believe—and this may surprise given my emphasis on the importance of aggression, hierarchy, authority, and even physicality in father-child relationships—that the answer to this question is a resounding "Maybe, but, very possibly, maybe not."

Here's what I mean.

A disciplining parent has available to him or her a number of potential modes of expression—calm words, firm words, punishment, consequences, lessons taught, and, of course, spanking. But to return to what is by now a familiar refrain, it is not parental behavior alone that leaves a lasting impression on one's child; what matters is the behavior plus the from-the-inside meaning of that behavior.

For each father, spanking will have a different from-the-inside meaning, based on his history, his constitution, and the meaning of spanking in any given circumstance. Is a spanking retaliatory? Sadistic? Poorly modulated so that it is too frightening? Overmodulated to the point of coldness and sadism? What's more, the meaning of a spanking will be different for each father, each child, and each father-child relationship. For a given father, will spanking a daughter have an eroticized element in a way that would be different for this same man with his son? For some fathers this scenario may be reversed. Will spanking an older child be more about a struggle for dominance than discipline? Will spanking a younger child be an act of control? What is the meaning of spanking a relatively aggressive child? A passive child? Do more aggressive and resilient children experience spankings differently than more sensitive children? Do boys experience spankings differently than girls? Each father *must*, repeat *must*, ask of himself these questions and more if he is to consider spanking.

Probably the one thing that can be said with absolute certainty is that no one should claim that spanking is a generally, or universally, legitimate and effective form of discipline. The fact is, there are simply some fathers who should *never* spank, regardless of the circumstances. They do not have the capacity to modulate and transform their impulses—their aggression, their sexuality, their inclinations for control, for sadism, for dominance, and so on—into legitimately and safely authoritative disciplinary responses when things get physical. Furthermore, each father, no matter how replete with self-knowledge and self-control, has conditions under which a spanking will edge over into the domain of the hurtful and even abusive. No father should be overly self-certain in this regard.

But I also believe, given these caveats, that spanking can, at times and for some, be a legitimate disciplinary response. I say this in part because of the potential value of spanking per se, and, even more, because of the profound importance of having a safe dialogue of physicality within the family. I'll say more about this latter idea shortly, but first, a few general guidelines for those who do spank.

Let's begin with what is relatively straightforward—some behavioral guidelines:

Controlled spanking does not mean hitting, slapping, or punching. It means one or two whacks, with an open hand, to the bottom. Never spank a child under the age of two. Probably don't spank after the age of ten. Spank in private to avoid humiliation. Always explain the reasons for this consequence. And, above all, keep in mind how easy it is for an adult to use too much force. Recently Dr. Sukhwinder Shergill and his colleagues from University College, London, found that when people are asked to touch back with the same force with which they are touched, they generally use more force than was used on them. In other words, we tend, perhaps for reasons of evolutionary imperative, to underestimate the degree of our physical impact on others.

But these "objective" guidelines are the easy part. The more complicated, and, in the end, the more important side of things, has to do with the from-the-inside aspect of this—with the matter of who you are when (and if) you spank.

A newspaper story from a few years ago comes to mind. A minister had been in the habit of using corporal punishment with some of his younger parishioners. When confronted, he argued that he never spanked in anger. He used a whip, and he read aloud from the Bible while delivering the "punishment." Well, this kind of self-deluded, self-righteous behavior is precisely what dangerous, indeed abusive, spanking is all about. You can't do something as emotionally intense and intimate as spanking without engaging powerful and potentially dangerous parts of yourself. One suspects the aforementioned minister of using his Bible reading as camouflage for control and sadism.

This story—which, in less blatant form, I have heard often—gives credence to the following advice. One man, a fine and committed father, told me of consulting with an older woman friend early on in his fatherhood. She had raised her own children, and he found her advice invariably sage. "She told me *only* spank in anger," this man told me. Implicit in her statement, he said, was that one should never spank as a cold afterthought. When such cold, apparently emotionless spanking occurs, the feelings that are invariably involved—anger, aggression, control, and even darker feelings like sadism and eroticism—are, in all likelihood, being expressed in an unacknowledged, and therefore even more dangerous, way.

I raise this point *not* to recommend that fathers, and parents, spank in anger. I raise it to underline the fact that the act of spanking a child invariably engages hugely powerful feelings. Better to know, and own, where one is coming from, than to submerge oneself in the illusion that one has somehow transcended one's own human nature.

In summary, a father, and a parent, always walks a fine line in the matter of spanking. On the one hand, spanking, like all matters of parenting and discipline, must come from a real and authentic place, one that can be felt; it should never be a cold and impersonal act. At the same time, the feelings involved are huge and combustible, and they need to be known, modulated, and transformed into something that is safely disciplinary, legitimately authoritative, and not narcissistic, self-serving, or, as is all too often the case, erotically or aggressively exciting.

The personal and individual decision that each father must make regarding spanking is, I submit, paradigmatic of the kinds of decisions that good fathers make all the time. One cannot abdicate one's responsibility for making these decisions by blindly following the advice of the experts, or by somehow not deciding at all. Here and elsewhere, a father's weight, and his legitimacy, derive from his willingness to know himself, his children, and his family, and then to use that knowledge to safely and generatively shape their minds and their lives.

Keeping Things Safe While
Still Being Real

As I mentioned, far more important issues lie beneath the lightning-rod matter of spanking itself.

Over the past twenty years, we have become more sensitive to the carnage that ensues when the sexuality of parents (and for that matter others in positions of authority) goes unregulated. More controversially, however, we have simultaneously become less attuned to the cost of oversuppressing this essential element of our human natures. Sometimes, for example, parents who fear the erotic aspects of their love and affection withdraw in order to protect their children. The distance that results can, as you will read in a later chapter, have the unintended effect of preventing a child from feeling loved and held, and it can inhibit the construction of a safe, developmentally useful space in which he or she can learn about his or her own growing sexual self.

Similarly, embedded in most anti-spanking positions lies an underappreciation, if not at times an outright rejection, of the many ways in which a child needs to experience a parent's aggressive, physical self. But again, does this mean that everyone should spank? Of course not! The fact is, children can feel their parents' meaning and intent through a wide variety of interactions—a fully present gaze, the sharpness of deeply felt words, a strong hand on the shoulder coupled with a direct look in the eyes—all of which and more are experienced through the body as well as the mind.

Good fathers, and good parents, appreciate the way in which physicality matters. They understand that through loving embraces, through rough-and-tumble play, through the modulated awareness of the sexual life of parents, through the contained eroticism of tickling and other modes of physical play, children encounter important truths within the persistent, undulating rhythm of physical life within the family. When eroticism is present (but experienced short of over-stimulation or violation), when aggression is available (but experienced short of trauma and abuse), children's minds grow, literally developing ever more useful and varied neural networks, immersed as they are in a medium of touch, affect, pulse, smell, and tone. Each father, therefore, would do well to make a safe place, within himself given his own individual predilections and capacities, and similarly within his family, for these deeply visceral, deeply formative, and deeply human interactions.

But this age-old truth—that parental physicality, and even parental aggression, is a normal and necessary part of family life—returns us, once again, to a now familiar refrain. Cain and Abel, Lear, Hamlet, Oedipus, Abraham and Isaac, and so many others—the myths and stories of our culture tell us that violence, overthrow, power, and even killing have long been embedded in the collective marrow of fathers, mothers, sons, and daughters. These stories remind us that we must be vigilant in our efforts to manage these basic instincts. If we are to discipline with both strength and fairness, we have to struggle with our aggression, and hence with the darker sides of our nature. We have to stay humble about our narcissism, and aware of our imperfections. We have to stay emotionally sensitive and engaged. And probably above all, we simply must make the commitment to struggle, in an ongoing and deeply personal way, with our ubiquitous proclivity to problematic expressions of aggression. Because when the aggressive forces that have to do with hurting, even killing, are not recognized and respected, *they still find expression.* And when these unacknowledged forces express themselves after having pushed their way through a strangle-hold of denial, they tend to emerge warped, and therefore even more dangerous.

We must never shrink from our commitment to monitoring and managing ourselves. We must, in other words, achieve authority over our own instincts and nature.

Dawdling

At the time my first son was born, I still carried, from the past, great
uncertainty about my weight and impact. So at first it seemed only
logical to me that my first son, Miles, would not really hear me. I don't
mean hear me with his ears. I mean hear me with his mind and heart,
hear me so that my intent would compel his action. When I'd ask him
to do something, and he wouldn't hop to it, his "Just a minute, Dad"
made sense to me, and I rarely called him on it. But slowly, gradually,
very imperfectly, I learned to get my words through to a place where
he could feel them.

I recall a day when I could see that I could make him hear me. He
was eight, and we were at our karate class. I brought him there hoping that he would learn to hit without hesitation or flinch. At first he
was uncertain, but he began to learn. His kicks were beginning to
sting me, and when his heel compressed my thigh muscle against the
bone I could feel his rising strength, and his lessening fear of my still
superior strength. It made me mostly proud, but also a little sad. For
reasons having to do with my history, I have always been intensely
attuned to the way in which the gap between my strength and his
relentlessly lessens. I am constantly aware of a bittersweet sense that,
barring catastrophe, the ascent of his trajectory will someday, shock-
ingly soon, cross the slowing path of mine.

A father must find and use the tools of his fatherhood, even while
he is being pulled into those crevasses that make him ineffective. For
me, the sadness that comes from seeing time move forward for those
I love has always engendered passivity. In feeling my children grow
older, I become awed by the power of time as I feel it relentlessly pro-
pel them forward, and, in the face of this power, I sometimes become
a child to their father. But this day Miles was dawdling, we were late,
and I needed him to hurry. Fighting the undertow of my passivity I
pushed: "C'mon, Miles, we've got to get going." He answered, "Just a
minute, Dad." "Not just a minute," I said, raising my voice a bit.
"Now." "I'm coming," he answered, but still, his pace did not

quicken, he had not heard my message of time. And then I found myself saying, in a voice that had alloys of both bite and calm, "Now means now, not 'just a minute,' not 'I'm coming.' Now."

To my surprise he focused, and he quickened his pace. As we walked out he took my hand, and he asked me what I thought of his spin-around back kick. Things were far from perfect. But they were better than they used to be.

8

No Violence! Fatherhood, Authority, and the Development of Self-Control

B Y NOW AN UNDERLYING and organizing theme has emerged from this exploration of fatherhood and authority. It's one that holds as much importance as the matter of authority itself, and it goes something like this:

Parenting involves shaping our children's raw constitutional endowments, their personal histories, their strengths, and their weaknesses, into unique characters best equipped to meet life's wide variety of opportunities and challenges. Our primary tool in this endeavor is, of course, ourselves. With those parts of us that were once primitive, and that now are transformed into something more civilized, lending liveliness, authenticity, and backbone to our efforts, we guide and accompany our children as they develop what will be their lifelong relationships with morality, kindness, ambition, diligence, and many, many more.

In this chapter I'll discuss the way in which fathers use basic elements of their masculine selves to help their children learn to use their aggression in constructive, not destructive, ways.

Joey

My colleague and I are playing with Joey, Chrissy, and Althea, three children at a preschool for abused infants and toddlers. We play a game in which we try to get the children to hit a drum. We have them hit hard, then soft, then very hard, then very soft. There is a method to this game. We want the children to feel their feelings, and think their thoughts, in a safe place. In this game we especially want them to learn about their forcefulness, with its alloy of anger, hurt, will, and aliveness.

We pay particular attention to Joey, a four-year-old boy from an economically disadvantaged family. His easy smile often gives way to sudden fits of fury. Joey pounds the drum relentlessly, enveloped in angry intensity, heedless of our ever more insistent efforts to help him soften and modulate. When he is not banging, Joey likes to place his head intentionally in the way of the two girls' flying arms, elbows, and drumsticks. We make protecting his head a part of the game.

Later we learn from the teachers that Joey has been hit in the head the night before by Manny, his much older brother. This does not surprise us: Children's play often expresses, with striking eloquence, the daily realities of their lives. We also learn that this hitting happens a lot to Joey, whose scars and bruises testify to the violence that he faces daily at home. The staff at the school tell us that Joey's development is showing the strain. His language acquisition is delayed, he is having trouble controlling himself with his peers, and his impulsivity is high.

Joey faces a daunting task. The daily dose of violence that he has known has both shattered and rigidified important aspects of his growing mind. Essential childhood capacities—to play, to connect, to reach out, to remember, to learn, to control impulses and more—have all been affected. Joey is desperately in need of help.

My colleague and I meet with Delores, Joey's mother, and Roger, his stepfather. Joey's biological father was abusive, and he left the home when Joey was two. Delores was granted custody of the children, and she subsequently became involved with Roger. Roger asks us for advice. He is frightened of Joey's biological father, he tells us, who, on those rare occasions when he weighs in about Joey, is highly critical of Delores and Roger over their parenting.

Roger goes on to tell us that things became more safe after Joey's biological father walked out on the family. Recently, however, Joey's brother, Manny, has gotten bigger and stronger, and has started acting violently himself. Sometimes when Manny hits Joey he even uses the same words as his abusive father; it is as if he has become a mirror image of the man. Delores now joins the conversation. She notes that Social Services is considering removing Joey's brother from the home, and she pleads with Roger to step in, to discipline Manny, to use his strength to stop the hitting. When Roger remains silent, she begins to goad him: "Be a man," she says. "What are you here for if you can't control the kids?"

We meet with Delores and Roger on several occasions. We try to help Roger see that it is important that he find a way to keep the peace in the house, even if it means physically restraining Manny. There has to be a bottom line: No *injuries, no matter what!* But it is nearly impossible for Roger to exercise his authority in this way. He can sleep in the same bed with Joey, cuddle, use him as a security blanket in a problematic inversion of the father-son relationship, but he can't use his own aggression and power to set limits, to keep the family safe. We ask him about his unwillingness to get more involved, and he tells us that he is frightened that Joey's "real" father will beat him up if he disciplines Manny. "He doesn't do anything for the boy himself," said Roger, "but he's always saying if you hurt that boy you'll be sorry." And it's not only fear of Joey's biological father that causes Roger to hold back. It is also fear of himself. "What if I lose control?" he asks. "What if *I* hurt the boy?"

This is, of course, an important question. We push Roger hard; he needs help with his concerns, and we want him either to talk with us, or with someone else, about them. But he never does, and so while the situation in Joey's house improves when Delores becomes more forceful in *her* response to the violence, Roger is never able to join in the important parental task of keeping family life safe.

Regulating Our Musth

Like so many fathers I have known, Roger needed to use his strength and his position—his paternal authority—for a good cause, in this case literally to protect his family. But he was so frightened of Joey's biological father, and so worried that he himself could be abusive, that he withdrew to a position of impotence and passivity.

He is not alone in his dilemma. As we have seen, authority, these days, is often compromised by a broad-based confusion over the relationship between aggression, forcefulness, and safety. Sometimes force and power are used in ways that are overly self-serving, arbitrary, or "over the top" (the wrong amount of power for the wrong reason), and the result is authoritarianism. At other times, aggression is seen as being narrowly synonymous with violence and primitivity, as colliding with the aims of civilization rather than potentially serving them, and so all expressions of aggression are renounced. Neither of these approaches is useful. Indeed, each is, in its own way, dangerous.

Clearly a more thoughtful integration is called for.

I'll begin with an admittedly unlikely analogy. Recently, South African game wardens became aware of a serious problem among herds of elephants in which poachers had killed older males. It turns out that the presence of these elder statesmen calms the herd's young males. Absent powerful father figures, the duration of the younger males' musth (a period of sexual aggression and excitement fueled by testosterone) increases dramatically, and the resultant increase in aggressively disruptive behavior is a threat to the herd.

While no one in his right mind would suggest that pachyderm and human behavior are equivalent, this anecdote illustrates a truth that can be found across species. The ritualistic fighting, and the creation of dominance hierarchies, common among most social animals, serves to channel and regulate the aggression of the group's males, while simultaneously creating a viable structure for all manner of social behavior—mating, hunting, affiliation, and more. What's more, such fighting promotes higher-order social behavior among the group's individual members. When one baboon slashes at another, more powerful member of the troop, for example, he gets immediate behavioral feedback—a return slash that tells him that his impulse was a bad idea. The learning paradigm is clear: Meeting aggression with modulated, nonlethal counteraggression teaches impulse control. And, as primatologist Robert Sapolsky notes, it is not necessarily the biggest, smartest, and most powerful baboons who do the best at spreading their gene pool, it is the ones with the most impulse control.

Now let's bring this all the way back to fathers.

Just as baboons learn to be less impulsive by coming up against the aggression of more dominant baboons, we humans learn about modulating our nascent force and power through our contacts with controlled, authoritative strength and aggression. The findings of psychiatrist Allan Schore are relevant here. Schore links the emergence of antisocial behavior in boys to an absence of "rough and tumble play" with fathers, and to an absence of paternal discipline, in particular physical discipline. Integrating his work with that of Jim Herzog, he argues that such physical interaction activates and establishes mental structures (the reader may recall the previous discussion of neural pathways) necessary for the governance of aggression, and hence for the regulation of violence.

I'm reminded of a brief story. A friend of mine recently told me about how his father responded when he and his brother fought. His dad would pick the worst offender up by the ankles, walk him over to his sibling, and, while hanging him upside down, say, "Pete, meet your brother, Ray. Ray, meet your brother, Pete. You guys are brothers. Cut it out." As my friend noted, "There wasn't anything abusive about it, it was all done with control, even humor. And it worked."

Children need to develop the neural pathways necessary for

impulse control and violence regulation. Or, as my friend put it, "At some point you've got to learn 'You don't tug on Superman's cape.'"

Joey's mother knew all of this intuitively. As a result, she was begging Roger to teach Joey's brother the following crucial lesson: "Life is not a video game, a movie, or a script of your own making. The person on the other end of your fist (your knife, your gun, even your words) is real, and your aggression and your violence really do injure him. You can't do that."

Ryan Clifton

Ryan Clifton, twelve years old when he first came to see me, was referred by his school. He had been bullying and taunting other boys in his seventh-grade class, on a couple of occasions shoving and threatening to start fights. He was quite intolerant, becoming furious, for example, over a disagreement during a recess basketball game. As the school psychologist told me about Ryan I also formed a picture of a boy with no real friends, though he had a bit of a following. In a way typical of kids in seventh and eighth grades, his contempt and arrogance led some kids to see him as "cool."

Before meeting Ryan I met with his parents.

Ryan came from a very wealthy family. Daniel, his father, now forty-five, had made a fortune starting a couple of high-tech businesses. He was smooth and self-assured, and during our initial interview he often interrupted my questions by telling me how the therapy should be conducted. Ryan needed to learn to control himself better, he acknowledged, but he also needed help understanding that it was not so easy to be privileged. Ryan, after all, would have to live with what his father repeatedly referred to as his "special stature" for the rest of his life.

I struggled to contain my annoyance at Ryan's father's arrogance, and, I'll confess, my envy of his wealth. I noted that this man, brilliant and successful in the world of technology and commerce, seemed virtually clueless about his boy's troubles.

Ryan's mother, Elaine, struck me differently. At times during this first meeting she was docile, nodding in agreement with her husband's pronouncements. But on a few occasions she showed another side. Both she and her husband came from relatively modest backgrounds, she told me, but, unlike her husband, she thought that there was something to be said for not having so much money. She noted that her husband had needed to work for everything they now had, and she wondered where Ryan, his younger brother, and his sister, would find motivation and ambition. She became quiet, however, when her husband said, dismissively, "Of course your view is naive. In this world it's always better to have money."

After meeting with his parents, I set out to get to know Ryan, a short, brown-haired, boyish kid who looked younger than his age. He arrived in my office, slouched into a chair, stuffed his hands into the pockets of his khakis, and, looking me right in the eyes, said: "Your house is not very big." Soon after he inquired about my credentials and training. This is an unusual thing for a thirteen-year-old to do, and what's more, his tone was arrogant and provocative. He noted that he had come to my office because the school had made him, and because his father had asked him to go along so as "not to make waves." When I asked him about the school's concerns regarding his bullying he responded with a detailed list of grievances against the other kids. They were "stupid," "annoying," and "boring." Early on, I'll admit, I found it hard to warm up to Ryan.

During our first year of talking together Ryan remained a problem at school, though interestingly, the school failed to intervene, never confronting him on his behavior. All they required was that he continue to see me. On occasion I sensed an unhappiness, especially a loneliness, beneath Ryan's arrogance, but by and large he steadfastly blamed his repeated flare-ups on the other kids' "stupidity" and "boringness." In our relationship Ryan continued to ridicule my house (too small), my training (not a real doctor), and my children (whom he occasionally saw when he came to my home office for his appointments).

Things reached a low toward the end of Ryan's eighth-grade year.

He and a group of other kids began picking on one of the weaker classmates in the locker room. The hazing escalated, and the boys, led by Ryan, pushed the classmate's head into a toilet.

A meeting was convened to discuss the incident. The principal reprimanded Ryan, but he failed to impose any serious consequences— neither probation, suspension, nor even the requirement that he write a letter of apology to the assaulted student. Nor would there be any communication about the incident to the prestigious high school to which Ryan had recently been admitted. The principal proposed that Ryan and his buddies get together with the school psychologist and the boy they had hazed. They'd all work it out together. He ended the meeting on a cheery note, suggesting that in the time left before graduation the kids get to know one another better, maybe play a game of basketball. Boys, he appeared to say, will be boys.

When I heard about the principal's decision I laughed a silent laugh of disrespect. The principal had caved in to the pull of Ryan's father's money, and what he proposed was woefully inadequate.

Sure, Ryan was a bully. And sure, he had probably become a bully because, as Pollack and others of the sensitive man movement tell us, he felt hurt and misunderstood. By now I had begun to see beyond the armoring of his arrogance to some of where that hurt lay—he felt isolated, insecure, lonely, and friendless, he didn't know whether he was smart, and he assumed that whatever success he had came because of who his father was, not because of his own hard work and abilities.

But there was another piece to this puzzle, one more immediate and basic. The fact was, Ryan was also a bully because he could be. He was a bully because no one had ever called him on his behavior—not his father, who seemed to need to instill in him a false sense of superiority; not his mother, who retreated in the face of her husband's bluster, and not the school, which seemed intimidated by his father's wealth.

The hazing occurred in March of Ryan's eighth-grade year. From then until June, when he left town with his family for their summer vacation home, Ryan and I struggled with what had happened. Or perhaps it would be more accurate to say that I struggled with him over what happened. As his therapist I tried to understand what had driven him, but I also confronted him quite a bit, asking him how he would feel were he in his victim's shoes, telling him that he was not above the rules, warning him that things would not go well for him if he did not make some changes. When he mocked me, as he was still wont to do, I told him that I actually didn't find his barbs so funny, and that I thought his disrespect of others was a big-time problem. I tried to be kind, but I'll admit I was also pretty fed up with Ryan. During this time he seemed largely unchanged, with two possible, and perhaps encouraging, exceptions: He kept arriving on time for sessions, even though he came to my office on his own and could have begun avoiding me. And he also seemed more quiet than usual, even, perhaps, unhappy.

The next fall Ryan, now fourteen, began at a new school. I had wondered whether he would return to talk with me. The confrontation between us had not been easy, and the school's recommendation that he be in therapy was no longer in effect. What was more, his father had voiced growing reservations about our relationship, even saying to Ryan, on occasion, "Do you think you still need the shrink?"

To my surprise, however, Ryan seemed, perhaps for the first time, more willing to talk. He admitted to being nervous about beginning his new school, and he allowed me to see a glimmer of self-doubt. He still gave me a hard time, but things had softened. On occasion he spoke of how important he imagined my children were to me, saying, with what even sounded like a touch of jealousy, "I bet you just can't wait to get back to the family, huh. They're lucky you have a home office, you're here all the time." And when he teased me about my house, my degree, or other aspects of my "less-than-his" life, a slight smile played around his lips. I felt, alongside his off-putting contempt, the hint of an invitation to play, to tease back. It even occurred to me that he, like Larry, the out-of-control father about whom I wrote earlier, might be goading me into giving him the kind of firm counter-response he needed.

About two months into his first year of high school, Ryan got into a familiar sort of trouble. This time he had mocked a classmate's performance in English class, saying to some other students "he doesn't seem like the sharpest knife in the drawer." The classmate, who was a scholarship kid from the projects, heard about Ryan's comment and confronted him. Ryan responded with a reflexive "fuck you," and a fight ensued. Ryan got by far the worst of it—a black eye, a fat lip, assorted bruises, and a wounded ego.

Ryan's new school responded immediately and firmly to both students. The boy whom Ryan had derided was disciplined for fighting, while Ryan, rather than being treated as a victim, was severely reprimanded for speaking so contemptuously of a fellow student. A faculty member was assigned to talk regularly with Ryan about his attitude. The fact that he had been beaten up afforded him no special license.

Ryan's father, incensed by the decision of the disciplinary committee, went into action mode. He contacted the school to arrange a meeting, insisting that I be present. He ordered me to inform the school that the fight ("beating," he called it) had been traumatic for Ryan, and to offer my professional opinion that it was inappropriate to discipline the boy.

I had no intention of going along with these demands, but before informing Ryan's father I spoke with Ryan. To my surprise, he was strongly opposed to his father's intentions. "The kids will think I'm a rich-boy wimp," he said. "Let's face it—I was a total asshole, I got beat up. Now let's move on."

I was impressed, and I saw a real opening. "Look, I think it's great that you don't want me to get you off the hook. It sounds like you're learning an important lesson. You're being responsible for yourself, and, what's more, you can appreciate what it feels like for a kid who's never had any money to be treated like he's less than you. If you can own what you did and deal with the consequences, kids will respect you. Teachers too."

"Yeah, yeah," he had said, interrupting my proselytizing this time with more justification than denigration. "That's all well and good. But I just don't want to be more of an asshole than I already am."

I admired Ryan a lot for the stand he was taking, but it wasn't so easy to convince his father of its value. Mr. Clifton continued to press for a reversal of the school's decision. But again Ryan took a stand. "I'm not doing it, Dad," he said, on the occasion of a family meeting, convened by his father, to pressure me to intervene with the school. "It's your thing, not mine. I've got to be at that place for the next four years, and I don't want everybody thinking I'm an asshole."

The incident, and Ryan's response to it, proved pivotal. Ryan handled things in a way that earned the respect of teachers and students alike, and he began to change his attitude. By his sophomore year he had some success, academically and athletically, and his school began to feel like a place in which he could find himself. For the first time, he felt that other students might like him for something about him, not because of his family's money. He gave up on the idea of having special stature and instead enjoyed feeling like one of the guys.

As Ryan moved into his junior year he felt increasingly solid in his sense of himself, and he began to talk more openly with me about things that had long troubled him. The hardest, and it seemed most important, of these had to do with his father. Not surprisingly, beneath Ryan's superficial embrace of his father's arrogance and conceit, the relationship was complicated. Ryan was pained by how uninterested his father had been in him over the years. He hated the way his father dismissed his mother, and it upset him that she had become so silenced and unhappy in the face of that tyranny. He told me that he knew that his father's bluster was a cover for insecurity. He admired his father's success, but he also knew him to be an unhappy man who felt friendless and empty behind his wealth, and who had never gotten over his own father's criticism of him. Ryan was, in fact, painfully disappointed in the father who so craved his admiration.

In a final twist, Ryan, who was by the end of high school showing himself to be a rather remarkable young man, began to talk to his father about his disappointment. He did so thoughtfully and respectfully. Ryan's father, however, found it hard to tolerate his son's attempts to break through to a more real engagement. Indeed, Daniel

Clifton proclaimed that the therapy with me had been a subversive experience, and he demanded that we resume the family meetings that had been suspended following my refusal to do his bidding with the school's disciplinary committee. He wanted to "monitor" our work.

These meetings were stormy at first, but Ryan held his ground, and his mother, Elaine, emboldened by Ryan's strength, also began to speak more openly. When Daniel realized that he could no longer bully his family he actually began to listen. He also agreed to meet privately with me a few times. During these sessions I encouraged him to take Ryan seriously. Ryan wasn't being disrespectful when he called his father on his bluster and remove; if anything he was asking his father for more of a relationship. "It's my sense that he's giving you something very special," I said. "Maybe you will be able to see yourself more clearly if you look through your son's eyes."

To his credit, Daniel Clifton was able to hear some of what his son and wife were saying. He could admit that he covered over a good deal of his insecurity with his presumption of superiority, and he could see that this might be a problem in his relationships. He even agreed to accept a referral to talk with someone himself. By the end of high school things were much better for Ryan, and they had even begun to improve at home.

On the occasion of Ryan's first vacation from college he came to visit me. "I was such an asshole at first," he told me. "How did you stand me?"

"You turned out to be a great guy," I answered. "In fact, I'd say that you turned things around about as much as anybody I've ever met."

"Things seem pretty good now, don't they?" he said. "But you know, I had a lot of help. The fact that my mother finally came out of her shell, that my father was able to give up some of that stuff about my being so much better than anybody else, the teachers at school, you. Thanks. But you know what else? That kid who beat me up. There was something about going into school the next day, fat lip, black eye, and all, and not whining about it. You know, I think that was the first time in my life I actually felt strong on my own. That was real, and it was mine. That's when things really started to get better."

"Cruising for a Bruising"

On important occasions over the years—when he graduated from college, when he began his first real job, when he became engaged—Ryan returned to talk with me. He never swayed from his belief in the value of the fight, and of the school's response. And, over time, Ryan came to recognize something else, something that is a fascinating aspect of the authority equation: He came to understand that his provocations had been an effort to elicit exactly what he had gotten: an authoritative response.

Children work hard to get what they need. Who can watch a baby nursing without being moved by his or her will to feed and grow? So is it for other basic developmental requirements—learning, protection, love, and more. You'll recall here the way that Devon was so tenacious, and so creative, in enlisting Eric into being a better father.

Along these lines, children who have been deprived of authority tend to look for it. Sure, they evade and resist, but they also seek out and find their parents' harder edges, they look for where the "no" is. And when they don't get what they need from their parents they look elsewhere. Just as love-starved children sometimes become promiscuous, discipline-starved children often provoke, looking for the formative and organizing aggressive counterforces that have been lacking in their lives. (Perhaps you'll recall here the way that Larry constantly tried to provoke me into disciplining him.)

Unfortunately, because provocation is more likely to elicit sadism and even brutality than the fair firmness that is needed, the discipline-starved child, like the love-starved child, often gets involved in hurtful encounters. But sometimes these gambits do work, particularly when a child has either the good fortune or the good sense to look for a disciplinary response from someone willing and able to transform his anger into something generative. Ryan, a case in point, got himself a pretty powerful kick in the pants, but he probably needed that extreme degree of force; when children are deprived of the authority they need, the volume needs to be raised in order for the message to get through. And because the fight, in addition to being a big-time wake-up call, occurred in the relatively safe environment of a savvy school, Ryan was not traumatized or injured. He got the kind of "neural jolt" necessary for jump-starting a process of change.

You might find it interesting to think about this idea the next time you are walking through the mall, and you have the impulse to give someone else's whining twelve-year-old a "good talking to." The irritation that his demand for yet another indulgence elicits may not be a sign of unreasonable intolerance or impatience. It may be a normative, developmental response to a kid who is, in his or her way, screaming out for some limits. Now obviously it is not our place to teach lessons to other people's children, but these moments illustrate critical discernments a father must make every day.

When our children annoy us, are we being intolerant or impatient for reasons of our own, or are we responding to the music of development? Part of becoming a good father, of becoming wise, means learning how to tell the difference. If it's the former, we need to deal with things within ourselves. If it's the latter, it's our job to transform our annoyance into affecting, shaping parental responses.

There is indeed something to the phrase "cruising for a bruising."

"You Bastards Meant Business"

As I noted when I discussed Jorge Rivas, the man who built a successful business from scratch, we can learn a great deal about fathering by looking at paternal relationships that do not involve fathers. Another example can be found in many of our social institutions, which, when they are working well, manifest a kind of paternal authority—that is, they use their legitimate, aggression-infused, hierarchical positions to protect those at risk, and, importantly, to ensure respect for their personhoods. I'll illustrate by returning to a critical moment in my work with Sam Burke, the man who was hospitalized after a drunk-driving accident, and who, more to the point, beat his wife and children.

Sam, you'll recall, eventually accepted our treatment recommendations—referral to Alcoholics Anonymous, a halfway house, psychotherapy, a program for abusive men, and ongoing monitoring by the Department of Social Services. But in order to gain his compliance, a unified show of force was required. The hospital staff, Sam's wife, Jane, a representative from the Department of Social Services, and I had informed Sam that he would not be allowed to return home until and unless he made some headway with the drinking and the violence.

As always, Sam had threatened and obfuscated, but we kept things simple and firm. He had been abusive, we told him, and he would have to change if he wanted to come home.

"How're you gonna make that happen?" he demanded.

"Very simply," we answered. "You can either agree, or we'll get a restraining order and enforce it through the courts."

"It'll never fly," Sam answered, but without the same degree of threat and bluster. Clearly this had not occurred to him. "You're kidding," he then said, turning to his wife.

"The kids are terrified of you, Sam," Jane answered. "Don't you see what you're doing? What did you think when you saw the bruise on Joel's cheek last month? Don't you notice that they're scared of you? Is that what you want?"

Sam didn't answer directly, but the words he did speak, something like a mumbled "I don't think I'm all that bad," indicated a clear shift in his demeanor. Sam had heard that we were serious about the restraining order—that Jane was going to stick to her guns, and that we were going to back her up. In subsequent meetings, a now more subdued Sam and I began to talk about what he would need to do in order to return home, and we put together his treatment plan.

Sam's response to our confrontation was something that I have now seen many times: Violence (and in Sam's case bullying) diminishes in the face of a sufficient show of controlled force. I vividly recall my introduction to this principle, which also occurred in a psychiatric inpatient unit. Time and time again patients would be out of control with psychotic fury and terror, and no amount of talk alone could calm them, or help them agree to take needed medications. Sometimes it was necessary to restrain them, both for their safety and for the safety of the unit. Naive as I was early on in my career, the notion of restraint struck me as uncaring, even barbaric. After witnessing several of these incidents, however, I changed my opinion. Almost without fail, whenever there was sufficient force available to make it clear that things were going to be made safe, no matter what, the patient became more organized. Subsequently he or she would invariably tell us that the restraint had engendered a feeling of protection. I recall one young man, a college student enduring his first manic episode. He had been escalating—screaming, pacing the hallways, threatening staff and patients alike, for the first few hours of his hospitalization. When it became clear that he could not respond to our verbal efforts to set limits, we restrained him. It took five of us to restore order. Two days later, now in better control as a result of medication and a room program, he admonished us by saying: "What took you guys so long? I was terrified I was going to kill somebody."

Sam, though a limited guy, came himself to understand this basic principle of violence and safety. Years later, during one of our painful check-in calls, he remembered the meeting: "I hated all of you, even Jane," he said. "But I looked around the room and I could tell that you bastards meant business. And when Jane said that stuff about what it did to the kids, I just felt like a piece of shit. But you guys were still treating me with respect—like a fucking person. Most people in my life haven't done that. And I thought—'Jesus, my kids are people too.' It may seem weird, but all the time I was drinking and hitting them, I never really thought about what I was doing to them."

Faced with the power that we wielded, through the Social Services, through the courts, and through our own resolve, Sam felt the weight of our authority. Because he did not feel completely crushed and humiliated (this was why our respect was so important), he came up against a nonnegotiable reality that had the power, through the consequences it could impose, to hold him accountable for his actions. He experienced, in an extreme way, what we all need to experience, albeit in more quiet and normative ways: His victims became real people to him, he felt the impact of his violence, and he began to accept some responsibility for his aggressive and abusive actions.

Aggression is often violent and destructive. But until and unless evolution radically changes human nature by eradicating aggression from our constitutional endowments, aggression will *also* continue to be a key player on the side of the social and civilized. On both the individual and the societal level, our freedom and safety depend on authoritative counterforces that modulate, direct, and structure our impulses. The fact is, if we did succeed in banishing aggression from the "civilized" side of the equation, and relegated it to a primitive biological realm from which we then distanced our more "evolved" modern selves, we would have little more than uncivilized anarchy on our hands.

Violence and a Father's Authority

Aggression—whether it is the deformed and alcohol-disregulated aggression of an abusive man like Sam, the crying-out-for-limits aggression of an overindulged and deprived boy like Ryan, or the normal busting-out-at-the-seams aggression of a rambunctious child—is an essential part of all children. This is true of girls as well as boys, though in girls aggression differs by quality and degree.

All children, therefore, must learn to use their aggression in constructive, and not destructive, ways.

And all parents have to help them to do this.

This is, of course, a task that falls to both mothers and fathers.

Parents in general need to keep their families safe. This means guaranteeing physical safety, and it also means teaching children to recognize and respect the fact that others are real and separate, that what they do (and say) can cause harm. Only with this recognition can children develop the capacity to feel empathy, guilt, compassion, and other civilizing feelings and attitudes, only then can they become responsible for moral decision making, and only then can they voluntarily honor social contracts, as opposed to being forced to do so.

While mothers have their own essential role in this task, fathers, by transforming their innate aggression into a constructive and shaping force, and by using their inclination to hierarchy in the service of well-intended guidance and leadership, have a number of critical, and at times relatively gender-specific, roles to play.

Through the kind of rough-and-tumble play that enlivens and engages the brain, fathers help their children learn, in a safe space, about the shape and contours of their own aggression.

By using their force-imbued authority as an effective counterforce (including, when necessary, their physical strength), fathers provide a necessary policing safety within the family.

By communicating standards and rules in a manner not only organized by love, caring, and respect, but also backed, when necessary, by confrontation, fathers teach their children that nothing short of respect for others is acceptable.

And by themselves learning to tame and channel their own instincts, fathers model inestimably valuable lessons about the creative and safe use of aggression.

In these ways, all of which involve bringing their very being, their "weight," into contact with the minds, and even sometimes bodies, of their children, fathers play a critical role in raising kids who will protect, rather than injure, their brothers and sisters.

9

Fathering from the Inside Out

———

USING CORE ELEMENTS of oneself to shape a child's mind: Once we get beyond questions of what a father's authority is, and what it does, we get into some pretty murky territory. If there are indeed no universal recipes, no quick-fix formulas, for parents and fathers, if answers, such as they are, are as much based on who one *is* as they are on what one *does,* then what in heaven's name must a man do if he is to become a better, indeed a good, father?

Let me approach this question via an unexpected path.

Because this is a book about men and fathers, it suffers from a most obvious omission: that of women and mothers. Let's take a moment, therefore, to make a necessary, and unequivocal, statement: Women and mothers matter, just as much as do men and fathers. And now let's try to remedy this omission, at least partially, by relating the story of a woman and a mother.

Susan and Jenny

Susan Jackson, a single mother, struggled to become a better parent, and in doing so she had to walk the same path that many men and fathers do: She had to come to a better relationship with her aggression, and her authority. I believe that her story sheds useful light on the topic of the moment: How can a man become a better father?

Susan, a professionally dressed woman of about forty, came to talk with me shortly after her husband, Phil, had left her for another woman. This was not, however, her greatest concern; indeed in many ways Susan was happy that Phil had left. Throughout their marriage of seventeen years he had been at best inconsistent in his economic reliability, sexual fidelity, emotional constancy, and overall decency. She, a successful college professor, had wanted to leave the marriage for some time, but she had stayed to keep the family together for her daughter.

As soon as we talked about her daughter, however, Susan's professional composure gave way to tension and uncertainty. Jenny was fifteen when Susan and I first met. Susan had worked full-time since Jenny was six months old, leaving much of the care of the girl to Phil, who had had the time, given that he ran an unsuccessful business out of their home. Phil had appeared to be an attentive father, though now Susan wondered whether what she had perceived as attentiveness had in fact been a path-of-least-resistance overindulgence. Since Phil had left the family he had moved to another state, making no effort to provide either regular contact or economic support to Jenny. Susan, relieved to be rid of him, had not pressed matters legally.

Susan came to talk with me because she wanted help with Jenny. The girl was a handful. She emanated a silent, sullen anger, and she made it clear to all that she didn't owe anything to the world of adults. Though smart, she did poorly in school. She was drifting into a bad crowd and a world of promiscuity, drugs, and alcohol.

Susan felt that she had almost no control over Jenny, and she wanted help establishing some basic rules about bedtime, phone calls, language, curfew, and schoolwork. The latter was particularly important to her. Susan had always been grateful for her career, feeling that, whatever happened with Phil, she had a foundation that she could fall back on. Now that she was on her own she was even more appreciative of her success, and she wanted Jenny to have a similar sense of independence. She believed that to get it Jenny needed to turn things around at school.

Susan knew what was needed: an authoritative parental hand. So what was stopping her from doing what she needed to do?

Susan told me that she was terrified of being more firm with Jenny.

"Terrified of what?" I asked.

"It's confusing," she told me. "Some days I feel like I'm afraid that I just hate her, that I'm being abusive if I set limits and make her do her homework. Other days I feel like she'll hate me—even, I know this sounds nuts, kill me."

Where, I wondered, did these ideas come from?

Over time Susan told me. She was the third oldest of six children, and all of her siblings were brothers. When she was a little girl her father's anger and depression had dominated the household. He had been a frustrated inventor, a man who worked in the basement, always, it seemed, one step away from his "great discovery." That discovery never came. As the years passed, and his frustration and despair increased, he began to take things out on the kids, seeming to hate their very presence. Susan remembered nights when he would rage to her mother: "Why can't they just be quiet? I can't think." Often money was a focus. He would scream, for all to hear, "No man should have to feed so many greedy little mouths."

Susan's father suffered from, among other things, a severe, angry depression. She recalled that when she was about six he had begun stomping loudly around the house at all hours of the night, muttering that everybody would be better off if he were dead. On several occasions Susan remembered hearing the garage door open, and the rattling of gravel as her father's car left the driveway. She wondered, fearful but (she guiltily admitted) half hoping, whether he was driving off to kill himself.

Finally, when Susan was in her early teens, her father sought help. He talked to his pastor, who referred him to a psychiatrist. He began to take antidepressant medication, which lessened his depression and helped him to stop his angry outbursts at the children and his ruminations about suicide. He concluded that his basement inventions were a pipe dream, and he got a job. The family's financial situation improved.

Unfortunately, a great deal of damage had already been done. Susan's brothers had, of course, grown up in the same impossible household that she had and by the time they hit adolescence they were wildly out of control. The household was filled with their relentless yelling and screaming; when talking with her friends, Susan referred to her house as "the zoo." As the boys reached their mid-teens the chaos escalated, first to brutal, knockdown, drag-out fistfights, and then to threats of murder. On a number of occasions neighbors called the police to the house. By the time Susan came to see me several of the brothers had severe drug problems and had landed in jail for drugs, assaults, and thievery.

Susan's mind was filled with the images and scripts of her family life. Later in our work she told me: "In a way, it's amazing I ever got married and had a child. I always figured I'd never marry. I had this picture that a husband would be, at best, a burden that I'd have to take care of—like my father and my brothers. That part proved to be true. And I imagined that if I had a child it would be a boy, and—I know this sounds crazy—I really figured he'd grow up to kill me. I was so relieved when Jenny came, that she was a girl. Ironic, isn't it? Now she's totally out of control, and I'm terrified. If I don't learn to deal with her better she'll be the death of us both."

In order to help Jenny, and in order to grow herself, Susan had to become more comfortable with her anger and her forcefulness. Indeed, she, like so many of the men whose stories I have told had to become more comfortable with her aggression.

Susan began with the obvious; she set limits on her daughter. She imposed a curfew. She insisted that Jenny call home if she was going to be late. She put her daughter on an allowance, one that was dependent on Jenny's doing chores and behaving well. And the cornerstone of this new regime was that Jenny had to do her homework and her studying before she could socialize.

When Susan told Jenny the new rules, the young girl threw a screaming fit. "There's no way that's happening," she yelled. "You can't tell me what to do. You haven't hardly been my mother for the past fifteen years, so forget it. I'm old enough to make my own decisions, and if you don't like it—fuck you." Jenny turned on her heel, retreated to her room, and slammed the door.

Susan told me about her response with fear and shame. "I think I did a terrible thing," she told me. "I got so angry at her. I pushed the door open, and I yelled at her. I told her, 'You can't talk to me like that. Things are going to change around here, like it or not—so get used to it.' That part was okay, I guess. But I said other stuff too. I told her she was a spoiled brat, that she was ungrateful, that she was messing up her life. I told her not to blame everything on me. I really went after her."

I had a much more positive view of what had happened between Susan and Jenny. To be sure, Susan had to work on being a little less retaliatory with her anger. But this was the real world, where interactions such as these are never perfectly conducted, and I trusted that the elements of authoritative safety were generally present (Susan was a thoughtful and caring person, and she was constantly checking out her responses with me and with her friends). I doubted that Jenny had been particularly damaged by the exchange; in fact, I expected that the young girl needed to feel the bite of her mother's anger in response to her constant provocation. So I responded (as I would many times over the next year) by saying, "I'm not sure it was so bad, if it was even bad at all. But we can find out. How did things go after that?"

"Well, that's what seems strange," Susan answered. "She came out of her room about fifteen minutes later, and we talked. We really talked. She said that sometimes she felt like her father was so easy on her because he couldn't be bothered. She wondered, sometimes, whether either of us really cared about her. And she didn't really come out and say this, but she kind of hinted—I think that one of the problems with her and school is that she's afraid that she's not really smart. I got the sense that she was willing to do things differently, even though every time I talked about a specific rule she got argumentative with me."

The battle, now joined, obviously wasn't won easily. Jenny was very angry at both her mother and her father, and the fighting over limits and studying gave her a forum to express that anger. She was angry a lot, and usually in ways that were difficult. Furthermore, she was afraid of taking herself seriously at school. She worried that if she tried and then failed she would find out that she was "stupid." Better not to try, then she could blame failing on not caring.

But Susan persisted. She continued to discipline Jenny, sometimes a bit too angrily, but generally, it seemed to me, in appropriate and useful ways. Still, her efforts didn't feel acceptable to her, and here was where our work lay. After each confrontation Susan would come to her sessions mortified and confused, imagining that she had been brutal and sadistic. Generally the horror she felt about her forcefulness led her back to the horrors of the past: "All I picture when I think of anger is these ugly, angry men. I remember one time my two oldest brothers were slugging each other, right in the kitchen. Their faces were bleeding, mucus coming out of their noses. I don't know why I remember that part of it. I think it epitomizes how gross anger is to me. My father was standing there, saying 'Stop' in this quiet voice, as if that was going to do anything. My mother was standing there too, and she had this look on her face like she wasn't even there. Then Jake picked up a kitchen knife. He said he was going to kill Frank. Somehow it spilled out onto the lawn, and a neighbor saw it, and called the police. It wasn't the first time. It was humiliating. The police knew my family by name. No one ever talked about it, and no one ever did anything about it. That's what I picture when I think of anger."

Hard as it was, remembering these times helped Susan to better distinguish between aggression used in the service of legitimate, disciplinary authority, and anger that was abusive and unmodulated. She could see that there was a difference between the then and the now.

Eventually she made her way to the feeling that she could be forceful, and even angry, without being hurtful. "I always thought anger was a dirty word," she said. "And aggression, you like that word. But I remember the first time you said 'aggression' I literally cringed. I thought it was even worse than 'anger.' But now I don't feel the same way. I can see it can be a good thing. It still makes me uncomfortable, but I can do it, be aggressive."

Susan had begun to establish a real foothold on being an authoritative parent and mother, and as she did, Jenny's experience, both at home and at school, became more organized and focused. Indeed, by the time Jenny was in her senior year she had turned herself around academically. She could even acknowledge her mother's help. Susan told me, with quite a bit of pride, about the day she and Jenny had been visiting a friend, and the friend had congratulated Jenny on making the honor roll. Jenny had patted her mother on the back and said, "It was because of you."

How Men and Women Construct
Internal Senses of Authority

Susan's story reveals a daily reality that some modern views of women's authority fail to capture: Women, and mothers, *do* use their aggression, and their positions of legitimate hierarchy, to be powerful and authoritative—at home, at work, and elsewhere.

This is hardly a surprise to most mothers. While men tend to be seen as the prototypical familial disciplinarians ("wait until your father gets home"), research demonstrates that it is, in fact, women, home alone with children, who do the bulk of the heavy lifting when it comes to discipline. As Natalie Angier, author of *Woman: An Intimate Geography,* points out, ignoring women's aggression leaves aggressive women feeling "like 'error variants' . . . wondering why we aren't nicer than we are, and why we want so much, and why we can't sit still."

But while Susan's story sheds light on the subject of women's aggression and women's authority, what is its relevance to how a man becomes a better father? Let's move further into this question by returning to two topics previously covered: the endlessly fascinating matter of gender, and the rapidly unfolding world of neurobiology and developmental psychology.

As you'll recall, our overall sense of self is built from the library of experience that lives, ever at the ready, in our minds. This is true in an ongoing way—our moment-to-moment consciousness is textured by our feelings that we are *like* the important people in our lives (identifications), as well as by embedded memories of how it felt to be *with* these same people (representations). And this textured self-awareness is often especially acute when we engage in particular activities. For example, when we act authoritatively, our minds reflexively call on the catalogued identifications and representations ("templates," to use another word from our earlier discussion) that are relevant to authority. We thus recall the experience, in an inchoate, background way, of how our mothers, our fathers, and other meaningful people seemed to us when they were being aggressive, hierarchical, empowering, altruistic, and so on. In this way each of our histories serves as a kind of mental software: a living, organizing, interpreting accompanier in everything we do.

Gender enters the picture because all of these stored experiences, all of these identifications and representations, are built from relationships with people who are, obviously, men and women. The most important of these tend to be mothers and fathers, but of course we also rely on experiences with all manner of men and women. Thus every facet of our lives—what it feels like to love, to depend, to fight, to achieve, to be authoritative, and so on—derives its feel and meaning from a panoply of experiences, each of which has both masculine and feminine associations.

Consider, now, what Susan was up against in her efforts to discipline and organize Jenny. She had to build a sense of herself as an authoritative woman from a pretty tough place; neither her mother nor her father offered a very hopeful example (she had few positive identifications to turn to), and it felt frightening to be with them both (her representations were loaded with anxiety and fear). When she needed, therefore, to use her anger and aggression, she found it to be associated with her father's temper and her brothers' out-of-control rage on one side, her mother's inability to be aggressive on another, and the fear she felt when she was with them on still another. Her mental palette offered her a poor, lose-lose choice: Either she could feel like an ugly, angry man, or she could feel like a passive, ineffectual woman. Susan's eventual solution involved freeing her aggressive side from these embedded experiences so that she could better use it in the service of being authoritative.

Like Susan, each of us has access to both masculine and feminine sides of ourselves when it comes to virtually all aspects of parenting. Support for this notion can be found in a fascinating corner of parenting research, one that illustrates just how adaptable and flexible our gendered selves can be.

As previously noted, fathers and mothers have been shown to be very different with their children. Fathers tend to be more physical, aggressive, and outgoing, while mothers tend to be more nurturing, caretaking, and mirroring. In single parent households, however, things are often quite different. When men are absent women frequently discipline in ways that could be thought of as prototypically paternal (as did Susan). Women, in other words, are more likely to play the role of father. Similarly, fathers who are primary caretakers are far more likely to behave in ways that resemble the stereotypic role of mothers.

I raise these issues for two reasons.

First, I suspect that some will argue that this book is simplistic, that it promotes the nostalgic image of an archetypal father. There is probably some truth to this critique: I believe that we cannot understand the true nature of fatherhood without considering the contribution of men's masculine psychologies and biologies, qualities that are the basis of traditional fathering. But, as these findings clearly demon-

...ate, fathers are not confined to acting in stereotypically "male" ways. Both men and women can call on different aspects of themselves, different masculine- and feminine-tinged identifications, depending on the requirements of the situation. Sometimes a man may act from a place relatively more associated with important women in his life; at other times he may act from a place relatively more associated with important men in his life. And so it follows that, when it comes to the matter of authority, each person's version will be relatively gendered, but it will never be absolutely, rigidly gendered. If we keep this in mind we may be able to hold on to what is vital and meaningful in our image of the archetypal father without becoming confined to an inflexible, anachronistic view of what fatherhood means.

Second, I raise the matter of identifications and representations yet again because it gives us a framework within which we can approach the question: How does a man become a good father? Simply put, if fathering (like parenting in general) is as much about who one is as it is about what one does, then the processes of gaining access to, and achieving relative control over, the library of defining experiences that lives within each of us gives us greater facility with the basic tools of fatherhood—namely those aspects of ourselves that we need to activate and express when we accompany, and shape, our children's minds and lives.

Susan did this, and so became a better mother.

So did Allen Tinsley, the man whose story I will now tell.

Allen Tinsley

Allen Tinsley came to me because he wanted to talk about how one becomes a better parent. Interestingly enough, however, it wasn't that Allen wanted to become a better father—he figured he had that down. He wanted me to talk with his wife, Janet, about how she could be a better mother.

During our first meeting, Allen was clearly the one in charge.

Fifty years old, with a boyish face but a serious paunch that made him look at least his age, he had made a fortune by applying his gifts as a mathematician to the stock market. He conveyed the sense that he knew the right way to do things, and that it was his duty to enlighten others as to his wisdom.

Early on in our work he directed his off-putting self-righteousness toward Janet, his wife. Like an experienced teacher, he organized his exposition around a catchword: "nurturant." Allen felt that Janet wasn't "nurturant" enough toward Max, their seven-year-old son. "I know you love him," he said to her, "but you need to show it more. The other day, when he skinned his knee, I know you washed it, you took care of it, you asked him if he was okay, but he needs more than that."

"I hugged him and told him I loved him," Janet answered, with a tired resignation that suggested she'd had this conversation before.

"Sure, but he needs more than that. He needs you to be more nurturant."

Janet was an attractive woman who lacked both Allen's paunch and his air of self-certainty. She too was successful in her field, consulting to businesses about issues related to gender and race. During our initial meetings she listened quietly as Allen put forward his agenda. Occasionally she defended herself, but by and large she remained silent and watchful, exuding a quiet strength that suggested that she had ideas of her own, quite different from those of her husband, about what was going on.

Over the first few meetings Allen stuck to his agenda and Janet to her stoic quiet. I was concerned. Clearly we weren't going to get very far (wherever that might be) if I went along with Allen's agenda of trying to make Janet into a more "nurturant" mother. Obviously things were more complicated. Allen seemed to be quite controlling, and I didn't have the sense that Janet wasn't a good mother. I didn't even sense that she wasn't warm and caretaking.

I began by asking her why she was so quiet in the face of Allen's critique.

Shedding her reserve for a now palpable wariness, Janet answered: "I have my reasons, but I'm not sure it's safe to talk about them."

Allen, to his credit, dropped his proselytizing and answered with obvious hurt and surprise: "Why ever would you feel unsafe with me?" A nerve had been touched.

It took us a few weeks, but Janet found her way to talking about her worry. Her parents had divorced when she was twelve, and, she told us firmly, she had resolved that she would keep her own marriage together. No matter what. Was keeping the marriage together a concern? Perhaps. Janet suspected that Allen couldn't tolerate her disagreement. "You need to have things your way," she said to him. "I don't always like it, but it's the way you are." Then, turning to me, Janet added, "It's not that I'm too weak to disagree, I'm a pretty strong person. But I don't think it will go so well between us—he needs things to be his way."

Allen, still surprised, pressed Janet about this. "What are you worried about? How can you believe that our marriage can't tolerate disagreement?"

"I never saw my parents' divorce coming," Janet said, still looking at me. "Allen is a good guy, he's been very successful, but he's just not very flexible. I'm strong enough to do it his way, but I'm not sure he's strong enough to tolerate my disagreements." Then, turning back to Allen, she added, her voice now softening, "There are things I understand about you that I don't talk with you about. You're stronger on the outside than you are on the inside. I make it okay for you by not rocking the boat."

With these words Janet had disrupted an unacknowledged arrangement within the marriage: that Allen would appear strong, while she would be strong. By taking this risk she had gotten our work going. On her side of things she recognized that what she had said about Allen—that he wasn't strong enough to tolerate her independent mind—had been true about her own father, who had left his marriage when Janet's mother had begun to fight against his intolerance and control. And things opened up even further when Allen, who was becoming more open (and more likable) as his wife emerged from her retreat, offered his reassurance: "I'm sorry you feel that way. I had no idea. I know I can be arrogant about my way sometimes, but I'd never leave you. I love you. I'm sorry you felt that you couldn't talk to me."

By now we could push for the real meaning behind Allen's opening agenda. What was this "more nurturant mother" stuff about? I wasn't certain, but I suspected that the stated agenda was problematic. Allen seemed to need to make Janet into the kind of mother that *he* believed she should be, and he wasn't so open to letting her find her own way. "Things in a marriage are almost always shared," I said. "If we're going to get anywhere we have to begin with that premise." Now, turning to Allen, I said, "Can we be interested in what your agenda for Janet says about *you*?"

Allen was willing. While he continued to hold to his idea that Janet should be more nurturing, he had been taken aback by her having felt "unsafe," and he became more curious about his own role in things. Instead of demanding that Janet change, he began to talk about himself. As it turned out, he had brought quite a history of his own into the marriage.

"My father was a Great Santini—I mean literally. He was a military man, though never very successful. He graduated from West Point at the top of his class, but his career stalled because of his personality. He was—I can think of no better word for it—an asshole. He was an asshole father too. He was brutal. We were never good enough. No grades were ever high enough. We were never good enough in sports. We were never good enough—period." As Allen spoke, his controlled, almost at times affected, demeanor dissolved. His face reddened, his speech quickened, and he leaned forward, taut and tense. "He'd punish us by hitting us, by yelling at us. He made our family into boot camp—long hikes, holding our arms out in front of us, days without anything to eat or drink but water. And when we couldn't cut it, when we complained, he'd ridicule us for being weak. 'Pansies,' he'd say. 'I'm raising a bunch of pansies.' None of us—I had two brothers—could do what he demanded, but I was the worst at it. I've never been very physical."

Allen had once told Janet the story of his childhood abuse, but, apart from that conversation, he'd never before spoken to anyone about what had happened, not even his brothers. Now we spent several months with Allen remembering and talking. During this time Allen became anxious, depressed, angry, and often he wondered whether it was a good idea to "let the cat out of the bag." But as he became more vulnerable he also became less controlling and more emotionally available, and Janet and I both encouraged him to, as she put it, "let the cat stay out." For the most part Allen did.

I never got the sense that there was much positive for Allen to reclaim in his relationship with his sadistic and abusive father. The work was simply to see his father in more human terms—as a failed man who had covered his insecurities by dominating and humiliating his children. This understanding by no means excused the abusive behavior, but it helped Allen to see his father as less of a Goliath; it helped him get out from under his father's enduring and oppressive shadow.

Obviously the knowledge that Allen had been beaten up—both emotionally and physically—contributed to our understanding of his single-minded emphasis on "nurturant mothering." But to fill out this picture we also had to understand the role of his mother. And talking about Allen's mother meant talking about something sacred.

"I survived because of my mother," Allen said. "She was a saint. My father was as abusive to her as he was to us. He would demean her, call her stupid in front of us. She told us later that if she stood up to him when he went after us it would only make matters worse for all of us, so she quietly went along, then in private she'd try to make it better. After he did his Great Santini thing to us she'd come and find us. She'd hold us, ask us how we were, sit by our beds and tell us that she loved us, that even if he was cruel and hateful she would always be there for us."

As I listened to Allen speak of his mother in such fiercely positive terms, I realized something about his and Janet's marriage. Each of them had resolved to be, and to not be, a certain way, based on what had been painful in the past. Janet had resolved never to leave the marriage, and she had resolved never to confront Allen. Allen had resolved to not be like his father, and instead had insisted that both he and Janet parent Max in the idealized image of his mother.

When I pointed this out, Allen, interestingly, became highly defensive, saying with an uncharacteristic edge: "Are you implying that there is something wrong with being like my mother?"

"Not necessarily," I answered. "But sometimes, within this arrangement, there doesn't seem to be a lot of room for either of you to find your own way to do things. It's like you're both walking along the edge of a cliff, fearful that if you let yourselves explore another line you'll fall off."

Allen paused for a moment, returning to his now more thoughtful self. "Is that your experience?" he asked his wife.

"Sometimes," Janet answered cautiously. Then, after pausing for a moment, she continued more forcefully: "I feel I have to be a certain way because of me, but I also feel like I have to be a certain way for you. Especially around these ideas you have about me as a mother. You want me to be like you. But I don't want to be like you. You're very attentive to Max and protective, sure, but sometimes I think you're too much so. Like you're fussy with him. I feel like if I'm the way you are he'll be suffocated. I feel like I have to hold back to counter the way you are." And then she added something that would prove important. "I think Dr. O'Connell's right that there's something in here about your mother. You try to be like her. You want me to be like her. But I don't want to be like her. I'm not sure that she was as perfect as you think she was."

The notion that his mother had not, in fact, been a "saint" represented, as you can imagine, a potentially excruciating paradigm shift for Allen. He wanted to disagree, to defend his mother, but he had also committed himself to an open-mindedness toward his wife's experience and toward his own past. So, fighting with himself, he

allowed some hard questions to emerge. Why had his mother not protected him better? Why had she never left his father? What were her
real motivations when she told Allen, after his father had abused him,
that she would always love him, even if his father did not?

During the course of these explorations Allen not only fought
through his own reluctance but sometimes fought with me. On occasion he accused me of "blaming the victim." His mother was, after all,
in an abusive relationship, wasn't the assumption that she could or
should have done differently unfair? "Probably," I would answer.
"But we're not talking about making moral judgments right now.
We're talking about the way that you've based your vision of parenting on who you imagine her to have been, and it seems important that
you know her as accurately as possible."

"I'm all for this," Janet would say, encouraging Allen in the hard
work of loosening his idealized view. "She's such a goddess to you, I
feel like I can never be half the woman that she was in your mind, and
I'm always coming up short in comparison."

Over time, with the help of his wife's constant support, through
talking in our therapy, and through visits to his mother in which he
spoke with her about his childhood (Allen's father had died some five
years before), Allen's view of his mother shifted. He came to realize
that her avoidance of his father, while perhaps necessary, had also
been the result of her weakness. And he also came to see that her post-
abuse kindness had been more complicated than he had previously
admitted. Those moments when she had fussed over Allen had also
been her covert way of getting back at his father, something that further infuriated the man and set Allen up for more abuse.

It was brutally hard for Allen to see his mother in more realistic
terms, and at one point he blurted, "My God, if I don't have her, who
do I have?" Then, realizing that Janet was in the room, he turned to
his wife and said: "Well, I guess I know the answer to that. I have you
and Max."

By now, Allen and Janet had gotten through the defensive crust of
their arrangements to a place from which they could begin to build

something that was more their own. Not surprisingly Janet wanted to talk about Allen's fussiness and control. "I know you really love Max," she said, "but you go overboard. Every time he gets hurt—a cut, a scrape, a spat at school—you react like it's a catastrophe. I think it's too much." Janet paused, and then she spoke with the reassurance that comes from surer understanding: "I understand something now. When you were a kid you were in danger all the time. And your mother fussed over you—maybe it wasn't as great as you thought, maybe she had other, more selfish motives, but it was the only love you got. But Max doesn't need all that fussing. Our family isn't like yours was. We're not an abusive family."

Allen let this sink in. Eventually I broke the silence: "There's this great irony in parenting," I told Allen and Janet. "We all try our best not to be like the parts of our parents that we felt were hurtful or unhelpful. But often the harder we try not to be like them, the more we end up being like them." Now turning directly to Allen I said: "I think that you do this with your fussiness. You feel like you're being protective, but I wonder if sometimes you end up being a kind of Great Santini of fussiness. You're not your father, for sure, but you can be awfully overbearing with your caretaking. And you insist that Janet be the same."

After a pause Allen answered, "Okay. But what should I do? Sometimes I feel like this whole therapy is about how I shouldn't be like my mother and my father. Well, who should I be like?"

"It's a good question," I answered, realizing that there was some truth to what Allen was saying: I had been intent on helping him let go of his insistence that Janet fashion herself along the lines of his idealized mother, and I hadn't been as focused on how he might find more acceptable, and perhaps more real, alternatives. I answered: "It's not as if you should be exactly like anybody else, you need to find your own way. All parents do. But who have you had for role models in your life?"

Allen thought for a moment. "One person. Jim Benson, my graduate mathematics advisor. He was my mentor, really to me he was a friend."

"What was he like?" I asked.

"He taught me how to think. He was absolutely opposed to letting thinking be governed by preexisting assumptions. He used to say: 'Don't think with your feelings. The beauty of numbers is that they don't lie; they are what they are. If you look at them and set your own assumptions aside, they'll reveal their own truth.' I made my money using his basic principle. Now everybody knows that buying and selling stocks based on what you feel is a mistake, but I understood that fifteen years ago. I began, back then, to make my decisions based on the numbers alone, without any emotional assumptions about what was going to happen. And," Allen noted, his face alive, his voice full of pride, "it worked."

Allen's economic approach—he had been among the new wave of investors who had understood that the markets operated within a set of discernible mathematical paradigms, and that these paradigms could be exploited—gave us, oddly enough, a way to talk about parenting. I pointed out that Allen violated his most cherished mathematical principle in the way that he approached his wife and son: While he appreciated and respected numbers for the inherent truths they held, for their independent reality, he expected his wife and son to conform to his emotion-based demands.

Allen liked this angle. We were now talking about parenting using a language that he could relate to, and, equally important, the idea that he might apply his mentor's principles to his fathering grounded him. At one point he said to me, with a teasing twinkle of a smile, "Max and Janet aren't exactly numbers, you know. That's where your analogy falls short." And then, turning more serious, he added: "But I do realize that he is his own person. I worry about him constantly, I feel like I should be looking over him all the time, but I also can see that some of my worry is about the hell that I grew up in, not his reality now. But Christ, the world still feels like a dangerous place to me, probably it always will, and it scares the hell out of me not to watch out for him all the time."

I wouldn't say that Allen ever became an authoritative father;

his own father had been so brutal that, at least in the time I knew him, Allen was never comfortable being firm with Max. To borrow from the language we have been using, he couldn't free himself enough from the identifications and representations created by his father's abuse. But he was able to let Janet discipline the boy without criticizing her for not being "nurturant" enough, and he worked with her to figure out appropriate rules and limits. As he put it: "My father was right in what he stood for, he just went about it the wrong way. And he was so terrible I could never do that. So we do it together."

Perhaps, in the years since I last spoke with the Tinsleys (Max would be fifteen as I write this), Allen has become more comfortable with the art and practice of paternal authority. Perhaps not; the damage done by his father was substantial. Either way, Allen made himself into a better father. By learning to love without being so fussy and controlling, and by backing off enough that Janet could come forward with her natural inclinations to take care of Max, he helped to create a family space in which each member could grow and could be.

Buried Pain

The story of how Allen became a far better father without ever feeling at home in his own authority illustrates a basic principle of fathering: Sure, authority is a core element of fatherhood. But it is equally true that there is no behavioral sine qua non, no objective and absolute set of actions and deeds that can confer upon a man the title "Good Father." Instead, the measures used to determine whether a father is a good father are individual, subjective, and relative.

What we can say, however, is the following: Good fathers (like good mothers) parent from authentic places within themselves. Which means that the parameters that determine successful fathering tend to be personal ones: Does a man work hard at his fathering?

Does he manage to parent as well as, or better than, his own parents? And, perhaps most important of all, is he willing to struggle with himself, with his own history, with his own pain, with his own compromises and solutions in the face of that pain? If he strives to follow these principles, he will be able to bring more of himself to the job, and he will also be more likely to avoid, at least to a relative degree, the most egregious error a parent can make: He will be less likely to conscript his children, and his family, into shouldering those burdens that are in fact his own to shoulder.

Most of the fathers about whom I have written became better fathers by engaging in precisely this kind of struggle.

Some men avoided the hurt they held inside by removing themselves from the real-world forum of competitive interchange, and from the complex but enriching realm of family life. Gary Palmer, the reader may recall, kept himself at arm's length from these things because to feel alive meant to feel the pain of his loss and his regret. Only when he could tolerate the pain of what he had not had with his father could he begin to live his life more fully.

Other men became like their fathers so as not to feel their own pain. This was the "solution" made by Larry Miller, the man who was overly harsh, perhaps even cruel, toward Charlie, his son. Larry could not tolerate acknowledging that his own father had been belittling and abusive, and he avoided the anger and hurt he felt toward his father by being like his father. In this way, his life became a tacit acceptance of his father's abusive methodology. In order to be kinder to his son he had to see his father more clearly; he had to acknowledge the damage that had been done him. Only then could Larry resolve not to act like his father in interactions with his own son.

Other men renounced important aspects of themselves so as not to be like their fathers. Allen Tinsley, for example, renounced his father's brutal authoritarianism and instead acted like a caricature of his "nurturant" mother. He had to go back and reexperience the pain of his father's abuse, and his mother's fallibility, before he could find his way to a more personal, authentic version of fatherhood.

And still others suppressed important masculine and paternal qualities because owning and embracing those qualities led to pain and conflict in their relationships with their fathers. Jeffrey Stanton, you may recall, watched helplessly as his father died of multiple sclerosis. In order not to remember what it had felt like to grow bigger and stronger while his father wasted away, he became soft, retreating from his aggression and his competitiveness (and, of course, his authority), both in the family and in the world. He had to journey back, to remember his father, to remember the pain of his father's demise, before he could stand to be more firm with his children, Phil and Lora.

All of these stories are different. But all, I submit, share a common theme: If a man is to be a good father, whether that involves forging a more solid relationship with his authority, or whether it means freeing himself to better love, understand, protect, husband, or any of the other myriad endeavors involved in good parenting, he must commit to making a deeply personal, and quite often painful, journey. He must, in his own way, return to the buried sorrow that burns in his history. He must make his own relationship with the library of identifications and representations that lives inside him, gaining perspective on those that seduce him with the appeal of easy answers, freeing himself from those that deprive him of needed elements of his endowment, and disempowering those that drive him to visit the pain of his own childhood upon his children.

In a physical sense our children live in the homes that we provide for them. On a deeper level, their home is simply who we, their parents, are. They grow up immersed in the enriching yet burdening solution of our psychologies, our values, our histories, our compromises, and, importantly, our optimally relentless commitment to healing our inevitable fault lines in order to be good parents. This is why there are no shortcuts, why there is no faking it with jury-rigged, from-the-outside answers. This is why being a father is less about what a man *does* than who he *is*. This is what is meant by "fathering from the inside out."

More Dawdling

The doctors were never very straight with my mother about my father's most serious problem—a liver pickled by years of drinking. As I understand it, he never drank after I was born, but the damage had been done. By the time I was four the bouts of hepatic encephalopathy, and the trips to the hospital, had become frequent.

I remember, from this time, my first spanking.

My mother and I were walking home, and she was in a hurry. I think she was nervous about my father and wanted to get home to him. Feeling my usual objection to her eagerness to see him, I slowed. She told me to hurry. I slowed more. She told me, now angrily, that I was in for a spanking if I didn't get myself moving.

I gritted my teeth and decided to test her—her loyalty to me, and her disciplinary resolve.

She failed the former test and passed the latter.

She told me quite clearly the number of whacks I had coming. I think it was ten, though I'm not exactly sure. I do remember that the number mattered a great deal to me. As she neared the end, I felt her resolve wilt a bit. I thought perhaps I'd get a break on the last couple.

But she persevered.

In later years, we talked about this and the few other occasions she spanked me. In my twenties I considered these spankings not to have been a good idea, though I forgave her for having been so stressed.

Now I see it differently.

I am aware now that, when I discipline my children, when I need to be in some way tough, it is not my father I find in myself, it is my mother. In my childhood it was she, not my father, whom I saw use her aggression. It was she who taught me about the harder edges of life—not only through her inarguable hand but also through her resolve, and through the fight she waged to make a life for us as a woman in the 1960s with no money and no real education. Ironically, given the subject of this book, it was my mother, not my father, who brought the essence of what I have been calling paternal authority—

the reality of the world, and the inevitability of its demands and expectations—into my life.

I know that I became a better father once I stopped trying to find my father in me—these fruitless efforts were, I suspect, a result of my unwillingness to admit how little of him I had. The fact is, my good father had been there all along. *My* good father is, ironically enough, my mother.

10

Sexuality and the Family:
Creating a Safe and Fertile Space

THREE O'CLOCK ON a fall Sunday in New England. A father and his fourteen-year-old son are watching the football game on television. Brady hits Brown over the middle for fourteen yards and a touchdown, and the two of them cheer. "Brown is so clutch," the boy says. The man nods. The two sit together, comfortable in their camaraderie, as the extra point goes through the uprights.

The scene on the television switches to a beer commercial. Young men and women dance and gyrate, perfect bodies scantily clad in tight T-shirts and tight jeans, mouths, eyes, and everything else open to one another. A party of seemingly random and easy partnering; it's all about sex.

For the father and son watching, the easy togetherness of the game has been replaced by something more strained. "Wow," the father mutters, but only because he feels he has to say something. The boy is silent.

Soon the game resumes. Manning hits Harrison on the sideline for twelve yards and a first down. "Our corners play so soft," says the boy, his first words since the commercial. "I know," the father answers. "It's not all their fault, though. We can't get any kind of pass rush." With this, father and son settle back into their togetherness, though now an unease gnaws at both of them.

All of us, children and adults alike, are saturated with sex these days. It comes at us from advertisements, from television and magazines, from billboards, from movies, from Victoria's Secret catalogs in the mail, from the Internet, and from the increasingly mainstream multibillion-dollar porn industry. Simultaneously and from every imaginable angle the message is that all things sexual are possible. Indeed, we are led to believe that we can and *should* have it any way we want, and if we don't there are enviable others out there who do.

Yet there is also something paradoxical about these sexually heightened times: We don't seem particularly happy or satisfied with this apparent cornucopia of sexual delight. If anything, there is strong anecdotal evidence that we are feeling quite the opposite. Husbands and wives seem frequently unsatisfied with their partners; cosmetic surgery and devotion to physical fitness don't give us bodies that are attractive enough; self-help books promise answers to sexually dormant relationships; and "sex addicts," to use the now common parlance, are driven from sexual experience to sexual experience without ever being sated. And, perhaps most disturbing, the problematic effects of sexual oversaturation extend to our children. Articles in the popular press tell us that oral sex is becoming a common practice among very young adolescents, fourteen-year-olds, twelve-year-olds, even younger. That these kids are so young (even, in some cases, prepubescent children) is disturbing enough, but the articles touch on something even more ominous. It's something that I hear about all the time in my office. Youngsters say things like, "It's just a thing to do. It doesn't mean anything." Sex for them has already become numbed and wooden.

Assaulted by a sea of overwhelming messages and images, these kids have retreated into a state of sexual numbness and meaninglessness. They imitate what they see, while leaving their genuine selves behind.

Probably these attitudes should come as no surprise. The sexual culture that generates them, pressured as it is by the often greedy sense that all should be possible, is not very much informed by the constraints and parameters of what can realistically be expected. Such a world becomes, inevitably, one of virtual sex, with all meaning being malleable and subjective. Such a world soon becomes devoid of personal feeling and connection.

In this chapter, I examine the question of how parents can raise children whose sexuality will be responsible, meaningful, and personal. In doing so, I'll be taking you through material that may seem a bit off-color for a book on fathers, families, and children. I believe, however, that the purpose is legitimate. We need to look candidly at sexuality—in both its constructive and destructive manifestations—because sexuality has a central, if often unmentioned, place in the interchange of family life.

As always, though development is unfathomably complex, my focus will be on the role of the father. I suspect that my argument will by now be familiar: As with violence, our children's relationship with sexuality is profoundly influenced by the way we bring our own modulated and organized instincts, our transformed sexual and aggressive selves, into appropriate engagements with those parts of our kids' minds that need to be protected, organized, and even sometimes opposed.

Tim and His Father

Tim Worrel, a twenty-year-old college junior, came to talk with me because he had to: Being in therapy was a condition for his remaining in college. Tim had made a series of obscene phone calls to a girl on the floor of his dormitory, explicitly sexual and vaguely threatening calls such as, "I know who you are, and sooner or later I'm going to get that blow job." As the college administrator to whom I talked put it, "I can't tell what kind of kid this is. Maybe he's an okay kid with really bad judgment and some problems with girls, in which case you might be able to help him straighten out. But sometimes I wonder if there's something really wrong with him. If that's the case, I'm worried that we'll be hearing from him again."

The story told by the administrator preceded Tim's first appearance in my office, and so I too wondered what kind of kid I was going to meet. My initial impression wasn't positive. Tim didn't have much trouble telling me the story of the obscene phone calls, which wasn't a good sign: He didn't appear to feel the shame and chagrin that I would have expected, indeed hoped for. "It was just a joke," he told me. "I wasn't the only one either. About three of my buddies were in on it. I'm the one who gets in trouble because I made the call, but it was everyone's idea."

I asked Tim to tell me more. How had they chosen the girl to call? How did he decide on what to say? Why had they done it?

"Like I say, the whole thing was just a harmless joke. The girl we called, she's really hot, and she knows it too. She's got a boyfriend, and she walks around like she's totally uninterested in anyone else. Yeah, I got a little too raunchy in what I said, and probably I won't do it again. But—who does she think she is? I just wanted to call her on her attitude, I guess."

I had known Tim for five minutes, and I already didn't like him very much. He was shallow, self-involved, arrogant, and irresponsible, and what was more, he had clearly taken a seriously wrong turn in his moral development. I felt like calling him on what he was saying, but I knew I'd be responding largely out of irritation. Truth be told, I felt like saying something that would make him leave my office and not come back. But it was my job to try to help him, so I put a lid on my impulse, and I inquired further.

"What do you imagine the girl—what was her name—felt?"

"Why do you want to know her name?"

"Because I imagine we'll be talking about her." I also wanted to see whether speaking her name might make her more of a real person to Tim.

"Tamara. She said she felt all scared and traumatized, but I think that was bullshit. I think she made a big deal out of it to get attention. It's not like we raped her or anything."

"Do you imagine there's any lesson in this for you?"

"Look, I know what I'm supposed to say, that 'I understand that what I did was scary to her, that I need to be more respectful of women,' all that. But the truth is, I think this is bullshit. I didn't force myself on her. I didn't put a drug in her drink. I didn't even grope her. It was just a joke."

So Tim and I moved forward from this rather disturbing beginning. Our work was hardly a great success. Tim was in many ways a hostage to the therapy; he came because it was a condition for his remaining in the dorm. At times he missed our scheduled sessions, and when the misses became regular I would inform him that I was going to tell the college that he was not participating. With this threat his attendance would improve, though his commitment remained minimal.

Tim had lots of troubles. He didn't care about academics, doing the bare minimum to get by. He drank too much, though by the norms of his college his drinking was not unusual. He didn't have very deep relationships with his male friends, whom he mostly hung out with because they were "good guys to party with." And, as you have heard, his relationships with women were deeply troubled. His went well beyond the usual late-adolescent uncertainties and conflicts. He was, for reasons you will hear shortly, furious with women, deeply insecure, and very frightened, and he kept all of this thinly wrapped by caustically devaluing anything remotely feminine. On the positive side, he did have some degree of popularity on campus; he played varsity hockey at a school that held that sport in high regard. He was by no means a star, but simply being on the team gave him a great deal of social clout. Unfortunately, he largely used this currency to "hook up" with women when he was drunk, and in the aftermath of these encounters his level of crudity and devaluation became, if possible, even greater.

Over the two years we worked together Tim was rarely forth-coming about himself. Nevertheless he did, dutifully if somewhat grudgingly, give me a sense of where some of his fury, and lack of moral development, came from. Tim was the younger of two chil-dren; he had a brother who was two years older. His mother had been, as he put it, a "sloppy drunk." "She'd start at lunch with the martinis," he told me, "and she'd take it from there. By five o'clock she was pretty much cooked. She never made dinner, but it didn't really mat-ter, my dad hired someone for that anyway. By dinnertime she'd either be in her room—since I was about eight my parents have slept in separate bedrooms—or maybe she'd make an appearance, eat a few bites, then stagger off, saying she didn't feel good. Everyone knew it was bullshit, she just wanted to keep drinking alone, but nobody ever said anything."

"Was she ever there for you as a mother?" I asked.

"No. I don't ever remember her putting us ahead of the drinking. And there's one other thing about her—you're a shrink, you'll prob-ably be interested in this. Maybe this is my Oedipus complex—is that what you guys call it? Actually it makes my skin crawl. She went through this period when she was kind of weird with me. I was thir-teen or fourteen. I'd come home from school, and she'd call me into her bedroom. She'd be in her nightgown—at four in the afternoon—and you could see too much of her. She'd want me to sit on the bed next to her, and she'd get all lovey-dovey with me. But it was weird, she wasn't wearing enough, she'd stroke my arm in this creepy way, and I'd just get the hell out of there as fast as I could. God, it makes me sick to talk about it."

Over the time that Tim and I spoke, I never had the sense that more overt abuse had occurred. But it was certainly clear that this wasn't any Oedipus complex. Tim's mother had been a severe alco-holic, her sense of motherhood had been completely lacking, and, whatever she was doing those afternoons in her bedroom, Tim had experienced it as frightening, disgusting, and overstimulating. His attitudes toward women had suffered accordingly.

Tim spoke much more positively about his father, though I must say that I didn't share his favorable sense of the man. His father had been trained as a physician but had left clinical medicine to become an executive at a pharmaceutical firm. In doing so he had become rather wealthy. Of him Tim said, "He's a good guy. Makes good money, we have fun together. He sure doesn't get along with my mother, but who would? He probably would have gotten divorced, but either he's too busy, or he's worried she'd take all his money, or maybe he wants to keep the family together, I don't know. He's had girlfriends on the side, so he's not doing too bad. I met one of them once. To tell you the truth, she was pretty hot."

I met with Tim's parents on a couple of occasions, when they came up to visit their son, and they were much as I expected. Mrs. Worrel seemed barely able to follow the conversation, occasionally adding, in seemingly random moments, "He's a good boy, isn't he, Doctor?" I wondered whether she was cognitively impaired by years of heavy drinking. Mr. Worrel, in contrast, was sharp in his mind, but he too seemed to be missing something—a moral compass. "Well, since we're paying for this enforced therapy," he said (with less of an edge, and more of a conspiratorial "we're all guys and we know what's really going on here" tone), "I hope he's making the most of it. Boy this is a strange world these days. When I was in college people let you have a good time."

I tried to enlist Tim's parents in the idea that Tim needed some help maturing, that he had a problem with his sense of action, consequence, and his attitudes toward women, but I suspected from the start that this would be a lost cause. Tim's mother seemed hardly to follow me, while his father became irritated and dismissive. "Look," he said, "he's a good kid. I know he's got to go through this thing with you. But he's an athlete, he's young, nobody got hurt, let's not get too bent out of shape about some touchy chick here."

Over our time together, I didn't get much further with Tim than I got with his parents. I failed completely in interesting him in the connection between his mother's absence, her odd and overstimulating approaches, and his anger and sadism toward women. He didn't see it as a problem that he had utterly no interest in having a relationship with a woman, that he thought of them as interesting only in regard to sex, and that he found them even more disgusting and undesirable in the aftermath of his intermittent "hookups." Perhaps at best I helped Tim graft on a slightly better sense of what right and wrong *should* be. Maybe he had an increased awareness that the calls had been frightening to Tamara, and that he had to think about being responsible. I never got the sense, however, that these understandings had become organic, that they had taken root from the inside. His idea of sexual responsibility was making sure that the girl said yes, and making sure she didn't get pregnant. He wasn't particularly concerned about her feelings.

Tim's parting words to me seemed rather telling: "Well, the truth is, I can't say I've enjoyed it, but you helped me to get through, and I'll try to be smarter about this stuff in the future."

Healthy Sexuality and the Respect for Otherness

Among his many difficulties, Tim, most obviously, had a very unhealthy relationship with sexuality. But this statement invites a complicated question. What, exactly, is "healthy" sexuality?

Sex can be lots of things. And at different life stages, different meanings may take center stage.

Sex for an adolescent may be about coming to terms with all that is stimulated by entering or being entered. It can be about beginning to deal with anxiety, shame, and guilt. It can be about knowing, and using, one's body. It can be about fun, a way to learn, a way to find one's self. Perhaps above all it can be about beginning to put together the overwhelming physical power of sexuality with an ongoing awareness of the personhood of others.

Sex for a young adult looking for a life partner can be about weighing the power and allure of physical attractiveness against the need for honesty, persistence, integrity, sincerity, and other qualities that make relationships work. It can be about finding a partner who will be a good father, or a good mother. It can be a mode of self-expression, a way (though interestingly no longer the only way) to generate new life, and, of course, a way of communicating intense emotions—hopefully love and affection, but also, at times, contained aggression.

Sex for a couple who have been together for a while, who already have children, or who have children who have grown and moved away, can be about refinding each other again and again in the timelessness that sex can momentarily provide. It can be about holding on to a sense of physicality that all too easily disappears in the face of life's multiple pressures and, over time, mounting losses.

Depending on one's predilections, and moral position, there may be a place for any, all, and even more of these meanings in one's own definition of "healthy" sexuality. But how can we corral these disparate possibilities into a definition of "health"?

Let me be completely presumptuous for a moment. What we all *should* want, for ourselves and our children, is to arrive at a place where sex is a pleasurable and meaningful way of sharing important and real aspects of oneself with another who matters. Expressivity, vitality, and connection ought to be the rule, not the numbness, over-stimulation, control, and disconnection that characterize so much of our present-day culture's version of sexuality. Seen in this light, the distinction between "healthy" sexuality and "perverse" sexuality is not based on what kind of sex one engages in: Straight-ahead missionary position sex can be perverse when undertaken with the intent of controlling the other, while the most apparently "deviant" sexual practices imaginable may not be perverse when they are undertaken in an atmosphere of mutually agreed upon, bilaterally respectful sharing and play. The bottom line is that sex is more likely to be "healthy" if it enhances liveliness, meaning, and connection. If it engenders deadness, disengagement, and constriction, one ought to be concerned.

This approach to healthy sexuality returns us to the theme of "otherness." As with violence, where recognition of and respect for personhoods outside of one's own narcissism and omnipotence prove critical to the matter of safety, so also is it the case with sexuality. In a sense, the question of whether sexuality is "healthy" can be distilled down to the following: Is the independent selfhood of one's partner respectfully preserved in the face of the complex emotions and powerful desires that sex engenders?

And in turn, the importance of developing and sustaining the capacity to recognize and respect otherness returns us to the matter of fathers and their authority.

At the heart of Tim's trouble lay a basic inability to understand his impact on Tamara. Indeed, in both his obscene calls and his more socially acceptable "hookups," he had no sense whatsoever of his hurtfulness toward the women involved. His sexuality was perverse, being, as it was, all about control and discharge, absent any sense of mutual, respectful relatedness. What Tim most meant to express in these encounters was not tenderness, caring, or even desire, but anger and control. Beneath his bravado he felt worthless and neglected, and he managed these feelings by making women feel the way he did. To him women were basically "things"—receptacles into which he deposited unwanted parts of himself.

Tim's difficulties illustrate a simple yet important truth: Men need to be solid in their aggressive selves if they are to be solid in their sexual selves. Without control over his aggression a man will be more likely to act hurtfully and sadistically. At the same time, if he does not have access to that aggression he will likely be rendered frightened, guilty, passive, deflated, overwhelmed, and ineffective in the face of sexual desire.

It goes without saying that mothers play a crucial role in helping children form a good working relationship with their aggression, their sexuality, and the way in which these core qualities work together. Clearly Mrs. Worrel, with her drinking, her withdrawal and neglect, and her disturbingly overstimulating behavior, was a textbook case in how a mother should not be. But our focus, as always, is on the role of fathers.

And Tim's father was as much a source of Tim's troubles as was his mother. From his own wife, whom he treated badly, to Tamara, whom he dismissed with the words "some touchy chick," to the overarching way he lived his life, Mr. Worrel failed woefully in a father's multilevel task of transforming his own biological and psychological endowment, and then bringing that endowment into meaningful contact with the mind of his child. As a result, he did not engender in Tim a basic sense of respect for women, and he did not help Tim learn to manage and control his aggression. He did nothing to ensure that Tim's sexuality would become tender, respectful, and recognizant of the "otherness," or "personhood," of a potential partner.

Tim's father's failure calls to mind an anecdote another father told me in the course of writing this book, one that illustrates how things *should* go between a father and a son. On coming home from work this man had found his twelve-year-old son in a foul mood. He noted, being well attuned to his son's daily life, that "girls are looming on the horizon." Later in the evening the father, though tired from a long day of work, found it in himself to wrestle with his son. He noticed that the boy seemed to feel a bit better afterward.

Through the physicality and scent of this wrestling match, which activated his boy's aggression and adrenaline in an organizing and loving interchange while simultaneously allowing the boy to discharge safely, this father, I suspect, gave his son just what he needed. He helped him to feel more solid, more focused, more robust, and more governed, as the boy began to foray out into what is, for young guys, the everdaunting, and ever-interesting, world of girls (and women).

This same structuring, organizing paternal presence can be found in most embodiments of paternal authority. Indeed, fathers teach enduring lessons about sexuality through everything from simple communications like "Pick up your room, your mother is not here just to serve you," to major communications like rules, curfews, expectations about boyfriends and girlfriends, and more. (Perhaps you will recall the man whose father told him that there were two unbreakable rules: "Don't drive drunk, and don't get a girl pregnant.") Such messages, all of which are about treating people with respect and concern, are a father's way of helping his children's developing (or, as often seems the case with adolescent boys, exploding) minds to recognize and respect the independent being of others. And when children learn to respect the selfhood of those whom they encounter, they will, as they grow up, be more inclined to experience sex as a meaningful, mutual experience, rather than an opportunity for control and even sadism.

Lisa Robey

Like Tim Worrel, Lisa Robey first came to talk with me when she was a junior in college. And, as with Tim, the now common phrase "hookup" was an important one for Lisa.

Lisa was a pretty twenty-year-old, and on first meeting she struck me as earnest and sincere, though shy and uneasy with herself. For the most part she seemed relatively unconcerned about her appearance, wearing no makeup, no jewelry, just jeans and a pair of sneakers. The one exception to her casual look, however, was a low-cut, tight-fitting tank top that revealed her midriff. This style was hardly noteworthy in this day and age, but it contrasted with the rest of her more asexual appearance, and it was unusually revealing for a patient coming to my office for the first time. Interestingly, I had the sense that Lisa was not very aware of the message of sexuality that this aspect of her dress conveyed; if anything, she seemed rather unaware of her body.

Immediately upon greeting me with a well-mannered "I'm glad to meet you, thank you for seeing me," Lisa poured out her story. She had been meaning to talk to a therapist for some time, she said, and her mother had been encouraging. Her father, however, had tried to dissuade her. "You're fine the way you are," he had told her. "What could you possibly need to talk about?" That father and mother disagreed was nothing new; Lisa's parents had divorced when Lisa was five, and they rarely agreed on anything.

"What made you finally take the plunge?" I asked.

Lisa burst into tears. Through her tears she said: "I'm so embarrassed, but it's what I'm here to talk about. I have this problem with sex. Maybe more with guys, I don't know. I don't understand it, but it's been going on since I got to college. I end up sleeping with these guys after parties. Probably it would be more accurate to say that I end up getting screwed by guys after parties. I'm usually a little drunk, they're usually really drunk, I tell myself each time that I'll just get hurt, that I'm not really interested in the sex, that I want something else. I tell myself not to do it, but I do it anyway. I hate myself for it, it's not who I am, or who I want to be—God, I've never told anyone about this. You must think I'm some kind of slut or something." With this the torrent of words and feelings stopped, Lisa sat back in her chair, and again cried, now more softly.

"Actually you seem like a nice kid who's really hurting about this," I said.

Lisa reached for a Kleenex. "I've been trying not to think about it, even though it's eating away at me. I figured it was my private thing. Yeah, right. What was I thinking, that this stuff doesn't get around the stupid, airhead school I go to? So what finally got me here was that I was hanging out with some friends of mine, and when I left their room I waited outside the door for a moment. I don't know why I did it, maybe in the back of my mind I'd been wondering what people really think of me. Anyway, this guy—actually this guy I like—says, 'There goes Lisa, nice kid, but the hookup queen of Boston.' 'THE HOOKUP QUEEN OF BOSTON!' I ran to my room, and, I know I'd never do this, but I actually thought about killing myself."

"I'm sorry," I said softly.

Lisa was silent but for her tears.

"Well, something's going on where you're acting in ways that you don't really want to be acting," I added. "Let's see if we can sort it out together."

Lisa nodded, and I thought she seemed relieved. But then a new look of worry crossed her face. "You live here in this nice house, you've probably got a family, I feel like you must think I'm disgusting."

I felt nothing of the sort toward Lisa. She seemed a sensitive and thoughtful young woman, deeply distressed with herself, and admirably willing to try to figure out what was going on. I offered a heartfelt antidote to her shame: "Not at all. We all do things that put us at odds with ourselves. We all live out of places that are hugely pressured, yet largely unknown. It's part of being a person. I admire you for your willingness to wrestle with these things."

And so we did.

Lisa was the younger of two girls born to parents who, as I mentioned, divorced when she was five. Her mother and father had negotiated joint custody, though Lisa had spent the majority of her time living with her mother. "She was—is—a good mother," Lisa told me. "She never remarried, only when I went off to college did she even start to date. She's worked since I was little, and she still found time to be a mom. My father's done pretty well financially since the divorce, but he wasn't making so much back then, and my mother never wanted to go back to court to change things. That's what she's like. She's just a good person. She'd say to us 'If your father wants to pay more he can, but it's not his responsibility. We're all responsible for ourselves. I can handle this.' She's such a decent person, that's why I feel sick to my stomach about this stuff I'm doing with guys. I could never tell my mother. She'd never understand it."

Throughout our work I had the sense that Lisa's mother had, indeed, been a good mother. Perhaps she wasn't very assertive, perhaps she was too self-sacrificing, but she had always tried to be there for Lisa and her sister. As I got to know Lisa better, I sensed that she operated from a foundation of feeling loved and lovable that so often comes from having had a good mother. Even in her darkest moments she held out hope for a better future.

Lisa's father was another matter.

During the first year of our work Lisa did not have much to say about her father. "He's just not that important a person in my life," she had said. "When I was growing up I'd see him every other week, now I see him once or twice when I go home for vacations. He's okay, he buys me presents, usually clothes, nicer things than I'd buy myself, but they're not really my style. What can I say, he's my father, I love him, but my world never revolved around him the way it did for some girls I know."

Playing a hunch, I asked Lisa what style of clothes her father liked to buy her.

"Oh, usually more sophisticated than I like. I don't care that much about dressing up. Sometimes I don't feel all that comfortable in the stuff he gets me. It's a little sexier than I tend to like. It doesn't feel like me. Does that seem odd to you, that I don't like sexy clothes, given what I came here for?"

I told Lisa that it seemed more interesting than odd.

"What's interesting about it?" Lisa asked.

"I'm not sure. But I can hear that you feel uncomfortable in what he buys you. And it makes sense to me, as I've gotten to know you, that sexy clothes aren't really your style. Maybe I get the idea that your father has ideas for who you are, or who you should be, that are different from who you really are, or who *you* want to be."

"I never really thought about it that way. He's always seemed like such a nonperson in my life. But it makes sense. I've never felt like he knows me."

"Does that ever bother you?"

"More like I'm just used to it," Lisa answered.

With this, Lisa and I started to circle around a place of great importance. Of course her father had mattered to her, but unfortunately, his mattering, his "weight," lay more in his absence than in his presence. Beneath Lisa's notion that her father was inconsequential lay a great deal of pain and longing, as well as a set of powerful, and problematic, ideas regarding who she was, and who she could be, to men. And, as you may have surmised, this business of "sexy clothes" was also a bigger issue than Lisa had realized.

We began to get at this when Lisa trusted me enough to talk, in some detail, about the "hookups."

"I'll be at a party, and some guy will be looking at me, or he'll start talking to me. The first thing is that I'm so surprised that someone is interested in me—I don't think that men are ever interested in me—that I get this surge of excitement. I start telling myself, 'It's two in the morning, this guy's drunk, he's a guy, you know what he's probably looking for, if he's really interested in you he can give you a call sometime when he's sober.' You know the saying: 'Fool me once, shame on you. Fool me twice, shame on me.' I know what to say to myself. But it doesn't matter, because there's this other thing going on inside me. I feel so happy that a guy is paying attention to me. I don't care about the sex, it always sucks, to tell you the truth. The guy smells of beer and cigarettes, he never looks me in my eyes, either he leaves as soon as its over, or he passes out and leaves the next morning like he can't wait to get away from me. Then I'll pass him in the hallway later in the week, and he'll act like I'm repulsive. God, it's horrible. I *know* it's going to go that way. But in the moment, that thrill that some guy is interested in me just takes over, and I *act* like a total whore."

Lisa, as you can hear, had a powerful and unfulfilled need for male attention. While her relationships with women were solid—she had good friends and she was a good friend—she had no sense whatsoever that a man could like her for herself. This recognition brought us back to this "unimportant" father of hers. Now she could see that there was more to her relationship with her father than she had realized.

"I remember, when I was a little girl, I would be so envious of my friends who had fathers. 'Daddies' was the way I thought about it back then. I'd be at their houses, their fathers would be there, playing with them, talking to them, just being around, and it seemed like having that must be heaven. It's funny that I didn't remember that when we first started talking, but that was such a big deal for me back then. For a while it felt like not having a father was the center of my life."

I wondered what had caused something that was such a big part of her mind to seemingly have vanished.

Lisa thought for a moment. "I never realized this. I think it got to where I couldn't stand it. I started to hate my friends for what they had. I stopped going over to their houses. It's almost like I just cut that part of me off. Now, when my women friends talk about their families, I listen, but I don't ask for them to tell me any more. It's a reflex now, I don't even realize I'm doing it, but I just turn off when I hear about fathers. Wow. Is that really weird?"

"Not at all. It's the kind of thing that people do when something hurts too much to bear. It sounds like there's a big hole where your father should be."

Once Lisa was able to break through to the pain and longing she felt over her absent father things began to open up. She could see that her hunger overwhelmed her when guys came on to her, that she was seeking attention she had needed, and missed. This understanding helped her to end the hookups, which, in turn, helped her to feel better about herself.

But now another question was raised.

"Why," Lisa asked, "are guys only interested in me when it's two in the morning and they're drunk? I don't think I'm gorgeous or anything, but my friends have boyfriends, and it's not like I'm super-picky or anything. I just want to be with someone who is a decent guy. I feel like no one ever talks to me at the library, on the bus, when it might be about something more than just getting laid."

I thought it unlikely that men were so uninterested in Lisa. She was pretty, feminine, kind, funny, and, while she was shy, I did not have the sense that her shyness was off-putting. What was more, she had men friends, a few of whom she thought she might like as "more than friends." So what was happening? Why had she never had a steady boyfriend? During the third and fourth years of our talking together, after Lisa had graduated from college, and, after she had taken a year off and then begun graduate school, we worked on this question.

As so often happens, we got some help from Lisa's real-world life.

One day, in the middle of our fourth year of talking to each other, Lisa came into my office with a huge smile on her face. She remained silent for two or three minutes, while her delight filled the room. Eventually we both laughed. "So tell me, what's going on?" I asked.

"I was talking to Gerry, this guy I've been telling you about.

Know how I said he'd never be interested in me? Well, guess what happened. I took this big risk. I asked him why guys like me as a friend but never want anything more. I even told him what I'd figured out about the screwing around. He's a nice guy, he never said anything to me, but I knew he knew about it. Christ, who didn't? So he says, 'Jesus, Lisa, all kinds of guys are dying to go out with you. They just figure you're not interested, or you just like guys who are assholes.' I almost fell off my chair, I couldn't believe it. 'Like who?' I asked. So he looks all uncomfortable and everything, and you know what he says? 'Like me.' So we talk, and he tells me he's had this crush on me, and he figured I wouldn't be interested in him. So you know what I've been doing the last two days? I've been hanging out with him. I can't believe it. I keep pinching myself to see if it's real."

Of course what had happened made sense, at least in hindsight. Over the last year of our work the pieces fit together in an unusually neat way. The key turned out to be the "sexy clothes" her father had bought her. In a fascinating twist, it turned out that the out-of-place tank top she had worn to her first appointment with me had been a gift from her father. She remembered that she had felt uncomfortable putting it on that morning, but she had worn it anyway. Now Lisa recalled that her father had at times noticed her, but always, it seemed, his noticing had been about her looks. "Sometimes he would talk to his friends about how I was 'growing up,'" she said, "but there was always a twist to the way he said 'growing up' that made me feel uncomfortable. Like everything else about my father I think I turned myself off to it, but I realize now that the one thing he always noticed was sex. When I'd be out on the street with him he was always looking at women. When he'd hug his friends' wives, it always seemed to me that he hugged them a little longer than he should. Even when he hugged me, it never felt easy. Wow. I have been so blind about this. You know, I've always felt that other women are interested in who I am, but men, that's another story. Until Gerry, I guess I really thought that—what is that old saying, 'Men are only after one thing'? Well, I guess that's what I thought. It's not really true, is it?"

Five years after we began, Lisa became engaged to Gerry and moved with him to another city. It was quite a gratifying thing to have helped her to learn that a man could love her for who she was.

Keeping Things Safe and Alive

Even with the advent of more egalitarian ways of judging men's and women's sexual behavior, there continue to be, for many of us, differing attitudes toward the idea of women having multiple sexual partners, and men acting in precisely the same way. Setting these biases aside, however, having multiple partners is, like most things, neither positive nor negative in and of itself, at least not from the point of view of psychological and sexual development. It is, as Tim's and Lisa's stories illustrate, the individual meaning of the behavior that is important.

For a boy, the experience of multiple partners may involve learning about his body, his sense of power, his desire, and more, in the face of how overwhelming girls and women can at first seem. Or, as was the case with Tim, promiscuity, or "hooking up," can be about conquering, controlling, and objectifying—relatively perverse ways of approaching women that may calcify as a boy moves into adulthood.

Similarly a girl may be learning about sex, about her body, about the alloying of feeling and desire, in situations that are more practice than the real deal. More problematically, she may, as was the case with Lisa, be searching for attention, for something that should have been supplied earlier but wasn't. Or, again as with Lisa, she may feel that sex is the only way a man will notice her. Such behavior may well be consistent with the intriguing findings of Bruce Ellis, a psychologist at the University of Canterbury in Christchurch, New Zealand, whose study team found that daughters of absent fathers tend to become sexually active sooner than girls raised with fathers.

Lisa's story illustrates yet another challenge faced by parents in their efforts to raise sexually healthy children. Not only must we teach our children to respect the independent personhood of others, we must take great care to create a "safe and fertile space" in which *their* own personhood is both respected and responded to.

Obviously the first key word in this effort is "safety." Authenticity, playfulness, vulnerability, surprise, respect, and other qualities essential to healthy sexuality have no chance to germinate if children feel overstimulated or assaulted. Thus boundaries need to be established and maintained, and safety needs to be respected.

On the extreme end of this issue, of course, lies the epidemic problem of the sexual abuse of children. As someone who has worked often and intensively with adult survivors of childhood sexual abuse, I have seen firsthand the devastation wrought when trusted adults violate children's minds and bodies. The damage is often irreversible, sentencing a child to a life of terror, fear of others, guilt, shame, and alienation from his or her body. Even with the best of help, sexuality and intimacy remain affected, and, in an often unrecognized consequence, the scars are frequently passed along to the next generation. This is an admittedly stark view, but, having had what is now a good deal of experience working with adults and children whose minds and bodies have been assaulted, I believe that the damage done by abusing adults is, if anything, understated. Almost invariably victims of early sexual trauma still suffer, years later, from an inability to "recontextualize." By this I mean that the shadow of abuse shapes all later interactions, and so a hug is never a safe hug, a lover's touch is never just a lover's touch. Even the most loving and benign of interactions are distorted by mental pathways disarrayed by the earlier abuse. As one woman put it: "When my husband touches me, even if it's just a kiss, it feels like when my father violated me. I hate it. It's like I'm just wired that way, and no matter how hard I tell myself 'He's your husband, he loves you, he means no harm,' it still feels like my father."

While outright abuse is the most obvious form of parental violation, there are also gradations to the problem of safety: Actions that fall far short of outright abuse can also do a great deal of damage.

Children need to have their privacy recognized and respected, and they need to be protected from intrusion and overstimulation—from sources outside the family (the Internet and the media included), as well as from parents themselves.

This is not as simple as it sounds. As we move away from the area of outright abuse, the business of what constitutes safety becomes less straightforward. The definition of privacy, for example, shifts with age; parents have different relationships with the bodies and minds of their nursing babies, their toilet-training toddlers, their latency age children, and their adolescents. One thing, however, is clear at all ages: As children grow up privacy becomes increasingly important. It is not helpful for parents to parade their own sexuality, and probably even their nakedness, in front of their children. And it is certainly important that parents take care not to make their children objects of their own sexual satisfaction, whether this be via physical violation or, as was the case with Lisa's father, via vicarious, intrusive sexual interest.

But there is a second half to the equation: a "safe and fertile space." Perhaps surprisingly to some, respect for safety, while necessary, is not sufficient. So now we get to the word "fertile."

Healthy sexual relationships are, as I have mentioned, characterized by authenticity (one is genuine in what one brings), vulnerability (what one shares tends to be intimate and tender), and surprise (the inevitable result when one does not control the mind of one's partner). Often these elements are modeled (not, importantly, paraded) within the family—through parents' tenderness, affection, and mutual regard, through loving embraces exchanged spontaneously in front of the kids, and through the values that parents themselves live by.

Simultaneously these things are also communicated directly to children. The lightly erotic rhythm of family life can include touching, tickling, roughhousing, teasing, and more. Things are, optimally, both safe and lively. One woman I know spoke wistfully of how comfortable her father was with play that had a lightly erotic feel to it. Games like bucking bronco, and a very special game that involved bouncing on his lap, always felt safe, but also always quite exciting.

Children need to be protected. But they also need to have their emerging physical and erotic selves met, and responded to, by parents who are comfortable with the physical, even erotic side of life. One woman told me the following all too familiar story:

"I remember when I reached puberty my father was like 'hands off.'" He was never that comfortable with me, but when I grew breasts, when my period came, he couldn't handle it. He was a nice man, but always pretty uptight. I never heard him tell a dirty joke, never saw him sneak a look at another woman, never saw him do anything with my mother other than peck her on the cheek. Now I know that was what *he* was like, but back then I didn't understand. I felt that there was something wrong with *me*. Like my body had become ugly and dirty. I'm still not completely over it. When I make love with my husband, I need him to reassure me a lot that he doesn't hate my body before I can relax enough to enjoy it. I love my father. But I have always wondered whether there was something dark in him, whether he just didn't trust himself."

Alex and Rachel

Here is the story of a father who struggled, and succeeded, at making a space that was not only safe but also fertile.

Alex Walker, a forty-five-year-old business consultant, came to talk with me about a general sense of dissatisfaction and mild depression. Over the course of our three-year therapy we spoke about many issues, including his lack of motivation at work, his disappointment in the sexual side of his marriage, and his feelings of insecurity about his masculinity. We also spent a great deal of time talking about his relationship with his daughter, Rachel, who was twelve when we began our work.

Alex described Rachel with an enthusiasm and brightness that he seemed not to feel for anyone or anything else in his life, his wife and son included. She was his "sweetheart" and his "sunshine," terms of endearment that he spoke out loud to her, and that he had never felt for Judy, his wife of now twenty years. Indeed Alex felt largely distant from Judy, and she complained about his lack of physical and emotional affection. Meanwhile Rachel made Alex feel alive and loving.

Around the time when we began working together, however, things with Rachel had begun to change. With the onset of puberty Rachel had become more distant and sulky, and for the first time Alex no longer felt that he knew what she was feeling and thinking. Always a good student, she began to let her schoolwork slip. She became more unpleasant at home, not doing what she was told, rolling her eyes, sometimes frankly demeaning Alex and Judy. She also became less purposeful, saying, when asked to do her work, "What's the point, anyway?"

"It seems like she doesn't care like she used to," Alex told me. "Like nothing matters to her."

Over the course of our conversations about Rachel, I learned that Alex had been a pretty good father to his son, Fred, now fifteen. While he felt less passionately drawn to the boy, he loved him, and he was involved with him, playing games, taking him places, talking with him about friends, sports, and school. He had also been a pretty effective authority figure on those few occasions when Fred had needed straightening out. And the boy was doing well—successful at school, reasonably polite by adolescent standards, with a system of values and hard work already beginning to develop.

"I feel like Rachel needs something like what Fred gets from me," he said. "Something firmer, some kind of kick in the pants or something. But you can't do that to a girl," he told me. "I feel like maybe I just have to accept it. Things have changed, she's just not my little girl anymore."

"Why do you have to accept it with a girl and not with a boy?" I asked.

"I don't know. It's just different. When I raise my voice, not terribly, just to be firm, I feel like I'm hurting her. I feel guilty like I never did with Fred. Like she's delicate, she can't take it. And touching her—if I even think of grabbing her by the shoulders, looking her in the eyes, which worked pretty well with Fred, I can't even tell you what that feels like."

"What does it feel like?"

"Touching her—just doesn't feel right. It doesn't even feel the same to hug her anymore. She's got a body now. I know this sounds terrible—but—if I grab her shoulders like I did with Fred, I feel like I'm—violating her."

"Do you feel aroused when you do it?"

"Not exactly—it's not like I'm really physically turned on or anything. Maybe there's a little charge, I don't know. The best way I can explain it is to say it feels wrong somehow."

Rachel had lost her way a bit, not in any great pathological sense, more like in the normal course of development. She needed her parents to step in so that a minor derailment did not move in the direction of becoming a major train wreck. And while she needed many things, both from Alex and from Judy, one thing she needed for sure was for her father to give her some of what he had given Fred.

Alex, however, was feeling too inhibited, too worried about his more visceral responses, to give Rachel what she needed. As it turned out, he was consumed with the kind of trouble I just mentioned: unrecognized and unresolved issues with his own sexuality had caused him to withdraw from Rachel as she reached puberty. So he and I tried to sort out what was going on.

Alex's father, I learned, had been a "pretty good father." "He was firm," Alex told me, "but not too hard. He had standards, but he could ease up when he had to. He was okay with me." But the man had also been a philanderer. "With my mother, he was a real louse," Alex told me. He recalled his mother spending most of his childhood depressed, quietly communicating her pain and hurt but never getting angry, never defending herself, never getting up the gumption to leave. She was, he told me, using a now familiar word, too "delicate" to get angry.

Through discussions such as this Alex began to get a handle on how he felt toward Rachel and Judy. He had the sense that men, and fathers, could treat each other reasonably well, but when it came to women men were reckless and thoughtless. Women, in turn, were "delicate." "I think women spend most of their lives trying to avoid getting hurt by men," he told me. Alex had resolved to not hurt women, to not be like his father, and so he swallowed his anger, and his sexuality, leaving him withdrawn and guilty toward both his daughter and his wife.

Alex and I worked on this, and, over time, he became better able to distinguish remembrances of the past from realities of the present. These understandings helped Alex to trust that being less inhibited would not turn him into a hurtful man. He became more comfortably direct and firm with Rachel, more able to look her in the eye and ask her what was bothering her, more able to occasionally take her by the shoulders and scold her when she became denigrating and cynical. He also became less frightened of hugging her.

"It still feels sort of weird to hug her, to get angry at her, all those things," he told me. "But it doesn't feel 'creepy,' and I don't feel like I'm being a pervert, or hurting her. It feels more part of life, a kind of weird part of life, but a good part of life."

By the end of our three years together, Alex had become more engaged, not only with Rachel but also with Judy. He realized that he had been treating his wife with kid gloves. Not only did this make him feel less alive with her, it meant that she could not find in him a vitality and presence to respond to. Similarly, he found he was playing with more of what we had come to call a "full deck" at work. Most important to him, Rachel was brightening. She got involved with a better group of friends and took on a significant role in the theater group at her high school. The talk of there being "no point to any of this" largely disappeared. It was a particularly gratifying moment when Rachel said to Alex one day, seemingly out of the blue, "You seem less quiet, less sad or something. I feel like you're feeling better. I felt like you went through a stage there where you just weren't feeling so good."

A Father's Caretaking Line of Development

Obviously it falls on both parents to create a "safe and fertile space" for a child's developing sexuality. But again, our focus is on the role of fathers.

By now it ought to be clear that a father must walk a fine line between the twin pitfalls of overstimulation and abuse on the one hand, and physical and erotic withdrawal on the other. This means that he must learn about himself in the dimension that child psychoanalyst Jim Herzog terms "caretaking." And, as with so many aspects of fathering, caretaking involves transforming more basic and raw urges and impulses into attitudes and responses that are generative and protective.

On the most basic level, this occurs through the way a father conducts his own sexual life. Here I will say something that may sound moralistic, but it is something I have found to be the case more often than not in the families with whom I have worked. While promiscuity may sometimes represent, in both men and women, a developmentally useful and even generative activity, fatherhood, optimally, involves suppressing one's inclinations to promiscuity. The channeling of sexuality into mutuality, into respect for one's spouse and for one's family, models for children critical lessons in alloying sexual urges and impulses into loving, protective, and mutual relationships.

On another level, caretaking occurs through the way a father acts toward his children. This leads us to raise some potentially hard questions.

What happens when a father sees his child's genitals? When he is faced with the bodily realities of puberty, the sweat and changing smell of his children, the body hair, the blood, the breasts, and other sexually evocative physicalities in his once "innocent" sons and daughters? And now, an even tougher question: What happens when a father feels, somewhere deep inside him, the responses to sexuality and bodies that are a natural part of being human?

It's not a simple moment. Some fathers overindulge their excitement and interest. This was true of Lisa's father, and I believe it was also true of Tim's father, who was vicariously aroused by Tim's sexual aggression toward women. Other fathers run away from what they are experiencing—mentally, physically, and often both. As Alex put it, once we had broken through to a place where we could talk openly and honestly, "I remember when Rachel was a little baby, and I'd change her diaper. I was fascinated by her body. But I'd find myself thinking about what she'd do with it someday, and I'd think I was a pervert. So I'd try to put it out of my mind, and while I was changing her diaper I'd try to make myself think about every golf shot I'd hit that weekend, or some other inane thing. I couldn't believe it was normal to be thinking about that stuff."

This business of creating a safe but generative family life in which children can develop a healthy relationship with their own sexuality involves fathering, indeed parenting, in its most elemental form. It requires being real and present, remaining aware of one's thoughts, feelings, and responses, and holding squarely to the recognition that what is happening in one's children's minds and bodies is theirs, not ours.

Sounds like a tall order, and it is. But before the task in front of us seems too daunting, a few supportive reminders are in order.

Thankfully, we don't have to be deadly serious all the time. Sometimes what is most real is also quite playful. I recall hearing about a running joke that one father had with himself. I bet it will be familiar to some. This man imagined that when his daughter's first boyfriend came to the door he'd be waiting there with a baseball bat. Horrifying? Hardly. This, I suspect, was his playful way of expressing his sense of rivalry and jealousy, while simultaneously expressing his commitment to the protection of his daughter.

What's more, we don't have to be perfect. We never will, and besides, children possess great resilience. If, therefore, we make our best efforts, and if we allow ourselves to be a little lively, fun, and real along the way, our kids will, in all likelihood, do the rest.

Walking Through the Castro

When my daughter was nine she, her mother, her uncle, and I took a walk through the city of San Francisco. Talking, mindless of our surroundings, we soon were walking through the part of the city known as the Castro. Blatant sexuality was everywhere, from the dildos in the window to the T-shirts that read, "If I wanted your opinion I'd take my dick out of your mouth." I looked at my little girl, meandering through this sea of pornographic sexuality. I wondered what we should do. The problem, of course, was not the homosexual nature of things; the same scene could have occurred in the Tenderloin, or any other district in which heterosexual culture prevails. The problem was that everything was so overstimulating. Usually wide-eyed and filled with questions, Chloe became quiet.

And then our daughter did something very creative. She took a stuffed mouse from her pocket and began a deeply engaged conversation with it.

When, that day in the Castro, our daughter retreated a few years back into her childhood safety zone, thus protecting herself from the onslaught, she did so because her parents had, for the moment, failed her in their authority. But perhaps her ability to turn to her mouse represented a kind of self-protection that grew from what we had previously given her, during more responsible times.

11

Father Time

———

"SORRY," LOU GASPED, breathlessly apologetic on arriving fifteen minutes late for our first session. "I'm always late. It's one of my many character flaws." I listened, interested in the way this gym-fit forty-five-year-old man seemed not really to be so genuinely sorry. If anything his words and tone suggested that nothing could or would be done to change the way that he was.

Lateness, it turned out, was an important theme for Lou Sutton. Big-picture lateness. My first thought on meeting him was that he seemed better preserved, less dinged-up, than most forty-five-year-old men I knew. Interestingly, age was on his mind too. "I know I'm approaching middle age," he said (I noted silently that forty-five seemed, to me at least, to be more than just "approaching" middle age), "but I don't feel it. My wife, though, she keeps telling me that I need to grow up. She says that with her, in my work, with the kids— I have two, Ethan, he's twelve, and Teresa, she's ten—I act like a big kid myself. For a long time I figured she was just complaining, which is something she does a lot of. But lately I wonder if there's something to what she says. I have this idea that my life will go on forever, but I'm not crazy, and I know it's not true. And if I take a harder look in the mirror I can see that the kids are growing up, that my marriage sucks, and that I'm stuck in a job where I make okay money but I'm not really going anywhere. I live for getting together with the guys on the weekend, playing golf, having a few beers. I'm not building any-thing. I keep saying 'I'll get to it next year.'"

Lou, I learned, had somehow put the cornerstones of a life in place—a marriage, children, a job—but he had no commitment to any of these. He claimed to have no interest in divorce, but he gave nothing to his marriage, he spent a great deal of time fantasizing about younger women, and he had had several of affairs, none of which his wife knew about. He claimed to love his kids, but his words seemed hollow. On weekends he would "go out with the boys" while his wife took the children to their baseball games, piano lessons, and so on. And workwise, though he had graduated with an MBA from a prestigious university, and soon after had landed a very good job, he had, over the past fifteen years, made little of his good start. After a few early promotions he had gone nowhere while his peers continued to be promoted around him.

Lou's life, lived as it was without passion or commitment, was dis-turbingly empty. And he was fast running out of time to change this.

Castles in the Sand

In 2000, the American psychoanalyst Stephen Mitchell died at the tragically young age of fifty-three. Among his many seminal contri-butions, Mitchell wrote eloquently about a core human task: How do we live in real time—with the omnipresent disparity between our deepest, private hopes and fantasies, and the often harsh truths of our actual lives? Dealing with this dilemma, Mitchell writes, is a bit like building sandcastles at the beach. To live well one must commit to the building, even though what one has built will soon be washed away by the incoming tide.

Some of us, Mitchell notes, throw ourselves into the building of sandcastles "oblivious to the incoming tide." We are then shocked when the tide comes in and washes away our creations. In general, when we operate this way we "ignore reality and [are] therefore continually surprised, battered, and bruised by it."

Others of us see "the inevitability of the leveling tide" and therefore don't build at all. Those of us who take this approach are crushed by finiteness and limit even before we begin, and in our anticipatory despair we hardly venture out to live.

And still others of us are "aware of the tide and the transitory nature of [our] productions, yet build [our] sandcastles nevertheless. The inevitable limitations of reality do not dim the passion with which [we] build [our] castles; in fact, the inexorable realities add a poignancy and sweetness to [our] passion." In this third option, Mitchell tells us, lies our best (though still imperfect) solution: to respect and recognize reality, to live fully within it without being crushed by it.

So what do these musings about sandcastles and tides tell us about fatherhood and time? I'll begin to answer this question by means of a brief story.

Chris, a fifty-year-old father who came to talk with me about his perpetual sense that his talents were never well enough appreciated, bragged to me that he had arranged for his son to take the college entrance exams "untimed." By "untimed" he referred to the fact that standardized tests now accommodate kids with learning disabilities by making sure they have enough time to complete their exams. Chris's son, however, needed no such exception: He was a good student with no special needs, and his father was doing something that many parents do these days—he was trying to secure for his son an unfair advantage. "Isn't that what a father does?" he said. "Help his kid get a leg up on the competition. It's a tough world out there."

Well, it is a tough world out there, but, as I explained to Chris, his approach, besides being unethical, was more likely to harm his son than help him. For one thing, I imagined that the boy felt guilty—he knew that he wasn't disabled and so was not entitled to special arrangements. On a deeper level, such paternal subversions of the rules undermine a child's sense of effectiveness and responsibility. Perhaps the reader will recall here how Ryan's father wanted me to get the school not to discipline Ryan for the fight.

I suspect that Chris never applied the message of our consultation to his son—after a few months he discontinued our work, feeling that I too had not well enough appreciated his abilities. The lesson of our encounter, however, is one I have learned over and over again. While wealth, an overreliance on cleverness, or a willingness to cheat can get your kid a free ride early on, these invariably result in long-term deficits in a child's sense of solidity and confidence. As fathers, we want something different for our children. We want them to build lives that recognize and respect the fact that life is not an untimed test, it is an experience that is absolutely shaped by rules, by tides, by *time*. We want them to use their talents, abilities, and persistence to build lives out of the world as it is. We want them to feel special because of what they achieve, not because of what they are given.

Lou's Father

The lessons that I had been unable to teach Chris were ones that Lou's father had likewise failed to impart to Lou.

Lou told me that his father had showered him with unconditional regard throughout his childhood and adolescence. Whatever Lou did seemed to be fine with his father. When he did poorly in school he was told that he was smart, that school didn't matter, and that things would work out. When he had trouble with friends his father told him that the difficulties were his friends' fault. When he underachieved in college his father used his connections to get him admitted to a prestigious business school. When he underachieved in business school his father helped him get a good job in a good finance firm. There were no rules, no expectations, and no consequences. As I mentioned, Lou had thought himself lucky to have had such a positive and supportive father. But now he began to see things differently.

This wasn't, Lou came to recognize, a message of unconditional regard, rather it was the ultimately false and disabling promise of an uninvolved father.

This promise was communicated not only through Lou's father's words but also his deeds. Though successful financially, Lou's father lacked integrity. He openly criticized Lou's mother, bragged to Lou about his affairs, and, when he eventually divorced Lou's mother, was erratic in his financial support. He took no responsibility for the family's troubles. Eventually he remarried and started a new family, but, as nearly as Lou could tell, things weren't very different.

Lou's father, the reader can see, did not respect the existence of tides, of time—of those life-realities that must be recognized and respected. And he didn't teach his son how to do this either. If anything, he, like Chris's father, had taught Lou to try to get around those realities. He had not possessed, to return to the words of Salman Rushdie, a "father's weight." And Lou, as a result, had become a forty-five-year-old man who had not learned that life is shaped by time and aging, that what one can have is at least in part made meaningful by what one can't, that one must make personal sacrifices in order to fulfill social and familial responsibilities.

Lou's difficulties could be seen most clearly in his relationship with women. Later in our work I had occasion to run into Lou with his wife, and she seemed an attractive woman who looked her age— if anything, a bit younger. But this was not how Lou saw her. He spoke of her in coldly disparaging terms, particularly in regard to her body. He spoke of her "droopy breasts" and her "leathery skin." He told me that he could not stand to make love with her, indeed he could hardly stand to look at her. Instead he was obsessed with younger women, both those whom he fantasized about incessantly, and those with whom he, like his father, had a series of affairs, unbeknownst to his wife.

It was through his relationship with women that Lou and I began to untangle his deeply problematic relationship with time, and, for that matter, with fatherhood, with his wife, indeed, with reality itself.

We learned that his affairs and masturbatory fantasies offered him a kind of sexual never-never land, one in which he could flee from growing up. Simply put, Lou looked obsessively at other women because he could not stand to look at his wife, and he could not stand to look at his wife because he could not stand to see, in the reflection of her changing face and body, the fact that his life too was moving relentlessly forward in time. He could not stand this because it brought him face-to-face with the fact that the limitless possibility of his youth, unrealistically promoted by his father, was vanishing, leaving him with nothing to show for his forty-five years.

A Father's "Muscle"

Truth be told, to the degree that I helped Lou I did so by being a pain in the ass. I respected his willingness to talk with me about hard things, but I also felt toward him the way I do toward those who push ahead of me in the checkout line at my supermarket—something like: "So where do you get off living by a different set of rules than me?" Fueled by my irritation, I pointed out that he was cheating his children by his absence. I talked to him incessantly about time, telling him, for example, that while his body might feel good now, he was perched on the edge of feeling significantly older, and that when things started to change they would change in a hurry. And most of all, I talked with Lou about women. I pushed him to think about the impact of his affairs on his wife and children, and I confronted him about the degree to which his obsession with younger women served to help him deny the reality of passing time. I was blunt, perhaps at times too blunt, but Lou was most adept at dodging reality, and I justified my bluntness with the thought that I was giving him the kind of authoritative presence he had so sorely lacked earlier in his life.

At first Lou simply dismissed me, but gradually, in part as a result of my persistence, in part because he had begun to see how his own father had come up short, and in part because he could feel his life slipping through his fingers, he became willing to take a harder look at himself. With this our contention began to lead to some common ground. Lou resolved to build something more meaningful than mind-numbing withdrawals into the faces and bodies of younger women, and empty, beer-fueled banter with the guys after a round of golf. Initially his resolve to change was largely self-centered. "I'm worth more than this," he told me. "Soon the girls will stop looking at me, and anyway, I'm damned if I'm going to my grave with nothing more than a few good fucks to show for my time here." Lou's words were not exactly life-affirming, but they were, at least, a start.

Not surprisingly, things did not go smoothly. Lou's resolve to change precipitated severe panic attacks. Sweating, terrified, his heart beating a mile a minute, he was at first certain that these episodes augured a heart attack. But after a few trips to his internist convinced him that his problem was not imminent death but terror, he asked me to help him understand what was going on.

It wasn't hard to figure out what made Lou so frightened. He had never taken the honest measure of himself in any way; rather he had always inflated himself with the view that whatever he did was, in the words of his father, "just fine—probably better than anyone else could do." These hollow words of support had begat in him a flimsy confidence, beneath which he doubted that he had the stuff to succeed as a father, a husband, a professional. Now, like a kid going to school on his first day, he was scared to death. He was scared of adult things that he had never faced—things like aging, like failing as a husband and a father, and, above all, genuinely trying to succeed on his own merit.

Lou persevered through his fear, and, over time, he eventually made some progress. He swore off affairs, he became less disparaging of his wife, and he tried to be a better husband. He spent less time at the gym perfecting and preserving his body, less time drinking with his buddies, and more time at work and with his family. Nevertheless, his solution was pretty incomplete. He still complained that he did not find his wife attractive, and he continued to obsess about other women. He also found relationships with his family to be more dutiful than joyful and satisfying. When our work ended it was with a grudging admission that captured both his gains and the disappointment he felt in their limitations. "I'm not sure whether to blame you or thank you," he said dryly, "but I sure wasn't going to get anywhere the way I was doing it."

The story of my work with Lou illustrates another source of a father's, indeed of any parent's, authority. When I spoke with him about time, about possibility tutored by realism, my weight lay less in my own personal qualities than in the immutable truths about which I spoke. I was, in a sense, but a messenger. Fathers, likewise, owe their authority not only to their personal qualities and their position, but also to the realities they communicate and mediate. We don't make pain, hopefully, but we fortify our children against it by titrating its early dosage. We don't create loss, but we prepare our children for its inevitability. We don't create finiteness, but we teach our children of its framing presence.

And we don't create time. But time is, one could say, a father's "muscle." Every time we say to our children "you have to do it—now" we invoke the weight and power of time. It is the same when, in a more gentle vein, we simply point out the reality of time by noting: "I know you're scared, but you know what? You're old enough to do this. It's time." Even when we say "You'll get 'em tomorrow," we are saying, all at once, that the time today has passed, but it will allow another chance. With all of these seemingly mundane communications we impart the inevitability of impermanence and loss. Of change and possibility. Of that which is finite. We encourage our children to build their sandcastles, even as we gently prepare them for losing what they have built to the relentless tides.

Jenny Birnbaum

I have the idea, perhaps fanciful, I'll admit, that I have a sixth sense for who among us has lost a father while still young. There is something vaguely unsettled about even the most apparently well adjusted of us. Never quite at rest, we constantly search for a comfortable place that we never quite find, we forever look at the world from angles that seem always the slightest bit off-kilter. Sometimes I've heard the same musing—it's really not quite a complaint—from others who are in some way or another fatherless. It is as if we are members of a secret club: We recognize each other, we know each other in that from-the-inside kind of way, and we find in one another, at least for the moment, a place in our shared placelessness.

Jenny Birnbaum was a member of this club. In her midtwenties, she came to talk with me about her relationship with Stephen, her boyfriend and future husband. "It's not like there's anything specifically the matter," she said. "It's funny I'm even here, because I think I'm really happy." She paused, curious about what she had just said. "'Think I'm happy,' that's a funny way to put it. I *am* happy. I love him, he's a good guy and I know he'll be a good father. I believe he loves me. Somehow, though, there's something about me that can never quite trust that. I always feel like I'm holding part of myself back."

I liked Jenny immediately. She was lively and earnest, she knew something wasn't right, and, even though she didn't know exactly what was wrong, she wanted to make it better. She wanted to do the right thing, by Stephen and by herself.

Jenny continued, "I've been in a few relationships, probably fewer than most people my age, but I've never been really serious about anyone like I am about Stephen. With other men it made sense to me that I held back. I knew the guy was never quite right for me. I figured 'things will be different when I meet the right one.' But Stephen is right for me, at least I think he is, and I'm still holding back. You know, sometimes he looks at me and says 'Where are you? Sometimes I think you go places I have no idea about.'"

"Where do you go?" I asked.

"I really don't know. I tell him I'm just going for a walk in my head, but I don't even know what that means. The words just come out, like they're from some unknown place inside. You know, most of the time I'm rushing around like a maniac. I never sit still. Stephen calls me his 'crazy lady.' I know he wishes I could relax a little more. But those times when I get all spacey and dreamy, I just stop. It's not like I relax, though, it's different. Time just stops. I feel like I'm hypnotized."

Jenny paused. She looked uncomfortable, as if she wanted to say something but wasn't sure she could say it.

"What are your thoughts?" I nudged.

"I think sometimes this thing, whatever it is, happens during sex. Making love with Stephen is great. But sometimes, not all the time, I get really excited and then I just turn off. It doesn't really bother me, it still feels good, I don't feel like I always need to have an orgasm or anything like that, and I like just feeling close to him. But I mention it because it feels a little like those other times when I go away. And another thing that seems weird: Lately, when I do have an orgasm I cry afterward. I have no idea what that's about."

"No idea?"

"Well, I'm not an idiot," she said playfully. "I figure it must have something to do with my father. I mean, I know it's not only that, but he's this huge thing in my life. Overall I've been pretty lucky. My mother's a good person, I grew up with enough money, I felt loved, but my father got cancer when I was twelve, and he died when I was fourteen. We never really talked about it as a family, we just moved on. But I know it must be part of all this stuff. I mean, here I am in love with this man, how could what happened with my father not fit in somehow? But while I get that in my head, I don't really get it in a way I can use it."

A Father's Death

Jenny began by talking about her present-day life. She talked a great deal about Stephen, who sounded like a kind and patient man. She talked about her intermittent sense of remove, sexually and emotionally. It wasn't a huge problem between her and Stephen, but Jenny wanted to know more about it. She talked about her plan to be a doctor (after getting a liberal arts degree she had gone back to school to take premed courses). She talked about her mother, who frustrated her with what she called her "inane, meaningless talk." And increasingly, as time went on, she talked about her father.

Jenny had no trouble remembering how much she loved her dad. He had been a warm and kind man, an engineer who loved to putter in his garage workshop. It hadn't been a hiding place for him, rather it was a place where Jenny felt welcome. As a girl of seven or eight she would find her way to the workshop, and, sitting on an old wooden bench that her father had made, she would watch him work. He would talk to her, and though she rarely understood his musings on his various projects, she loved to listen. Often he would interrupt what he was doing to make things for her. "Go get that stuffed bunny of yours," he'd say, "we're going to make a wagon for it." "You'd think that a guy like my dad, shy, mechanical, always in his own head, wouldn't necessarily know what to do with a little girl," Jenny noted, "but he was a great dad. I had all these things that he made out of whatever was lying around. Great stuff. I still have a lot of it. Every now and then I take it out, look at it, try to remember him."

"He sounds like a good guy," I said.

"He was a great guy. Quiet, kind of shy, but there was much more to him than people knew. He was always there. I remember when I was about seven I got really sick—some kind of weird pneumonia, and I had to be in the hospital almost a week, and I couldn't go to school for three weeks after that. Every day he came to see me, he read to me, brought me ice cream. My mom is a good person, she tries to *do* the right thing, but my dad, he just *was* the right thing."

Talking to Jenny about her dad felt like talking to my wife about her father, who also died when she was thirteen. I could feel Jenny's father when she spoke of him. It wasn't just that she described him vividly, though she did, it was something deeper than that. I felt that I could sense him living in her, and, as with my wife, Jenny's talk of her dad made me want to cry—more than I ever did on thinking about my own seemingly harder-to-find father. Jenny, however, did not cry. She spoke of her father wistfully but still factually, and I often imagined that I could feel the presence of her father better than she could. This was so even when she spoke of his death.

"I remember the day it all fell apart. It was the last day of seventh grade. He had been tired for a few months, run-down, but I hadn't been worried or anything. That day he and my mother were in the kitchen, and my mom was crying. He had his arm around her, and she was sobbing. He was telling her it was going to be okay. That's the same thing he said to me later that day. He said that he had been to the doctor, that he was sick, but that he was going to be okay. I wanted to believe him, I always trusted him, but for the first time ever something felt off about him. I knew that my mom was way too upset for something that was going to be 'okay,' and while my dad's words said 'don't worry' I knew that there was something in his voice, in the way he held me, that said the opposite: 'No, you should worry.'"

Jenny had been right. Her father had been diagnosed with colon cancer, and on that last day of seventh grade he learned that it had metastasized. During the next year he endured largely ineffective surgery and chemotherapy, which left him run-down, tired, but still the father Jenny had remembered. By the second year, however, he became more obviously ill. He still spent time in his garage, but he was less talkative. After a year and a half he became thinner and weaker, and he stopped working. "I feel so guilty about this," Jenny said, "but it got to where I couldn't stand to look at him. My mother kept saying it was going to be okay until the very end—God, I must have heard those words a million times—'it's all going to be okay.' But it wasn't okay. My dad got sick, he died, there was a funeral, and you know what? Nobody in my family has talked about it since."

Living with the Inevitability of Impermanence

No one wants, or expects, to lose a parent when still young. But the idea that a loss like Jenny's is unexpected is a relatively modern phenomenon.

In his book *Western Attitudes Toward Death,* the French historian Philippe Aries traces the near total transformation that has occurred in our relationship with mortality. From the Middle Ages, when "death was readily accepted by the living and the dying as a destiny collectively shared," up to our modern age, in which death has been "banished from life reconceived in terms of short-run earthly satisfactions," we have moved from seeing death as an inevitable, necessary, and even meaningful event, to one that is seen as an unexpected and unwanted intrusion on our "right" to live as well and as long as we want.

This transformation speaks to our overall relationship with pain. These days we are often not so good at accepting life's losses, regrets, and hardships; instead we cocoon ourselves in omnipotent scripts (consumerism being one), thus extruding painful inevitabilities into illusory oblivion. This notion—that we should somehow lead painless lives— is the force behind our present-day "cult of victimhood," a term coined by social critic Wendy Kaminer to refer to the proliferation of grudge and grievance, and to the increasingly common notion that one's pain and misfortune make one an exception, entitling one to special consideration. Life should be limitless and pain-free, many of us believe, and when it is not, something has gone wrong, and someone is to blame.

This reference to grievance and entitlement returns us to the matter of time. If we are not to be made victims by the simply expectable, if we are to live honorably with the inevitability of pain, loss, and hardship, we have to accept the fact that things move forward in time. That things change, that they are endlessly impermanent; this is perhaps the one constant on which we can always rely. What's more, such impermanence gives our lives meaning. We see this on the cellular level, where, as microbiologist Ursula Goodenough reminds us, in her book *The Sacred Depths of Nature,* complex life forms are possible only because of the creative patterning that derives from cell death. And we see it on the human level. As Adam Phillips writes in his reflections on Freud's 1916 essay "On Transience": "Love at its strongest . . . is an acknowledgment of transience, not a willful denial of it. Death makes life lovable; it is the passing of things that is the source of our happiness." Or, to be a bit more contemporary, as Joni Mitchell says, "You don't know what you've got till it's gone."

Time passes. Death and loss approach. The painful awareness of the impermanence of our lives, and of those we love, often tempts us to retreat into blunting illusions, as did Lou with his time-denying maneuvers of promiscuity with younger women. One of our jobs as fathers is to lend our children the strength to live with their eyes open, to appreciate and respect time, to know that pain, loss, and disappointment are not unexpected guests at the party. They are, if anything, our hosts: inchoate, authoritative presences that, both for better and for worse, give our lives their meaning.

Cryogenic Memories

For the most part, Jenny had formed a solid relationship with time. By the age of twenty-five she had found the man she wanted to marry, and she had decided on a career. She worried, realistically, about how she would manage being both a physician and a mother. "Women are supposed to be able to do it all these days," she noted, "but I don't expect it's easy. It's not just that there isn't enough time in the day. There isn't enough room in our minds." There were, however, a few telling glitches in her overall effective temporal arrangement. There were those moments when, as she put it, she went for a walk in her head, when time just seemed to stop. And there was what happened when she made love with Stephen.

"I like sex, but it's not a simple thing for me," she said. "I have to work at it a little. It feels really good, especially with Stephen, because he's attentive, and it feels personal. But sometimes, when I feel really turned on, something weird happens. My body, my breasts, wherever he touches me, it feels like too much in those places."

Curious but not fully understanding, I asked Jenny to try to say more.

"I almost feel at odds with myself when sex feels physically powerful. Sort of like I'm doing something wrong. Not so much morally wrong, more like I'm violating some kind of natural order. It's as if those places where I'm feeling so excited, I'm not supposed to have them yet—like I'm still a little girl. I work on it, I remind myself that I'm a grown woman, and that what I'm doing is normal and good. But I feel pulled into two places at the same time, like the little girl and the grown woman don't fit together. God, I sound like I have a multiple personality, or something."

These thoughts took Jenny directly back to the time of her father's dying. Twelve and thirteen years old, her body was emerging from its girlhood. She remembered her breasts growing, her period starting. In the way that it normally is for kids, it had been an exciting, scary, and disorienting time. But there had also been an added layer. "Everything just seemed off," she said. "Time seemed wrong. My body felt wrong. My father weighed ninety-five pounds when he died. When he got sick he was a man and I was a little girl. By the time he died I weighed more than he did. I went through this period of not eating just before he died. My pediatrician said I was becoming anorexic, but that wasn't what it was. I had the idea that if I stayed small, maybe he would stay big."

In the years after her father's death Jenny's field of struggle expanded from her own changing body to her relationship with boys. "I'd be on a date," she said, "and all of a sudden, in this really calm, almost cold way, I'd tell the guy I wanted to go home. God, those boys must have thought I was psycho. But I'd go home, sit at the kitchen counter, and I'd eat ice cream. Sometimes I'd find myself sitting on that bench in my dad's workshop. I don't even remember how I got there. I think I just wished I could be a little girl again. It's funny, it sounds so sad when I talk about it, but at the time I just felt numb."

Talking like this, Jenny and I began to sort things out. While most of her had moved forward in time, through college, through relationships, and through other aspects of building a life, a part of her had remained stuck in the time of her father's death. She had kept her father, and with him parts of herself, frozen; cryogenic memories suspended in time. Now her mind began to thaw. She realized that when she lay with Stephen after making love, her crying was, without her quite knowing it, a way of remembering her father. When she stopped herself from feeling excited during sex she was stopping herself from feeling her body, pulsating and alive, moving forward, out of her control, toward being a woman. By dousing her excitement she controlled this movement, and so she never entered into the moment when her little-girl self came together with her adult-woman self, the moment in which her body and mind felt the way they did when her father died, the moment in which she had felt unbearably sad.

These understandings reflected a process through which Jenny grew to feel less at odds with her body, and more in touch with her memories of her father. By the end of our work she had embraced her sadness, and the way her body could lead her to it: "I wish my father were still alive," she said. "He wouldn't be that old, even though it seems like a lifetime since I talked to him. But at least it's nice when I'm lying in Stephen's arms, crying, to know that I'm remembering him. I used to feel, when I had an orgasm, that I was growing up, and that I was losing him. Now I can let it happen more easily, because I know afterward, if I cry, I'll be thinking of him. Actually it's kind of nice. I feel like I'm lying there with the two men that I love."

Mourning involves a great paradox: It is not about forgetting and moving on, rather it is about remembering, and still loving, those one has lost. We hold the smells, voices, images, and experiences of those we love in a timeless place in our minds. If we can stand the pain, we can return to them time and time again, even as time moves relentlessly forward around us. Jenny had not been helped through time by her father, he had not been around to help her learn to live in its pace.

And so she hurtled forward too fast away from the moment of his death, all the while she remained frozen in it. By crying, by finding him again, she began to live at one speed.

"The Optimum Distance for Seeing One's Father"

"Perhaps," the narrator of Jane Smiley's novel *A Thousand Acres* tells us, "there is a distance that is the optimum distance for seeing one's father, farther than across the supper table or across the room, somewhere in the middle distance: He is dwarfed by trees or the sweep of a hill, but his features are still visible, his body language still distinct. Well, that is a distance I never found. He was never dwarfed by the landscape— the fields, the buildings, the white pine windbreak were as much my father as if he had grown them and shed them like a husk."

Over time, if all goes reasonably well, children gain perspective on their fathers, compiling and shaping inner experiences of them into a size that neither looms nor vanishes. Some of this making of perspective is, of course, the eventual responsibility of the child, who must come to terms with his or her idealizations and disappointments, thus arriving at a view that realistically appreciates, for better and for worse, his or her father (and of course mother). It's a job that extends well into adulthood. Probably it's one that never ends.

Much of how a child achieves perspective is determined by how well a father lives up to his end of the bargain. And much of this depends on a father's relationship with time.

Fatherhood requires that a man activate his masculinity, and also that he control it. This means committing to a relationship with one's partner, as well as with one's family. I don't intend this to be moralistic or admonishing; that we must all do battle with our elemental natures means that we are all, by definition, imperfect. Nevertheless, fathers must struggle with this "imperfection." Being a father means trying to sublimate many basic masculine inclinations—for self-centeredness, for acquisition, and, in fact, for promiscuity—in order to concentrate our life force and to use it constructively within our families. In this regard, time challenges us to channel our energies and resources away from the illusions that impulses like promiscuity embody, toward the more grounded choices that come with being a husband and a father.

Then there is the matter of how a father negotiates his own aging, in particular his acceptance of death, and, when the time comes, his preparation for it. It cost Jenny that her family never talked about her father's death. "I know it's a lot to ask," she once said, "but it would have meant a great deal to me if my father could just once have acknowledged that he was dying."

And there is also the way that fathers, indeed parents in general, serve as familial timekeepers. Families tend to become stuck in time. They hold on too hard to those moments that feel good, that feel emblematic of their preferred image of family life, and they move on too fast from those moments that feel bad or seem foreign. Fathers must learn to hold on appropriately when children are younger, and similarly must let go when the time is right. Some fathers fail at this because they are driven by a Lear-like insistence on dependence and submission, one that denies the reality of time's progression. Others fail because they force independence too early. The father of one family I know could not stand to think about the eventuality of his children's leaving home, and so he began preparing them for this event when they were still toddlers. "Our job is done when you're eighteen" was the family mantra. Unfortunately, these words only served to make the children feel that their parents couldn't wait to be rid of them.

In these ways and many more, fathers and parents teach children, inductively and indirectly, to live successfully in time.

And then, alongside the lessons a father imparts through how he lives his own life, there are the lessons he teaches directly.

Before discussing this, let's return, for a moment, to a familiar theme: Isn't the matter of living in and teaching about time an issue for both parents? Do fathers have some unique relationship with time that in some way privileges them in this domain? As always, the answers to these questions are relative. Fathers are certainly not privileged over mothers when it comes to this matter. Both have roles. But fathers, by virtue of their hierarchical, from-the-outside mode of relatedness, and their paternal inclination to introduce reality in ingestible doses (tools and proclivities that spring from their masculine biologies and psychologies), can make a distinctive contribution to the shared endeavor of helping children to live in time.

Consider the following story, told to me by a father about the time one of his children developed a medical problem. The treatment recommended was going to be expensive and time-consuming, and the family was given the option of putting it off a while, even though this probably would not have been optimal for the child. "We took care of it right away," the man said, "and now the whole issue has basically disappeared into the past. Everybody was great. My wife devoted herself to the therapy afterward, the doctors were good, it all came out well. My role was to say 'we're going to deal with it *now,* and money is not going to be an issue.' I knew we had to get right on it—it was a critical moment." By using his aggression to make time work *for* him, and not *against* him, the father not only helped his child, he also helped his wife by easing her understandable anxiety.

This story is reminiscent of the one I told several chapters earlier about my daughter and the bees. My wife's responses, you'll recall, were, in a sense, timeless. She operated in homeostatic attunement with our daughter, staying awake with her, attending to her, doing what needed to be done in a way that was organized around our girl's needs. I, meanwhile, operated with a different sense of time, one dictated by when the store where I could buy bee poison opened, by when the bees would be asleep, by the fact that I wanted to kill them while my daughter was still hurting, and so on. Thus we were able to replace some of my daughter's fear with the strength that comes from being effective and proactive.

These two stories are, among other things, stories about learning to live in real time. Indeed, most of this book's fathering stories feature the defining presence of time. When Bill made Oliver get the testing while still early in his school career, when you tell your running-across-the-street child to be instantly alert, when you tell your child he's ready for that driver's test—all these and more are events in which fathers focus and strengthen their children with the help of time's purpose-making, urgent presence.

Optimally, time organizes our lives, providing a steadying frame within which we can build lasting meaning. It disciplines us without crushing our spirits. But for a child to benefit from this truth, he or she must learn the language of time. This language, of temporal sequence, of critical moments, of cause and effect, is a language that fathers are well equipped to teach. The simple words "do it now" disrupt complacency with an incisive message: "Know that when you do something, something then happens because of what you did. Same if you do nothing—this causes that. Know that the moments in which you must act do not extend indefinitely. Know these universal laws, feel them, get them inside of you. If you do you will have more freedom of choice. If you do you will be less likely to feel paralyzed in the face of immovable forces. If you do you will be more likely to own a sense of responsibility and power. And if you don't you will be vulnerable to grievance, helplessness, and despair."

While writing this chapter, I realized something quite obvious about children and sandcastles: Kids build elaborate moats and sluice-ways, in recognition of the inevitable waves, thus making the impermanence of their creations part of their joy. In other words, they build because of the tides, not in spite of them. As adults, we have much to learn from children. Our lives, too, are made out of the tides of time, not in spite of them.

Bolinas

In and out of daydream, I push myself back into the anesthesia of semisleep, dimming my awareness that our last day here has begun.

Forty feet below us, the waves murmur, build, crash and are silent; murmur, build, crash and are silent.

A house in Bolinas, just up the coast from San Francisco. It sits on a cliff at the most western edge of town, and at seven in the morning our room lies in a pocket of sunshine. To the west the sun glints and glimmers off the Pacific. To the south, San Francisco is shrouded in luminescent fog. And eastward, the green and gold hills hide the bustle of Marin County, as the everyday world gets ready for work. The beauty is so extreme it seems almost virtual, and my wife jokes that the cormorants that swoop and splash outside our window must be our "screensaver."

In a few minutes our day will begin, and with it the housecleaning that signals the end of our time here.

I sit up and watch my wife as she lies reading. When I look at her face I see layers of time. I see her as I met her. I see her before that, as the young girl whom I have imagined, and whom I have seen in the family photo albums. I see her today, and in her face I see the twenty years accumulated between us, time filled with children, fights, celebrations, pleasures and pains, losses and gains. I see in her my own graying hair, my softening and thickening body, my aching knees. I see the time that we have had, and I regret the time that I could have had, had I not wasted it with petty and self-serving hurts and grievances. And finally I see her ten, twenty, and, with luck, thirty years and more from now. She doesn't believe me, but the hard part of seeing her in the future has nothing to do with "looks." It has to do with recognizing that the time that is gone will keep expanding, while the time that is left inexorably shrinks. It has to do with the awareness—sometimes pressing, sometimes dim, always lurking—that it all ends. It ends for me, it ends for her.

And, worst of all, it even ends for our children. This truth textures every moment of forward-moving joy—the voice of my older son, suddenly so deep that I don't know it is him when he answers the phone, my daughter standing back to back with her mother, now an inch taller, my younger son pushing through pain and fatigue on the soccer field because, for the first time, he thrills to the competition. Each of these moments signifies the ever-strengthening hold our children have on their own lives, and so each is to be celebrated. But each moment also carries the shadowing reminder that time will never stop moving, and so each, also, is to be mourned.

Marriage and raising children allow men and women to perceive, in the mirrors of each other, the relentless passage of time. When things go poorly, the reflection is harsh, and time's passing feels brutally finite. But when things go well, the time we see in our loved ones' faces can hold more hopeful, and more fluid, meanings. To be sure, it all ends. But the present is still open-ended—inviting. The future, though dwindling, is undecided. And even the past has fluidity. What's done is done, but there is a great deal that we don't yet know about that will affect what will come. So even within the harsh confines of time there is some room, not infinite, but enough to create and to not despair.

Father time. If a father is charged with teaching his children about reality, then, more than my father himself, time has been my father. In time I have found the closest thing that I have known to an immutable other. I ceaselessly press myself against his unyielding presence, and in the contact I find and find again my being.

12

Real Hope

HARRY FRIEDMAN first came to see me when he was fourteen. Referred by his school counselor, he was described as a boy who was "more self-centered and entitled" than anyone his high school guidance department "had seen in years." He rarely did his homework, spoke to teachers and other elders with flagrant disrespect, and interrupted conversations without hesitation. As the psychologist who referred Harry to me said: "Some of the things this kid says make you want to laugh, they're so outrageous. Except you end up wanting to strangle him instead." During the first two years of our work Harry lived up to his billing many times. On one noteworthy occasion soon after we had begun he stood up in the middle of class, berated his teacher for her "idiocy" and "incompetence," and, on walking out of the classroom, told her that when he became a "multi-billionaire," which of course he would, his first act would be to buy the school and have her fired. This threat was all the more remarkable for the fact that his was a public high school.

Early on, when things were still rocky, I met not only with Harry but also with Harry's parents. Decent and compassionate people, Jill and Gordon Friedman described their situation with thoughtfulness and concern. The first thing they told me was that Harry was adopted. Then, quite guiltily, they told me that they had had it with him. He seemed to care about little other than video games and television, he refused to do any work for school or around the house, and he threw screaming fits when things did not go his way. Any interest he had in others seemed strictly related to what they could do for him. Jill and Gordon were exhausted and exasperated by the nightly battles with Harry—to do his homework, to pick up after himself, to in some way take some responsibility for his life. Harry would have none of their entreaties for better behavior, and what was more, he had a trump card that he played often: He used the fact of his adoption against Gordon and Jill, screaming, "You're not my real parents. You can't make me do anything."

Like many parents of adopted children, Gordon and Jill hoped that they could make up for the painful loss that Harry had endured. Moreover, they were both, by nature, guilty and self-critical people, and, as a result, while their parenting featured kindness and understanding, it was harder for them to be stern and say no. Both parents needed to ease up on their guilt and self-criticism; they needed to use their parental authority to insist that Harry take more responsibility for himself, and that he contribute more positively to family life.

I won't tell all the details of Jill and Gordon's efforts, which paralleled many of the stories I have told thus far. But I will give you a glimpse into their eventual solution by relating an anecdote that occurred some three years after we began working together.

Harry had been insisting that he be allowed to watch television, even though Jill and Gordon had instituted a rule prohibiting this on school nights. Jill, who had been working very hard to get better at saying no, set a limit. Harry responded with a screaming, defiant, and insulting fit. Jill tried her best to intervene, insisting that Harry stop screaming, punishing him with grounding, and sending him to his room. Harry, however, continued his tantrum unfazed.

Eventually Harry stopped screaming, but the battle was far from over. He next left a note for his mother in which he proclaimed himself to be worthless and unlovable, and in which he informed her that he planned to run away from home. Here he expressed the seldom seen flip side of his rage: his guilt and shame over being so angry and destructive.

At this point Jill called Gordon, who was heading home from work. Forewarned, Gordon anticipated the scene at home. "I kept thinking about what was the best thing to do. I thought back on all the times that I tried to get Harry to do what I wanted, only to have him give me a great big 'Fuck you, Dad.' I'd just get angry and frustrated, and I'd end up either yelling or giving in. So this time, I decided that I was just going to stand by what I thought was right. Harry could like it or not, but I wasn't going to yell, or scream, or get all caught up in the fight. When I do that with Harry he says, 'See, you do hate me,' and then it's like he wins. I resolved that I just wasn't going to go there. Whatever he said or did, I was going to stick quietly but firmly to my guns."

Gordon arrived home calm and resolved. "I started out by reminding him that he's a kid, that his life is about things like doing homework, having friends, and getting to sleep on time. And then I told him three things: First, you cannot run away. Second, if you do we will find you, and if we need to call the police to do that we will. And third, when we find you there will be consequences. He yelled and screamed, like he always does, but I just stayed with it. And you know what? He started to calm down."

Gordon smiled and then continued: "I know that we'll have to go through this again and again with him. But I learned something. I had to give him something he could come up against." With this Gordon pressed his fists together to illustrate how the confrontation had felt. "I realized that he might scream at me, tell me I wasn't his real father, do all the stuff he does, but I didn't have to negotiate with him. I didn't have to control him. I just had to be strong about what I knew was right. I just had to be his father."

Harry, like so many of the rest of us, had to come to terms with a significant hardship, in his case having been given up for adoption. As a young teenager, he hadn't come close to dealing with how he really felt about this. His provocations were, more than anything, a common but misguided way of deflecting attention away from pain that he could not stand to feel, and his entitlement, his stated belief that he was special and therefore due special considerations, served as covering fire for his deep-seated sense that he did not have the wherewithal to make things better himself.

Jill and Gordon used their authority to help Harry change. They spoke firmly to him about the truths of the past: Harry's biological parents had indeed not been able to care for him, but this had not been his fault. They also spoke to him about truths in the present and future: Harry was still a child, more powerless than powerful; Gordon and Jill were now his parents; and they would take good care of him.

By speaking so clearly and firmly, Jill and Gordon began to create a safe arena in which Harry could begin to deal with what pained him. Now our individual work became more productive. Harry and I grew to understand that he had long covered over a deep-seated fantasy that his biological parents had gotten rid of him because he was unlovable. Sure that he would be rejected again, he provoked in order to test Jill's and Gordon's love and patience, as well as to elicit their anger (better, in his mind, to make them hate him than to wait helplessly for the inevitable). What was more, certain that he lacked the stuff he needed to make his own life better, he retreated to a position of absolute entitlement ("do it for me, since I can't do it myself").

By the time Harry was a senior in high school the family was much more solid and effective, and I had stopped meeting with Jill and Gordon. Harry started to care about his life. He began to do his homework, he felt less entitled, the fighting stopped, and he became an excellent student. In an ironically positive development, he became, for a period of time, depressed and sad—this often happens when a person has enough strength, and enough help, to stop behaviors and gambits designed to flee from pain. Harry became better able to stand feeling badly; he even, to his credit, could use these painful feelings to better understand himself.

Harry and I spent the next six years talking together; in fact he didn't stop talking with me until after his college graduation. At the end of our last session he thanked me with words that I will never forget. "I think I'm finally happy with where I am," he said. "And part of it is that I can see that I've not only built my life *in spite of* my pain, I've built it, in no small part, *out of* my pain."

Of all the things that people have said to me over the years, Harry's parting words remain among the most powerful. They reveal, I believe, the essence of real hope.

Hope, as we all know, is founded upon feelings of desire, possibility, optimism, promise, and imagination, all of which come together in the belief that "things will work out." These feelings and wishes live timelessly in the mind, a locale that gives them a certain freedom; there they have room to grow unconstrained by the demands and exigencies of reality.

Simultaneously, however, the timeless and ungrounded conditions that are characteristic of this mind-only locale impose a limitation. If hope is to be something more than private, untested wishing, then the feelings noted above must also be tempered by the challenge of real time, real others, and real life. This requires moving the timeless fantasies and constructions of one's imagination into a relationship with outside-the-mind reality. As Winnie the Pooh wisely noted, "You can't stay in your corner of the forest waiting for others to come to you. You have to go to them sometimes."

When Gordon spoke firmly to Harry about the reality of his adoption, the need to do homework, and the inevitability of consequences, he said, in essence: "Things were what they were, you can't change that. Sure, you have lots of feelings about it, but if you want to have a life, you'll have to build what you need to build out of the hand that you were dealt. We'll help you to the best of our ability, but in the end it's up to you." With these words he conveyed a father's message of real hope.

Shoulders and Handkerchiefs

In the beginning, everything still seems possible. Our shiny, newborn children have yet to emerge from being pure-form creations of our own hopes, dreams, and, of course, thwarted wishes. They can, in the freedom of our untested imaginings, still score the goal that we never scored, ace the test that we never aced, find their way to that natural popularity that we never found.

Soon enough, however, things change. Their skin absorbs that first cut, and that cut turns into their first enduring scar. We see, for the first time, another child run faster, and play more deftly, on the soccer field. They come to us struggling with a math problem that just will not give way. Perhaps they even find themselves in that same outside-looking-in place with other children at school that we so painfully recall. Now their real bodies and minds, complete with potentials and limitations, have begun to emerge.

Our children must now deal with a complicated truth. They also, in a sense, must deal with a broken promise, even if one made only implicitly. The world in which they will live will be harder than the idealized one that we imagined for them, and that we subtly, and without meaning to, told them they could expect. They will have to work hard if they want to run faster, and even then they likely will not be the fastest. They will have to struggle with that math problem. And socially, if they grow up to be their own man or woman, they will have good friends, but not everyone will like them.

The *real* work has begun.

It has begun for the child, who must bring the hopes incubated in the protected womb of that early parent-child relationship into meaningful contact with a complex, and often unrelenting, world.

And it begins for the parents.

One summer day, my daughter, Chloe, then twelve, came to me in tears. She probably came to me because her mother, whom she finds more helpful when things are really tough, was elsewhere. She had a problem with a friend—a simple, everyday problem. She wanted to swim, her friend didn't want to. She wanted to walk into town to buy some candy, her friend didn't want to. She was willing to do pretty much anything, but she couldn't get her friend to go along. Usually she handles these things pretty well, but she had burned her hand that morning, she was in pain, nothing seemed to be going right, and she was in a terrible mood. Probably she needed the space to just be miserable. But, burdened as she is with the family neurosis of feeling overly responsible for anyone and anything that crosses her path, just being miserable wasn't an option for her. Everything in this twelve-year-old moment was a mess; she was mad at herself, mad at her friend for making her mad at herself, and guilty about being mad at her friend because she knew that none of this was her friend's fault. She just wanted to get out of the whole darn thing, but she was too responsible to let herself do that. She was, we agreed, in "a yucky tangle."

Probably my daughter didn't need much more than a shoulder, an ear, and a handkerchief. But it wasn't so easy for me to leave it at that. The fact is, every time I talk with her I see her as my still seven-year-old girl skipping off into the morning sun, with her bright aliveness extending out into the future. In the part of my mind where this image will always live there is no burn on her hand, there are no friends with whom hard negotiations are necessary, and there is no burdening sense of overresponsibility. In this part of my mind there will always be an aching wish for her to have a painless and unfettered life.

When memories like these kick in, something problematic happens: My sense of reality subtly erodes. Perhaps, I think, my daughter's friend is to blame; she's stubborn and demanding, and somehow, by virtue of some flaw in her twelve-year-old character, she has made my daughter unhappy. What's more, my Chloe shouldn't have to worry about these things; the world is, after all, her oyster, and she should be able to do whatever feels right to her, whenever she feels like it.

Of course these mental gambits of mine are wrongheaded. Chloe is not *my* Chloe, and this problem is not the fault of her friend. Chloe does have to worry; solving dilemmas like these is part of being a friend, part of being a trustworthy and connected person. I can help my daughter, but I can't make her pain vanish by blaming, by evading, by reconfiguring in my own mind the world that *she* has to encounter. She has to come up against it—burned hand, messy friendship, and so much more. Which means that today, a shoulder, a handkerchief, an ear, and a kind acknowledgment that the world is often not so easy are all that I have to offer. I have no magic; under these circumstances magic would be only alchemy.

And so we sit together for a few minutes. Eventually we'll come up with some ideas of what she can say to her friend, and we'll acknowledge that the burn will feel better by tomorrow, but these are not the point. What matters is the sitting together in the realization that there is no quick fix, that things are what they are. And then the slightest of smiles touches the corners of her lips. It's not a happy smile, nor is it an ironic smile of resignation. More like acceptance, even surrender. I can't make the mess vanish, and neither can she, but she, and maybe to some small degree we, will find a way to deal with it.

A Quiet Business

As the book has progressed, I have tried to describe a quality of fatherly authority that moves beneath, around, and through the relatively traditional, and relatively overt, authority of forcefulness, hierarchy, and announcements to "clean up your room." This quiet, beneath-the-surface sort of authority lies more in our natures than in our words and deeds, and it infuses our more visible acts of authority—louder, more forceful, more in a given moment—with the strength and resolve of its authenticity. It also serves as a constant presence in our children's lives, and then, as it becomes their own, an organizing, structuring fiber in their emerging minds.

This quiet, omnipresent authority of parental being is one that can only be arrived at from the inside out. It comes from being wise enough so as not to be conscripted into naive or self-serving agendas. It comes from how a man subdues his inclinations to omnipotence and narcissism enough to live realistically, honestly, and generously. It comes from how a father moderates the erotic elements of his love and affection when he hugs his children. It comes from transforming and using anger and aggression when a child goes out in the middle of the night to do drugs. It comes from owning and managing competitiveness and ambition in order to foster his children's success. It comes from channeling fear into a protective response when his child runs out into the street. In sum, it comes from coming to honest terms with one's own self.

This inner quality of authority owes its power to one of life's great paradoxes: We parents are not only first and foremost in teaching our children about the challenges of the world, we are also, ourselves, their first and foremost worldly challenge. This paradox creates both a potential problem and a potential opportunity: A problem because those things we have not worked out can't be hidden. An opportunity because, since our kids know who we are, since they feel us, sense us, and smell us at all times, every act of doing and not doing carries meaning, and each moment of our parental being is itself an act of authority. It's because of this that, as Gordon demonstrated with Harry, we don't have to be loud and forceful to be authoritative. We don't even have to try to act authoritative in order to be that. The fact is, timely silence often carries as much weight as loudly spoken words. A decision not to intervene can have the power of an active action. A simple act of patience communicates a world of trust ("You will get through this"). And our resolve speaks volumes about our love and commitment.

Whatever the dimension—love, protection, discipline, mothering, fathering—our parenting is as much defined by who we are as it is by what we do. Thus, while our fatherhood, our authority, indeed our "weight," are forged from strength, power, love, caring, and a commitment to the safety and well-being of those we love, we would do well to temper these ingredients with a certain humility—an acceptance of the inevitability of change, for example, a respect for limitation, a tolerance of uncertainty and fallibility. The fact is, our self-understandings are always fluid and imperfect. Same with our very selves. Our solutions, precisely because they are deeply personal and hard-earned, are invariably flawed. Our fatherhood and our authority, therefore, do not lie in "right" and definitive answers, nor do they reside in unassailable power or opinion. It lies in our ever-evolving selves. Our children feel our efforts to grow, to do our best, as much as they feel our answers. They take in who we really are, not who we think we are.

Real children live in *real* bodies, and they need *real* help with their *real* struggles. If they are to meet the world outside themselves with strength and conviction, if they are to bring their minds, their selves, their hopes and wishes to the relentless challenge of living—they must be allowed, encouraged, indeed sometimes even forced to collide repeatedly with the often hard edges of reality. Absent such collisions, they will not learn how to be architects and movers of their own destinies, and they instead will be hamstrung by the entitled and ultimately self-defeating belief that the world will, indeed should, shape itself to their wishes and fantasies.

Fathers, in the ways I have described, help their children with just this. By bringing his very being, his "weight," into his relationship with his children, a father conveys, ideally in a way that can be absorbed and then used, the sometimes reasonable, sometimes brutal, always inescapable rules, expectations and inevitabilities of life. He does this by using elements of his own transformed masculine endowment, including both his instincts and his psychology, to teach his children about the immutable nature of time and limit. He does this by being a palpable "other," one whose independent selfhood cannot easily be conscripted. And he does this by helping his children understand, in an environment of safety and caring, that the world does not lie in their omnipotent control. In all of these ways and more, a father inoculates his children against retreating into a muffled, daydream world of fantasy, omnipotence, and self-involvement. And he helps them find the essential stuff of their own selves.

Changing

Several years ago, when the thoughts that would eventually form this book were first starting to move through my head, I secretly hoped that my writing would help me find more of my father. Back then I believed in rather more dramatic and absolute cures and solutions, and I thought I might be able to strengthen myself along those fault lines where my authority, my fatherhood, indeed my very masculinity, felt soft, and brittle, and wanting. Maybe then I would be able to respond with a strong calm when angered, rather than a bristly irritation. Maybe then I wouldn't hide behind my eyes when I felt things deeply. Maybe I would stop seeing myself as a little smaller, a little younger, and a little less than I really am.

These were grand wishes. Too grand, as it turns out.

Writing this book didn't help me find my father, as I had hoped it would, but it did help me understand my relationship to his loss differently. I now see that my insistence about his absence was, at least in part, a facilitative self-deception, one hard to distinguish from the truth that lay alongside it. By imagining myself to be absolutely fatherless I made my father real and palpable. I gave him substance and presence through the way I knew him best—his absence and his death.

The knowledge that this was my solution brings with it a subtle change. Now, in unexpected moments when I am not looking so hard, when I shed the oddly grounding certainty of my fatherlessness, I sense a shadow that was not there before. It's a feeling that the man I am growing into is oddly familiar, a perception that I am building my fatherhood and masculinity on less foreign ground. I hesitate to say that what I feel in myself is my father, because when I do, when I look directly, the presence that is there recedes. Still, I am glad for the suggestion of something, however faint, that I could not previously find.

We are always changing.

Notes

Children make fictions of their fathers: S. Rushdie, *The Moor's Last Sigh* (New York: Vintage, 1997), p. 331.

1. A Father's Weight

PAGE

5 *father hunger*: The term "father hunger" is now part of our common parlance. It was originally coined by Jim Herzog in a paper entitled "Sleep Disorder and Father Hunger," *Psychoanalytic Study of the Child* 135 (1980). It is also the title of his recent book: J. Herzog, *Father Hunger* (Hillsdale, NJ: Analytic Press, 2002).

6 *Webster's defines "authority"*: *Webster's College Dictionary* (New York: Random House, 1991), and, in a different edition, *Webster's New International Dictionary of the English Language,* second edition (Springfield, MA: C. & C. Merriam, 1950).

6 *Machiavelli's assertion that it is better for a prince to be feared than loved*: N. Machiavelli, *The Prince,* ed. and trans. Peter Bondanella (Oxford: Oxford University Press, 1998).

6 *Weber's belief that the power of authority derives from its legitimacy*: From Richard Sennett, *Authority* (New York: Norton, 1980), and M. Weber, *Basic Concepts in Sociology,* trans. H. P. Secher, (New York: Citadel, 1962).

13 *The gods visit the sins of the fathers upon the children:* Euripides, *Phrixus,* 970.

16 *as Ann Hulbert notes*: Ann Hulbert, *Raising America: Experts, Parents, and a Century of Advice About Children* (New York: Knopf, 2003).

16 *as Susan Faludi puts it in her popular book* Stiffed: Susan Faludi, *Stiffed* (New York: William Morrow, 1999).

2. The Great Masculinity Debate

PAGE

23 *Then Carol Gilligan*: C. Gilligan, *In a Different Voice: Psychological Theory and Women's Development* (Cambridge, MA: Harvard University Press, 1982).

23 *Nancy Chodorow, Judith Jordan, Irene Stiver, Janet Surrey, to name a few*: Nancy Chodorow, "Family Structure and Feminine Personality," in *Woman, Culture and Society,* ed. M. Z. Rosaldo and L. Lamphere (Palo Alto, CA: Stanford University Press, 1974); J. Jordan, "The Relational Self: A New Perspective for Understanding Women's Development," *Contemporary Psychotherapy Review* 7 (1992): 56–71; I. Stiver, "The Meanings of Dependency in Female-Male Relationships," in *Women's Growth in Connection,* ed. J. Jordan et. al (New York: Guilford, 1991); and J. Surrey, *Relationship and Empowerment* (Wellesley, MA: Stone Center Publication #30, 1987).

23 *"If boys in early childhood"*: C. Gilligan, "The Centrality of Relationship in Human Development: A Puzzle, Some Evidence, and a Theory." In *Development and Vulnerability in Close Relationships,* ed. Gil Noam and Kurt Fischer Majwah (Hillsdale, NJ: Erlbaum, 1996).

24 *The psychiatrist Eli Newberger*: Eli Newberger, *The Men They Will Become: The Nature and Nurture of Male Character* (Reading, MA: Perseus Books, 1999).

24 *Terrence Real*: Terrence Real, *I Don't Want to Talk About It* (New York: Fireside, 1997).

24 *Olga Silverstein and Beth Rashbaum*: Olga Silverstein and Beth Rashbaum, *The Courage to Raise Good Men* (New York: Penguin, 1994).

24 *And William Pollack*: W. Pollack, *Real Boys: Rescuing Our Sons from the Myths of Boyhood* (New York: Random House, 1998).

25 *Ron Levant*: Ron Levant, *Masculinity Reconstructed: Changing the*

Rules of Manhood—At Work, in Relationships, and in Family Life (New York: Plume, 1996).

25 *Dan Kindlon and Michael Thompson*: Dan Kindlon and Michael Thompson, *Raising Cain: Protecting the Emotional Life of Boys* (New York: Ballantine, 1999).

25 *As Susan Faludi writes*: Faludi, *Stiffed,* p. 26.

25 *As Michael Kimmel*: M. Kimmel, *Manhood in America: A Cultural History* (New York: Free Press, 1996).

28 *men are from Mars*: John Gray, *Men Are from Mars, Women Are from Venus: A Practical Guide for Improving Communication and Getting What You Want in Your Relationships* (New York: HarperCollins, 1992).

32 *Betty Friedan's* The Feminine Mystique: Betty Friedan, *The Feminine Mystique* (New York: Dell, 1963, 1983).

33 *books like John Rosemond's* Parent Power!: J. Rosemond, *Parent Power! A Common-Sense Approach to Parenting in the '90s and Beyond* (Kansas City, MO: Andrews McMeel, 1991).

33 *"Christ wasn't effeminate"*: Falwell quote taken from Kimmel, *Manhood in America*. Credit to Frances Fitzgerald, *Cities on a Hill* (New York: Simon & Schuster, 1986), p. 166, and Leon Podles, "Men Not Wanted," *Crisis,* November 1991.

33 *Asa Baber*: Asa Baber, *Naked at Gender Gap* (New York: Birch Lane Press, 1992).

33 *Richard Doyle*: Richard Doyle, *The Rape of the Male* (St. Paul: Poor Richard's Press, 1986).

33 *Nicholas Davidson*: Nicholas Davidson, *The Failure of Feminism* (Buffalo, NY: Prometheus, 1987).

34 *Probably the best-known author in this genre is Robert Bly:* Robert Bly, *Iron John* (Reading, MA: Addison-Wesley, 1990).

34 *Lionel Tiger, originator of the term "male bonding"*: Lionel Tiger, *The Decline of Males* (New York: St. Martin's Griffin, 1999).

34 *As Kimmel astutely points out*: References to William Blaikie's *How to Get Strong and How to Stay So* (1879), Macfadden's *The Virile Powers of Superb Manhood* (1900), Edgar Rice Burroughs's *Tarzan*, Teddy Roosevelt, Jack London, Frederic Remington, and Billy Sunday and the "Muscular Christians" taken from Kimmel, *Manhood in America*.

35 *At that time, a hypermasculine image*: It is worth noting that there

was, at the time, a move from a largely agricultural society to a predominately industrial one. As is the case today, there was a sense that women could do many of the jobs that were once the relative purview of men.

36 *a finding that leads Steve Jones to write*: Steve Jones, *Y: The Descent of Men* (Boston: Houghton Mifflin, 2003).

36 *a* New York Times *article*: Donald McNeil, "Are Men Necessary?" *New York Times,* November 11, 2003.

3. Harnessing a Father's Aggression

PAGE

42 *With her groundbreaking 1976 work:* Jean Baker Miller, *Toward a New Psychology of Women* (Boston: Beacon, 1976, 1986).

42 *Over the past twenty years a significant body:* Among others: Ballard, *Equal Engagement*; Fletcher, *Disappearing Acts*; Gilligan, *In a Different Voice*; Helgeson, *The Female Advantage*; Rosener, *America's Competitive Secret*; and Surrey, *Relationship and Empowerment*.

45 *When we think of power, we think along the lines of the dictionary definition:* Webster's College Dictionary.

45 *proposed by the American psychoanalyst Otto Kernberg:* O. Kernberg, "The Analyst's Authority," *Psychoanalytic Quarterly* 65 (1996): 137–57.

46 *In study after study:* Eleanor Maccoby and Carol Jacklin, *The Psychology of Sex Differences,* vol. 1 (Palo Alto, CA: Stanford University Press, 1974); Deborah Niehoff, *The Biology of Violence* (New York: Free Press, 1999); Janet Hyde, "Where Are the Gender Differences? Where Are the Gender Similarities?" in *Sex, Power and Conflict: Evolutionary and Feminist Perspectives,* ed. D. Buss and N. Malamuth (New York: Oxford University Press, 1996), pp. 108–18; and A. Eagly and V. Steffen, "Gender and Aggressive Behavior: A Meta-Analytic Review of the Social Psychological Literature," *Psychological Bulletin* 108 (1986): 309–30.

46 *it seems at this point a safe research bet:* Linda Mealey, *Sex Differences: Developmental and Evolutionary Strategies* (San Diego: Academic Press, 2000).

46 *The same goes for brain-based cognitive abilities:* Among others, D. F.

Geary, "Sexual Selection and Sex Differences in Mathematical Abilities (with Commentary and Rejoinder)," *Behavioral and Brain Sciences* 19 (1996): 229–84; D. F. Halpern, *Sex Differences in Cognitive Abilities,* 2nd ed. (Hillsdale, NJ: Erlbaum, 1992); E. Hampson and D. Kimura, "Sex Differences and Hormonal Influences on Cognitive Function in Humans," in *Behavioral Endocrinology,* ed. J. Becker, S. M. Breedlove, and D. Crews (Cambridge, MA: MIT Press, 1992).

47 *As James Dabbs tells us*: James Dabbs, *Heroes, Rogues and Lovers: Testosterone and Behavior* (New York: McGraw Hill, 2000).

47 *one Freud spoke to when he wrote*: S. Freud, "Civilization and Its Discontents," *The Standard Edition of the Complete Psychological Works of Sigmund Freud,* ed. J. Strachey (London: Hogarth Press, 1930).

47 *To again draw on James Dabbs*: Dabbs, *Heroes, Rogues and Lovers*.

48 *what Robert Sapolsky refers to as a "permissive" effect*: R. Sapolsky, *The Trouble with Testosterone (and Other Essays on the Biology of the Human Predicament)* (New York: Touchstone, 1997).

49 *man, as Stephen Mitchell aptly puts it*: Stephen Mitchell, *Hope and Dread in Psychoanalysis* (New York: Basic Books, 1993).

49 *Over the past hundred years*: E. Fromm, *The Anatomy of Human Destructiveness* (New York: Holt, Rinehart & Winston, 1973); H. Sullivan, *The Interpersonal Theory of Psychiatry* (New York: Norton, 1953); H. Kohut, *The Restoration of the Self* (New York: International Universities Press, 1977).

49 *No longer do we see ourselves as "guilty man"*: Mitchell, *Hope and Dread in Psychoanalysis*.

49 *As Bill Pollack said to Maria Shriver on the* Today *show*: From C. Hoff-Sommers, *The War Against Boys: How Misguided Feminism Is Harming Our Young Men* (New York: Touchstone, 2000), p. 145.

52 *a "prewired potential"*: This phrase is taken from Mitchell, *Hope and Dread in Psychoanalysis*.

54 *To quote the primatologist Frans de Waal*: F. de Waal, *Good Natured* (Cambridge, MA: Harvard University Press, 1966).

59 *listed in the American Psychiatric Association's* Diagnostic and Statistical Manual: American Psychiatric Association, *Diagnostic and Statistical Manual of Mental Disorders IV* (Washington, DC: American Psychiatric Association, 1994); Herzog, *Father Hunger*.

4. Fatherhood and the Music of Masculinity

PAGE

63 *These hierarchies not only reflect competitive success and failure*: See Clifford Geertz, *The Interpretation of Cultures* (New York: Basic Books, 1973).

63 *Workers become unmotivated when there is no hierarchy to climb*: R. Crawford, "Reinterpreting the Japanese Economic Miracle," *Harvard Business Review* 76 (1997): 179–84.

66 *The British psychoanalyst Donald Winnicott*: D. W. Winnicott, "Mirror Role of Mother and Family in Child Development," in *Playing and Reality* (Harmondsworth, England: Penguin, 1967, 1980).

66 *The noted pediatrician T. Berry Brazelton*: T. B. Brazelton et al., "Early Mother-Infant Reciprocity," in *Parent-Infant Interaction,* CIBA Foundation, Symposium 33 (Amsterdam: Elsevier, 1975).

66 *child psychoanalyst Jim Herzog*: J. Herzog, "Early Interaction and Representation: The Role of the Father in Early and Later Triangles and Triads" (Stuttgart: Schottaur, 1998), pp. 162–79, and J. Herzog, *Father Hunger.*

66 *and others have also observed that mothers*: D. Ehrensaft, *Parenting Together: Men and Women Sharing the Care of Children* (New York: Free Press, 1987); M. Lamb, "Mothers, Fathers and Child Care in a Changing World," in *Frontiers of Infant Psychiatry,* vol. 2, ed. J. Call, E. Galenson, and R. Tyson (New York: Basic Books, 1984); R. Parke and D. Sawin, "The Family in Early Infancy: Social Interactional and Attitudinal Analyses," paper presented to the Society for Research in Child Development, Denver, 1975; R. Rabain-Jamin, "The Infant's 'Sound Envelope' and Organization of Parent-Infant Communication," in *Frontiers of Infant Psychiatry,* vol. 2; D. Stern, *The Interpersonal World of the Infant* (New York: Basic Books, 1985); and others.

66 *As psychologist Judith Jordan notes*: Jordan, "The Relational Self," p. 63.

67 *It "privileges" it*: The notion of "privileging" another's reality is taken from G. Gabbard, "A Reconsideration of Objectivity in the Analyst," *International Journal of Psychoanalysis* 78 (1997): 15–26.

71 *We now recognize, from intensive study of mothers, fathers, and infants*:

K. Clarke-Stewart, "The Father's Contribution to Children's Cognitive and Social Development in Early Childhood," in *Father-Infant Relationship: Observational Studies in a Family Setting,* ed. F. A. Pedersen (New York: Holt, Rinehart & Winston, 1980); R. Corwyn and R. Bradley, "Determinants of Paternal and Maternal Investment in Children," *Infant Mental Health Journal* 20 (1999): 238–56; Ehrensaft, *Parenting Together*; Lamb, "Mothers, Fathers and Child Care in a Changing World"; Parke and Sawin, "The Family in Early Infancy"; Y. Yogman, "The Father's Role with Preterm and Fullterm Infants," in *Frontiers of Infant Psychiatry,* vol. 2; Herzog, "Early Interaction and Representation"; and Herzog, *Father Hunger.*

71 *He will lead the way and ask his child to follow. He will even, at times, see his children not only as they are, but as he wishes them to be.* Paraphrase from Rushdie, *The Moor's Last Sigh,* p. 331.

71 *"benevolent disruption,"to borrow a phrase*: Steven Cooper, *Objects of Hope: Essays on the Limited Possible* (Hillsdale, NJ: Analytic Press, 2000).

71 *"Sweet are the uses of adversity."* W. Shakespeare, *As You Like It* (New York: Washington Square Press, 1997).

71 *J. M. Coetzee's novel*: J. M. Coetzee, *Disgrace* (New York: Penguin, 1999).

5. "So Who Put You in Charge?"

PAGE

98 *With one third of all children born out of wedlock and half of all marriages ending in divorce*: R. Schoen and N. Standish, *The Footprints of Cohabitation: Results from Marital Status Life Tables for the U.S., 1995,* Population Research Institute, September 2000.

6. Keeping Things Safe

PAGE

105 *we fathers give our children a weight with which they can "collide"*: The word "collide" is borrowed from literary critic Harold Bloom, who writes of how writers "collide" and "swerve" with the authors,

or fathers, of previous generations. Harold Bloom, *The Anxiety of Influence: A Theory of Poetry* (New York: Oxford University Press, 1997).

110 So *writes social psychologist Roy Baumeister*: Roy Baumeister, *Evil: Inside Human Violence and Cruelty* (New York: W. H. Freeman and Company, 1997), p. 15.

110 *"Boys are more likely to be physically abused by a parent"*: M. Gurian, *The Wonder of Boys* (New York: Penguin, 1997).

111 *As historian Robert Griswold notes*: R. Griswold, *Fatherhood in America: A History* (New York: Basic Books, 1993).

112 *Psychoanalyst Otto Kernberg answers this question clearly and succinctly*: Kernberg, "The Analyst's Authority."

112 *As Stanford psychologist William Damon observes*: William Damon, *Greater Expectations* (New York: Simon & Schuster, 1995).

7. Discipline

PAGE

129 *In their reworking of Benjamin Spock*: Benjamin Spock, *Dr. Spock on Parenting: Sensible Advice from America's Most Trusted Child-Care Expert* (New York: Simon & Schuster, 1988).

130 *As Newberger sees it*: Newberger, *The Men They Will Become*.

130 *Newberger and others review the relevant data*: See also: T. Gordon, *Teaching Children Self-Discipline at Home and at School: New Ways Parents and Teachers Can Build Self-Control, Self-Esteem, and Self-Reliance* (New York: Random House, 1989); I. Hyman, *Reading, Writing, and the Hickory Stick* (Lexington, MA: Lexington Books, 1990); T. Real, *I Don't Want to Talk About It*.

131 *Dan Kindlon and Michael Thompson, for example*: Kindlon and Thompson, *Raising Cain*.

131 *All too often they arrive at positions like that of Thomas Gordon*: Gordon, *Teaching Children Self-Discipline at Home and at School*.

133 *The dictionary tells us that "to discipline" means*: *Webster's College Dictionary* and *Webster's New International Dictionary of the English Language,* 2nd ed.

133 *the usually male and often Christian authoritarians*: James Dobson, *Dare to Discipline* (Wheaton, IL: Tyndale, 1970); James Dobson, *The Strong-*

Willed Child (Wheaton, IL: Tyndale, 1988); Rosemond, *Parent Power!*;
Kevin Ryan and Karen Bohlin, *Building Character in Schools: Practical
Ways to Bring Moral Instruction to Life* (San Francisco: Jossey-Bass,
1998).

133 *Consider these words of Rosemond*: Bolotin, S. "The Disciples of Discipline," *New York Times Magazine,* February 14, 1999.

134 *Consider again the words of Rosemond, in this case his thoughts on
spanking*: Rosemond, *Parent Power!*

135 *Its generally acknowledged leader is Stanford psychologist William
Damon*: Damon, *Greater Expectations*.

135 *Thomas Lewis, the coauthor*: T. Lewis, F. Amini, and R. Lanon, *A
General Theory of Love* (New York: Random House, 2000).

139 *Infant researchers and theorists*: Stern, *The Interpersonal World of the
Infant*; B. Beebe and D. Stern, "Engagement-Disengagement and
Early Object Experiences," in *Communicative Structures and Psychic
Structures,* ed. M. Freedman and S. Grand, (New York: Plenum,
1977); E. Tronick, H. Als, and T. B. Brazelton, "The Infant's
Capacity to Regulate Mutuality in Face-to-Face Interaction." *Jour-
nal of Communication* 27 (1977): 74–80.

140 *As Thomas Lewis puts it*: Lewis et al., *A General Theory of Love,*
p. 128.

140 *As the mind collects a library of experience*: Solms and Turnbull
describe a two-step process. First, as Donald Hebb discovered in
1949, experience leads to "reverberating circuits—groups of inter-
connected cells firing together in closed (self-reactivating) loops."
Subsequently, as Eric Kandel's Nobel Prize–winning discovery
showed, such repeated reverberations lead to, as Solms and Turnbull put it, a "more permanent, anatomical process—the growth of
new synapses at the site of these reverberating neurons." These are
the processes by which new experience leads to the formation of
new "neural networks." Donald Hebb, *Organization and Behavior*
(New York: Wiley, 1949); E. Kandel, J. Schwartz, and T. Jessell,
Principles of Neural Science (Norwalk, CT: Appleton & Lange,
2000); Mark Solms and Oliver Turnbull. *The Brain and the Inner
World* (New York: Other Press, 2002).

140 *Repeated experiences, experiences with important and loved people*:
This is described by Joseph LeDoux, *The Emotional Brain* (London:

Weidenfeld & Nicolson, 1996); and Solms and Turnbull, *The Brain and the Inner World.*

141 *There appear to be, as neurobiologist Joseph LeDoux has noted*: LeDoux, *The Emotional Brain.*

141 *as Richard Brockman points out*: Richard Brockman, *A Map of the Mind* (Madison, CT: Psychosocial Press, 1998), p. 164.

142 *(again to quote Brockman)*: Brockman, *A Map of the Mind,* p. 164.

142 *and not as inarguable hard science*: There remains quite a bit of uncertainty regarding the actual relationship between the chemical and anatomical phenomena we are now able to observe in the brain, and the behavioral phenomena thought to result from these. Much of what is written about this relationship ought to be considered hypothesis rather than fact.

143 *When you first respond from that adrenaline surge*: Obviously the child's memory is not directly enhanced by the *parent's* adrenaline response, but rather by the way a child's autonomic system is aroused by the parent's emotions, which in turn affects the child's remembering brain.

143 *You want his mind to remember your voice, urgent and intense*: The work of Jim McGaugh and Larry Cahill is relevant here. McGaugh and Cahill had subjects read two stories. In one story, a child rides his bike to visit his father. The ride is uneventful. In the other story, the child is hit by a car. All things being equal, subjects tended to remember more details from the traumatic story. When, however, subjects are given an "adrenaline blockade," thus minimizing the effect of emotional arousal, there is no difference between the number of details recalled. LeDoux quotes this experiment to demonstrate the "memory-enhancing effects of emotional arousal." From: LeDoux, *The Emotional Brain*; J. McGaugh et al., "Involvement of the Amygdala in the Regulation of Memory Storage," in *Plasticity in the Central Nervous System: Learning and Memory,* ed. J. McGaugh et al. (Hillsdale, NJ: Erlbaum, 1995).

143 *Now you are speaking the language of your child's limbic brain*: In this regard, it is important to note that matters of degree are important. While the release of adrenaline, the activation of the autonomic nervous system, can influence memory centers in the brain in such a way as to enhance memory, extreme examples of this can lead to

dysfunctions in the memory system. As Schacter notes, there is convincing evidence that prolonged and extreme stress, as occurs in war traumas and childhood abuse, leads to elevated glucocortico-steroids. Prolonged exposure to such steroids leads to memory abnormalities. As Solms and Turnbull note, this may be one of the reasons that traumatized individuals reveal decreased hippocampal volume on brain-imaging studies. The point here is a simple but important one: Fathers, and mothers, must manage their level of reponsiveness. While real and emotional responses are valuable to a child, responsiveness that is overwhelming or traumatizing is clearly detrimental. D. Schacter, *Searching for Memory* (New York: Basic Books, 1997); and Solms and Turnbull, *The Brain and the Inner World*.

143 *a child will, over time, build inside himself*: Joseph LeDoux refers to the "unified" experience of declarative and emotional memory. LeDoux, *The Emotional Brain*.

144 *In the 1990s two popular books*: Hyman, *Reading, Writing, and the Hickory Stick*; M. A. Straus, *Beating the Devil Out of Them: Corporal Punishment in American Families* (San Francisco: Jossey-Bass, 1994).

144 *As leading spokesman Rosemond writes*: Rosemond, *Parent Power!*, p. 12.

145 *Diana Baumrind, a research psychologist*: Diana Baumrind, www. fractaldomains.com/devpsych/baumrind.htm.

145 *More recently a number of studies*: In addition to Baumrind, other researchers, prominent among them Marjorie Gunnoe, a psychologist, and Robert Larzelere, director of residential research at Boys Town in Nebraska, have also reviewed the data that Straus, Hyman, Newberger, and others use to support their anti-spanking position. They conclude that these data are both inconclusive and methodologically flawed. As Lynn Rosellini, in a *U.S. News & World Report* article on the subject, notes: "When Larzelere and others presented their research at the 1996 AAP conference on spanking, it prompted a quiet wave of revisionism. The two conference organizers, S. Kenneth Schonberg and Stanford B. Friedman, both pediatrics professors at Albert Einstein College of Medicine in New York, wrote afterward in *Pediatrics,* 'We must confess that we had

a preconceived notion that corporal punishment, including spanking, was innately and always "bad."' Yet by the end of the conference, the two skeptics acknowledged that 'given a "healthy" family life in a supportive environment, spanking in and of itself is not detrimental to a child or predictive of later problems.'" From Lynn Rosellini, "When to Spank," *U.S. News & World Report,* April 13, 1998, p. 198. See also R. Larzelere et al., "The Effects of Discipline Responses in Delaying Toddler Misbehavior Recurrences," *Child and Family Behavior Therapy* 18 (1996): 35–37; and M. Gunnoe and C. Mariner, "Toward a Developmental-Contextual Model of the Effects of Parental Spanking on Children's Aggression," *Archives of Pediatrics and Adolescent Medicine* 151 (1977): 768–75.

147 *Let's begin with what is relatively straightforward—some behavioral guidelines*: Interestingly, despite all of Rosemond's sarcastic and provocative rhetoric, his guidelines for how to spank (don't threaten, don't act out of frustration, use an open hand, start a dialogue) are relatively sensible. Rosemond, *Parent Power!*

147 *Recently Dr. Sukhwinder Shergill and his colleagues from University College, London*: S. Shergill et al., "Two Eyes for an Eye: The Neuroscience of Force Escalation," *Science* 301 (July 11, 2003): 187.

150 *Because when the aggressive forces that have to do with hurting*: The words of Melvin Konner come to mind: "Whatever cultural conditioning we may do, we must remain cognizant of the fact that human beings who have been trained and conditioned to be nonviolent retain the capacity for violence; as constrained as that capacity may be in certain contexts, it can come out in others. It is subdued, reduced, dormant, yes. But it is never abolished. It is never nonexistent. It is always there." Melvin Konner, *The Tangled Wing: Biological Constraints on the Human Spirit* (New York: Holt, Rinehart & Winston, 1982).

8. No Violence! Fatherhood, Authority, and the Development of Self-Control

PAGE

156 *Recently, South African game wardens*: Reuters, "Musth," November 2000. Note also a study in *Nature* magazine, in which researchers

found that introducing older male elephants into a herd decreased the rampant killing of rhinoceros by younger males. These researchers note that "Young male [elephants] lose the physical signs of musth minutes or hours after an aggressive interaction with a higher-ranking musth male." Chun-ru Wang et al., "Older Bull Elephants Control Young Males," *Nature,* November 2000, pp. 425–26.

157 *And, as primatologist Robert Sapolsky notes*: "A Bozo of a Baboon: A Talk with Robert Sapolsky," www.edge.org/3rd_culture/sapolsky03/sapolsky_print.html.

157 *The findings of psychiatrist Allan Schore are relevant here*: This synopsis of Schore's thinking comes from his chapter "Effect of Early Relational Trauma on Affect Regulation: The Development of Borderline and Antisocial Personality Disorders and a Predisposition to Violence" in his book *Affect Dysregulation and Disorders of the Self* (New York: Norton, 2003). Meanwhile, the "rough and tumble play" idea refers to his thoughts about Jaak Panksepp's article "Socially Induced 'Fertilization': Play Promotes Brain Derived Neurotrophic Factor Transcription in the Amygdala and Dorsolateral Frontal Cortex in Juvenile Rats," *Neuroscience Letters* 341 (2003): 17–20. Schore writes: "My extrapolation of [Panksepp's] results is that regulated rough and tumble play with fathers acts as a growth facilitating environment for the experience-dependent maturation of the boy's dorsolateral prefrontal cortex, starting in the second year, a critical period of growth of this prefrontal structure." Also acknowledging the work of Jim Herzog, Schore notes that he proposed this idea in his 1994 book, *Affect Regulation and the Origin of the Self: The Neurobiology of Emotional Development* (Hillsdale, NJ: Erlbaum, 1994). (Schore, personal communication.)

9. Fathering from the Inside Out

PAGE

177 *research demonstrates that it is, in fact, women*: Griswold, *Fatherhood in America: A History.*

177 *As Natalie Angier, author*: Natalie Angier, *Woman: An Intimate Geography* (New York: Anchor, 1999), p. 264.

179 *In single parent households, however*: J. Raphael-Leff, *Psychological Processes of Childbearing* (London: Chapman & Hall, 1991), pp. 372, 533; and A. Samuels, "From Sexual Misconduct to Social Justice," *Psychoanalytic Dialogues* 6 (1996): 295–322.

180 *Sometimes a man may act from a place*: Both the sensitive man movement and the real man movement recognize the importance of feminine and masculine identifications: The sensitive man valorizes the former, the real man the latter. Neither group, however, appreciates the importance of fluidity and flexibility in regard to these identifications. Instead each substitutes a politicized view of how men "should be" for pragmatism and realism.

180 *If we keep this in mind we may be able*: Andrew Samuels notes that fathers are "culturally constructed creatures of relationship." Fatherhood, in other words, derives its meaning and definition not only from biology's relatively constant influence, but also from the rather more immediate and variable pressure of culture and context. Samuels, "From Sexual Misconduct to Social Justice."

10. Sexuality and the Family:
Creating a Safe and Fertile Space

PAGE

201 *Sex can be lots of things*: Psychoanalyst Jim Herzog has proposed a tentative scheme for the varieties of psychological meaning found in male intercourse in his book *Father Hunger*. Men, Herzog notes, engage in declarative intercourse ("I am a man, I can do it"), recreative-interactive intercourse (which stresses the "hedonic and social aspects of the act"), procreative intercourse (which is aimed at making a baby), parentogenic intercourse (which couples the wish to make a baby with the intent to care for it), and integrative intercourse (which results in a feeling of oneness and wholeness with one's partner).

202 *Seen in this light, the distinction between "healthy" sexuality*: A number of years ago, Supreme Court Justice Potter Stewart's efforts to articulate the essence of pornography led him to utter the now famous phrase, "I know it when I see it." Stewart's words are evocative, but he could have been more specific in his definition if he had

referenced the French psychoanalyst Joyce McDougall, who writes, "It seems to me that one important differentiating factor [between pornography and erotic art] is to be found in the extent of imaginative space that the artist leaves the public. Erotica, if it is to be judged art, should stimulate the fantasy of the onlooker, whereas pornographic inventions leave next to nothing to the imagination, whence their lack of artistic merit." McDougall goes on to note that perversion involves, by definition, "a conspicuous lack of fantasy and imaginative freedom." J. McDougall, *A Plea for a Measure of Abnormality* (New York: International Universities Press, 1980).

203 *In a sense, the question of whether sexuality is "healthy"*: See M. Parsons, "Sexuality and Perversion a Hundred Years On," *International Journal of Psychoanalysis* 81 (2000): 37–52.

212 *Such behavior may well be consistent*: Ellis and his team studied nearly eight hundred girls from New Zealand and the United States, tracking the girls from early in life to age eighteen. The study revealed that the absence of the biological father from the home was an overriding risk factor for early sexual activity and teenage pregnancy, and the earlier father absence occurred, the greater the risk. Father absence emerged as a major pathway to risky sexual behavior, even for girls who came from otherwise socially and economically privileged homes. Ellis notes: "Father absence was so fundamentally linked to teenage pregnancy that its effects were largely undiminished by such factors as whether girls were rich or poor, black or white, New Zealand Maori or European, cooperative or defiant in temperament, born to adult or teenage mothers, raised in safe or violent neighbourhoods, subjected to few or many stressful life events, reared by supportive or rejecting parents, exposed to functional or dysfunctional marriages, or closely or loosely monitored by parents." Ellis cautions that the path between cause and effect needs to be further investigated. B. J. Ellis et al., "Does Father Absence Place Daughters at Special Risk for Early Sexual Activity and Teenage Pregnancy?" *Child Development* 74, 2003.

213 *"It's like I'm just wired that way"*: The damage that results from childhood abuse is now understood to include not only behavioral sequelae but also significant, observable changes in brain chemistry

and anatomy. M. Teicher, "Wounds That Won't Heal: The Neurobiology of Child Abuse," *Cerebrum* 2 (2000): 50–67.

219 *that child psychoanalyst Jim Herzog terms "caretaking"*: Herzog, *Father Hunger.*

11. Father Time

PAGE

223 *Among his many seminal contributions*: Stephen Mitchell, *Relational Concepts in Psychoanalysis* (Cambridge: Harvard University Press, 1988).

234 *In his book* Western Attitudes Toward Death: Philippe Aries, *Western Attitudes Toward Death* (Baltimore: Johns Hopkins University Press, 1974). Quotations from Patrick Hutton in: P. Hutton, "Of Death and Destiny: The Aries-Vovelle Debate About the History of Mourning," in *Symbolic Loss: The Ambiguity of Mourning and Memory at Century's End,* ed. Peter Homans (Charlottesville: University Press of Virginia, 2000).

234 *a term coined by social critic Wendy Kaminer*: Wendy Kaminer, *I'm Dysfunctional, You're Dysfunctional: The Recovery Movement and Other Self-Help Fashions* (New York: Vintage, 1992).

234 *as microbiologist Ursula Goodenough reminds us*: Ursula Goodenough, *The Sacred Depths of Nature* (New York: Oxford University Press, 2000).

235 *As Adam Phillips writes in his reflections*: On Life Stories and Death Stories (New York: Basic Books, 2001).

238 *"Perhaps," the narrator of Jane Smiley's novel*: Jane Smiley, *A Thousand Acres* (New York: Fawcett Columbine, 1991).

12. Real Hope

PAGE

248 *This requires moving the timeless fantasies*: Or, as Steven Cooper puts it, hope involves "carrying the imagination . . . into an act of collaboration . . . with another." Cooper, *Objects of Hope.*

Sources

American Psychiatric Association. *Diagnostic and Statistical Manual of Mental Disorders IV*. Washington, DC: American Psychiatric Association, 1994.

Angier, Natalie. "Are Women Necessary?" *New York Times,* November 11, 2003.

———. "Canary Chicks Not All Created Equal." *New York Times,* January 25, 1994.

———. *Woman: An Intimate Geography*. New York: Anchor, 1999.

Appleby, Scott. "Unflinching Faith: What Fires Up the World's Fundamentalists?" *U.S. Catholic* 11 (1989).

Aries, Philippe. *Western Attitudes Toward Death*. Baltimore: Johns Hopkins University Press, 1974.

Baber, Asa. *Naked at Gender Gap*. New York: Birch Lane Press, 1992.

Ballard, Nancer. *Equal Engagement: Observations on Career Success and Meaning in the Lives of Women Lawyers*. Stone Center Publication #292. Wellesley, MA, 1998.

Baumeister, Roy. *Evil: Inside Human Violence and Cruelty*. New York: W. H. Freeman, 1997.

Baumrind, Diana. www.fractaldomains.com/devpsych/baumrind.htm.

Beebe, B., and D. Stern. "Engagement-Disengagement and Early Object Experiences." In *Communicative Structures and Psychic Structures,* ed. M. Freedman and S. Grand. New York: Plenum, 1977.

Bem, Sandra. "The Measurement of Psychological Androgyny." *Journal of Consulting and Clinical Psychology* 42 (1974): 155–62.

Benjamin, Jessica. *The Bonds of Love: Psychoanalysis, Feminism, and the Problem of Domination*. New York: Pantheon, 1988.

————. *Like Subjects, Love Objects*. New Haven: Yale University Press, 1995.

Bloom, Harold. *The Anxiety of Influence: A Theory of Poetry*. New York: Oxford University Press, 1997.

Bly, Robert. *Iron John*. Reading, MA: Addison-Wesley, 1990.

Bolotin, S. "The Disciples of Discipline." *New York Times Magazine,* February 14, 1999.

Bourke, Joanna. *An Intimate History of Killing*. New York: Basic Books, 1999.

Brazelton, T. B., et al. "Early Mother-Infant Reciprocity." In *Parent-Infant Interaction*. CIBA Foundation, Symposium 33. Amsterdam: Elsevier, 1975.

Brockman, Richard. *A Map of the Mind*. Madison, CT: Psychosocial Press, 1998.

Celan, Paul. *The Poems of Paul Celan*. Translated by M. Hamburger. New York: Perreia Books, 1972.

Chasseguet-Smirgell, J. *Creativity and Perversion*. London: Routledge, 1985.

Chodorow, N. "Family Structure and Feminine Personality." In *Woman, Culture and Society*, ed. M. Z. Rosaldo and L. Lamphere. Palo Alto, CA: Stanford University Press, 1974.

Clark, R. *Family Life and School Achievement: Why Some Black Children Succeed and Some Fail*. Chicago: University of Chicago Press, 1983.

Clarke-Stewart, K. "The Father's Contribution to Children's Cognitive and Social Development in Early Childhood." In *Father-Infant Relationship: Observational Studies in a Family Setting,* ed. F. A. Pedersen. New York: Holt, Rinehart & Winston, 1980.

Clendinnen, I. *Reading the Holocaust*. Cambridge: Cambridge University Press, 1999.

Coetzee, J. M. *Disgrace*. New York: Penguin, 1999.

Cooper, Steven. *Objects of Hope: Essays on the Limited Possible*. Hillsdale, NJ: Analytic Press, 2000.

Corwyn, R., and R. Bradley. "Determinants of Paternal and Maternal Investment in Children." *Infant Mental Health Journal* 20 (1999): 238–56.

Crawford, R. "Reinterpreting the Japanese Economic Miracle." *Harvard Business Review* 76 (1997): 179–84.

Dabbs, James. *Heroes, Rogues and Lovers: Testosterone and Behavior*. New York: McGraw Hill, 2000.

Damon, William. *Greater Expectations*. New York: Simon & Schuster, 1995.

Darwin, C. *The Descent of Man, and Selection in Relation to Sex*. Vol. 1. London: John Murray, 1871.

Davidson, N. *The Failure of Feminism*. Buffalo, NY: Prometheus, 1987.

DeSalvo, L. *Virginia Woolf: The Impact of Childhood Sexual Abuse on Her Life and Work*. New York: Ballantine, 1989.

Dobson, James. *Dare to Discipline*. Wheaton, IL: Tyndale, 1970.

———. *The Strong-Willed Child*. Wheaton, IL: Tyndale, 1988.

Doyle, R. *The Rape of the Male*. St. Paul: Poor Richard's Press, 1986.

Eagly, A., and V. Steffen. "Gender and Aggressive Behavior: A Meta-Analytic Review of the Social Psychological Literature." *Psychological Bulletin* 108 (1986): 309–50.

Earley, T. *Jim the Boy*. Boston: Little, Brown, 2000.

Ehrensaft, D. *Parenting Together: Men and Women Sharing the Care of Children*. New York: Free Press, 1987.

Eldridge, Sherrie. *Twenty Things Adopted Kids Wish Their Adoptive Parents Knew*. New York: Dell, 1999.

Ellis, B. J., et al. "Does Father Absence Place Daughters at Special Risk for Early Sexual Activity and Teenage Pregnancy?" *Child Development* 74 (2003).

Ensler, Eve. *The Vagina Monologues*. New York: Villard, 1998.

Faludi, Susan. *Stiffed: The Betrayal of the American Male*. New York: William Morrow, 1999.

Fisher, Helen. *The First Sex: The Natural Talents of Women and How They Are Changing the World*. New York: Ballantine, 1999.

Fitzgerald, Frances. *Cities on a Hill*. New York: Simon & Schuster, 1986

Fletcher, Joyce. *Disappearing Acts: Gender, Power and Relational Practice at Work*. Cambridge, MA: MIT Press, 1999.

Freud, S. "A Child Is Being Beaten." *The Standard Edition of the Complete Psychological Works of Sigmund Freud,* ed. J. Strachey. London: Hogarth Press, 1919.

―――. *Civilization and Its Discontents. The Standard Edition of the Complete Psychological Works of Sigmund Freud,* ed. J. Strachey. London: Hogarth Press, 1930.

―――. *Three Essays on the Theory of Sexuality. The Standard Edition of the Complete Psychological Works of Sigmund Freud,* ed. J. Strachey, London: Hogarth Press, 1905.

Friedan, Betty. *The Feminine Mystique.* New York: Dell, 1963, 1983.

Fromm, E. *The Anatomy of Human Destructiveness.* New York: Holt, Rinehart & Winston, 1973.

Gabbard, G. "A Reconsideration of Objectivity in the Analyst." *International Journal of Psychoanalysis* 78 (1997): 15–26.

Garmezy, M., and M. Rutter. *Stress, Coping and Development in Children.* New York: McGraw Hill, 1983.

Geary, D. F. "Sexual Selection and Sex Differences in Mathematical Abilities (with Commentary and Rejoinder)." *Behavioral and Brain Sciences* 19 (1996): 229–84.

Geertz, C. *The Interpretation of Cultures.* New York: Basic Books, 1973.

Ghiglieri, M. *The Dark Side of Man: Tracing the Origins of Violence.* Reading, MA: Perseus Books, 1999.

Gilligan, C. "The Centrality of Relationship in Human Development: A Puzzle, Some Evidence, and a Theory." In *Development and Vulnerability in Close Relationships,* ed. Gil Noam and Kurt Fischer Majwah. Hillsdale, NJ: Erlbaum, 1996.

―――. *In a Different Voice: Psychological Theory and Women's Development.* Cambridge, MA: Harvard University Press, 1982.

Gilligan, Jim. *Violence: Reflections on a National Epidemic.* New York: Putnam, 1996.

Glasser, M. "On Violence." *International Journal of Psychoanalysis* 79 (1998): 887–902.

Goldberg, C. "Of Prophets, True Believers and Terrorists." *Cerebrum* 3 (2001): 21–24.

Goodenough, Ursula. *The Sacred Depths of Nature.* New York: Oxford University Press, 2000.

Gordon, T. *Teaching Children Self-Discipline at Home and at School: New Ways Parents and Teachers Can Build Self-Control, Self-Esteem, and Self-Reliance.* New York: Random House, 1989.

Gray, John. *Men Are from Mars, Women Are from Venus: A Practical Guide for Improving Communication and Getting What You Want in Your Relationships*. New York: HarperCollins, 1992.

Griswold, R. *Fatherhood in America: A History*. New York: Basic Books, 1993.

Gunnoe, M., and C. Mariner. "Toward a Developmental-Contextual Model of the Effects of Parental Spanking on Children's Aggression." *Archives of Pediatrics and Adolescent Medicine* 151 (1977): 768–75.

Gurian, M. *What Could He Be Thinking? How a Man's Mind Really Works*. New York: St. Martin's, 2003.

———. *The Wonder of Boys: What Parents, Mentors, and Educators Can Do to Shape Boys into Exceptional Men*. New York: Penguin, 1997.

Hall, G. Stanley. *Adolescence: Its Psychology and Its Relations to Physiology, Anthropology, Sociology, Sex, Crime, Religion and Education*. 2 vols. New York: Appleton, 1904.

Halpern, D. F. *Sex Differences in Cognitive Abilities*. 2nd ed. Hillsdale, NJ: Erlbaum, 1992.

Hampson, E., and D. Kimura. "Sex Differences and Hormonal Influences on Cognitive Function in Humans." In *Behavioral Endocrinology*, ed. J. Becker, S. M. Breedlove, and D. Crews. Cambridge, MA: MIT Press, 1992.

Hanley, C. "Reflections on Feminine and Masculine Authority: A Developmental Perspective." *Psychoanalytic Quarterly* 65 (1996): 84–101.

Hebb, Donald. *Organization and Behavior*. New York: Wiley, 1949.

Helgeson, Sally. *The Female Advantage*. New York: Doubleday, 1995.

Herzog, J. "Early Interaction and Representation: The Role of the Father in Early and Later Triangles and Triads." Stuttgart: Schottaur, 1998: 162–79.

———. *Father Hunger*. Hillsdale, NJ: Analytic Press, 2002.

———. "Fathers and Young Children: Fathering Daughters and Fathering Sons." In *Frontiers of Infant Psychiatry,* vol. 2, ed. J. Call, E. Galenson, and R. Tyson. New York: Basic Books, 1984.

———. "Sleep Disorder and Father Hunger." *Psychoanalytic Study of the Child* 135 (1980).

Herzog, J., and M. O'Connell. "Children Are Being Murdered: How Do People Live and Play in the Aftermath of Atrocity?" In *Children, War and Persecution: Rebuilding Hope*. Proceedings of the Conference on the Effects of War and Persecution on Children at Maputo, Mozambique, December 1–4, 1996.

Hinde, R. "Study of Aggression: Determinants, Consequences, Goals, and Functions." In *Determinants and Origins of Aggressive Behavior,* ed. J. DeWit and W. Hartup. The Hague: Mouton, 1977.

Hoffman, I. "Some Practical Implications of a Social-Constructivist View of the Psychoanalytic Situation." *Psychoanalytic Dialogues* 2 (1992): 287–304.

Hoff-Sommers, C. *The War Against Boys: How Misguided Feminism Is Harming Our Young Men.* New York: Touchstone, 2000.

Hulbert, Ann. *Raising America: Experts, Parents, and a Century of Advice About Children.* New York: Knopf, 2003.

Hutton, P. "Of Death and Destiny: The Aries-Vovelle Debate About the History of Mourning." In *Symbolic Loss: The Ambiguity of Mourning and Memory at Century's End,* ed. Peter Homans. Charlottesville: University Press of Virginia, 2000.

Hyde, J. "Where Are the Gender Differences? Where Are the Gender Similarities?" In *Sex, Power and Conflict: Evolutionary and Feminist Perspectives,* ed. D. Buss and N. Malamuth. New York: Oxford University Press, 1996, pp. 108–18.

Hyman, I. *Reading, Writing, and the Hickory Stick.* Lexington, MA: Lexington Books, 1990.

Jacoby, R. "The Politics of Narcissism." In *The Problem of Authority in America,* ed. John P. Diggins and Mark E. Kann. Philadelphia: Temple University Press, 1981.

Jones, Steve. *Y: The Descent of Men.* Boston: Houghton Mifflin, 2003.

Jordan, J. "The Relational Self: A New Perspective for Understanding Women's Development." *Contemporary Psychotherapy Review* 7 (1992): 56–71.

Kaminer, Wendy. *I'm Dysfunctional, You're Dysfunctional: The Recovery Movement and Other Self-Help Fashions.* New York: Vintage, 1992.

Kandel, E., J. Schwartz, and T. Jessell. *Principles of Neural Science.* Norwalk, CT: Appleton & Lange, 2000.

Kernberg, O. "The Analyst's Authority." *Psychoanalytic Quarterly* 65 (1996): 137–57.

Kimmel, M. *Manhood in America: A Cultural History.* New York: Free Press, 1996.

Kimura, D. "Sex Differences in the Brain." In *Scientific American* special issue: *Men: The Scientific Truth About Their Work, Play, Health, and Passions* 10 (1999): 26.

Kindlon, D., and M. Thompson, *Raising Cain: Protecting the Emotional Life of Boys*. New York: Ballantine, 1999.

Kohut, H. *The Analysis of the Self*. New York: International Universities Press, 1971.

————. *The Restoration of the Self*. New York: International Universities Press, 1977.

Konner, Melvin. *The Tangled Wing: Biological Constraints on the Human Spirit*. New York: Holt, Rinehart & Winston, 1982.

Lamb, M. "Mothers, Fathers and Child Care in a Changing World." In *Frontiers of Infant Psychiatry,* vol. 2., ed. J. Call, E. Galenson, and R. Tyson. New York: Basic Books, 1984.

Larzelere, R., et al. "The Effects of Discipline Responses in Delaying Toddler Misbehavior Recurrences." *Child and Family Behavior Therapy* 18 (1996): 35–37.

LeDoux, Joseph. *The Emotional Brain*. London: Weidenfeld & Nicolson, 1996.

Lepper, M. R. "Anthropology and Child Development." *New Directions for Child Development* 8 (1983): 71–86.

Levant, R. *Masculinity Reconstructed: Changing the Rules of Manhood—At Work, in Relationships, and in Family Life*. New York: Plume, 1996.

Lewis, T., F. Amini, and R. Lanon. *A General Theory of Love*. New York: Random House, 2000.

Lorenz, K. *On Aggression*. New York: Harcourt, Brace & World, 1966.

Maccoby, E. and C. Jacklin. *The Psychology of Sex Differences*. Vol. 1. Palo Alto, CA: Stanford University Press, 1974.

Machiavelli, N. *The Prince*. Edited and translated by Peter Bondanella. Oxford: Oxford University Press, 1998.

Marty, M. and S. Appleby, eds. *Fundamentalisms Observed*. The Fundamentalist Project, vol. 1. Chicago: University of Chicago Press, 1991.

McDougall, Joyce. *The Many Faces of Eros*. New York: Norton, 1995.

————. *A Plea for a Measure of Abnormality*. New York: International Universities Press, 1980.

McGaugh, J., et al. "Involvement of the Amygdala in the Regulation of Memory Storage." In *Plasticity in the Central Nervous System: Learning and Memory,* ed. J. McGaugh et al. Hillsdale, NJ: Erlbaum, 1995.

McNeil, Donald. "Are Men Necessary?" *New York Times,* November 11, 2003.

Mealey, Linda. *Sex Differences: Developmental and Evolutionary Strategies.* San Diego: Academic Press, 2000.

Miczek, K., and J. DeBold. "Hormone-Drug Interactions and Their Influence on Aggressive Behavior." In *Hormones and Aggressive Behavior,* ed. B. B. Svare. New York: Plenum, 1983.

Miller, Alice. *The Drama of the Gifted Child.* Rev. ed. New York: Basic Books, 1997.

Miller, J. B. *Toward a New Psychology of Women.* Boston: Beacon, 1976, 1986.

Minow, M. *Between Vengeance and Forgiveness: Facing History After Genocide and Mass Violence.* Boston: Beacon, 1998.

Mitchell, Stephen. *Hope and Dread in Psychoanalysis.* New York: Basic Books, 1993.

———. *Influence and Autonomy in Psychoanalysis.* Hillsdale, NJ: Analytic Press, 1997.

———. *Relational Concepts in Psychoanalysis.* Cambridge, MA: Harvard University Press, 1988.

Money, J. *Sex Errors of the Body and Related Syndromes.* Baltimore: Brookes, 1968, 1994.

Murdoch, I. *Metaphysics As a Guide to Morals: Philosophical Reflections.* New York: Viking, 1994.

Newberger, E. *The Men They Will Become: The Nature and Nurture of Male Character.* Reading, MA: Perseus Books, 1999.

Niehoff, D. *The Biology of Violence.* New York: Free Press, 1999.

Nouwen, H. *Life of the Beloved.* New York: Crossroad Publishing, 1992.

O'Connell, Mark. "Subjective Reality, Objective Reality, Modes of Relatedness, and Therapeutic Action." *Psychoanalytic Quarterly* 69 (2000): 677–710.

Ogden, T. *The Primitive Edge of Experience.* Northvale, NJ: Jason Aronson, 1989.

Panksepp, Jaak. "Socially Induced 'Fertlization': Play Promotes Brain

Derived Neurotrophic Factor Transcription in the Amygdala and Dorsolateral Frontal Cortex in Juvenile Rats." *Neuroscience Letters* 341 (2003): 17–20.

Parke, R., and D. Sawin. "The Family in Early Infancy: Social Interactional and Attitudinal Analyses." Paper presented to the Society for Research in Child Development, Denver, 1975.

Parsons, M. *The Dove That Returns, the Dove That Vanishes*. London: Routledge, 2000.

———. "Sexuality and Perversion a Hundred Years On." *International Journal of Psychoanalysis* 81 (2000): 37–52.

Pellegrini, A., and J. Perlmutter. "Rough and Tumble Play on the Elementary School Playground." *Young Children* (January 1988): 14–17.

Phillips, A. *Darwin's Worms: On Life Stories and Death Stories*. New York: Basic Books, 2001.

———. *On Flirtation*. Cambridge, MA: Harvard University Press, 1994.

———. *On Kissing, Tickling, and Being Bored*. Cambridge, MA: Harvard University Press, 1993.

Podles, Leon. "Men Not Wanted." *Crisis* (November 1991).

Pollack, W. *Real Boys: Rescuing Our Sons from the Myths of Boyhood*. New York: Random House, 1998.

Rabain-Jamin, R. "The Infant's 'Sound Envelope' and Organization of Parent-Infant Communication." In *Frontiers of Infant Psychiatry,* vol. 2, ed. J. Call, E. Galenson, and R. Tyson. New York: Basic Books, 1984.

Raphael-Leff, J. *Psychological Processes of Childbearing*. London: Chapman & Hall, 1991.

Real, T. *How Can I Get Through to You: Reconnecting Men and Women*. New York: Scribner, 2002.

———. *I Don't Want to Talk About It*. New York: Fireside, 1997.

Resnick, P. "Risk Assessment and Liability: Violence, Stalking and Suicide." In *Innovations in Improving Women's Mental Health*. Irvine, CA: CME, 2001.

Restak, R. "Profile or Preconception?" *Cerebrum* 3 (2001): 33–37.

Reuters News Service. "Musth." November 2000.

Rosellini, Lynn. "When to Spank." *U.S. News & World Report,* April 13, 1998.

Rosemond, J. *Parent Power! A Common-Sense Approach to Parenting in the '90s and Beyond.* Kansas City, MO: Andrews McMeel, 1991.

Rosener, J. *America's Competitive Secret: Utilizing Women As a Management Strategy.* New York: Oxford University Press, 1995.

Ross, J. *What Men Want: Mothers, Fathers and Manhood.* Cambridge, MA: Harvard University Press, 1994.

Rutter, M. "Psychosocial Adversity: Risk, Resilience and Recovery." *Southern African Journal of Child and Adolescent Psychiatry* 7 (1985): 75–88.

Ryan, Kevin, and Karen Bohlin. *Building Character in Schools: Practical Ways to Bring Moral Instruction to Life.* San Francisco: Jossey-Bass, 1998.

Samuels, A. "From Sexual Misconduct to Social Justice." *Psychoanalytic Dialogues* 6 (1996): 295–322.

Sapolsky, R. "A Bozo of a Baboon: A Talk with Robert Sapolsky." www.edge.org/3rd_culture/sapolsky03/sapolsky_print.html.

———. *The Trouble with Testosterone (and Other Essays on the Biology of the Human Predicament).* New York: Touchstone, 1997.

Schacter, D. *Searching for Memory.* New York: Basic Books, 1996.

Schoen, R., and N. Standish. *The Footprints of Cohabitation: Results from Marital Status Life Tables for the U.S., 1995.* Population Research Institute, September 2000.

Schore, Allan. *Affect Regulation and the Origin of the Self: The Neurobiology of Emotional Development.* Hillsdale, NJ: Erlbaum, 1994.

———. *Affect Dysregulation and Disorders of the Self.* New York: Norton, 2003.

Sennett, Richard. *Authority.* New York: Norton, 1980.

Shabad, P. "The Most Intimate of Creations." In *Symbolic Loss: The Ambiguity of Mourning and Memory at Century's End,* ed. Peter Homans. Charlottesville: University Press of Virginia, 2000.

Shakespeare, W. Sonnet 138.

Shay, J. *Achilles in Vietnam: Combat Trauma and the Undoing of Character.* New York: Touchstone, 1994.

Shergill, S., et al. "Two Eyes for an Eye: The Neuroscience of Force Escalation." *Science* 301 (July 11, 2003): 187.

Siegel, A., and H. Edinger. "Role of the Limbic System in Hypothalamically Elicited Attack Behavior." *Neuroscience and Biobehavioral Reviews* 7 (1983): 395–407.

Silverstein, O., and B. Rashbaum. *The Courage to Raise Good Men*. New York: Penguin, 1994.

Smiley, Jane. *A Thousand Acres*. New York: Fawcett Columbine, 1991.

Solms, Mark, and Oliver Turnbull. *The Brain and the Inner World*. New York: Other Press, 2002.

Spock, Benjamin. *Dr. Spock on Parenting: Sensible Advice from America's Most Trusted Child-Care Expert*. New York: Simon & Schuster, 1988.

Steinem, Gloria. Foreword. In *The Vagina Monologues,* by Eve Ensler. New York: Villard, 1998.

Steiner, J. *Psychic Retreats*. London: Routledge, 1993.

Stern, D. "Affect Attunement." In *Frontiers of Infant Psychiatry,* vol. 2., ed. J. Call, E. Galenson, and R. Tyson. New York: Basic Books, 1984.

———. *The Interpersonal World of the Infant*. New York: Basic Books, 1985.

Stiver, I. "The Meanings of Dependency in Female-Male Relationships." In *Women's Growth in Connection,* ed. J. Jordan et al. New York: Guilford, 1991.

Stoller, R. *Porn*. New Haven: Yale University Press, 1991.

Straus, M. A. *Beating the Devil Out of Them: Corporal Punishment in American Families*. San Francisco: Jossey-Bass, 1994.

Sullivan, H. *The Interpersonal Theory of Psychiatry*. New York: Norton, 1953.

Surrey, J. *Relationship and Empowerment*. Stone Center Publication #30. Wellesley, MA: 1987.

Teicher, M. "Wounds That Won't Heal: The Neurobiology of Child Abuse." *Cerebrum* 2 (2000): 50–67.

Tiger, Lionel. *The Decline of Males*. New York: St. Martin's Griffin, 1999.

Tronick, E., H. Als, and T. B. Brazelton, "The Infant's Capacity to Regulate Mutuality in Face-to-Face Interaction." *Journal of Communication* 27 (1977): 74–80.

Ulirch R., and N. Azrin. "Reflexive Fighting in Response to Aversive Stimulation." *Journal of the Experimental Analysis of Behavior* 5 (1962): 511–20.

Waal, F. de. *Good Natured*. Cambridge, MA: Harvard University Press, 1966.

Wade, N. "What's It All About, Alpha?" *New York Times,* November 7, 1999.

Wang, Chun-ru, et al. "Older Bull Elephants Control Young Males." *Nature* 408 (November 2000): 425–26.

M. Weber, *Basic Concepts in Sociology.* Translated by H. P. Secher. New York: Citadel, 1962.

Webster's College Dictionary. New York: Random House, 1991.

Webster's New International Dictionary of the English Language. 2nd ed. Springfield, MA: C. & C. Merriam, 1950.

Werner, E. "Protective Factors and Individual Resistance." In *Handbook of Early Childhood Intervention,* ed. S. J. Meisels and J. P. Shonkoff. Cambridge: Cambridge University Press, 1990, pp. 97–116.

White, G., J. Katz, and K. Scarborough. "The Impact of Professional Football Games on Violent Assaults on Women." *Violence and Victims* 7 (1992): 157–71.

Whitebook, J. *Perversion and Utopia*. Cambridge, MA: MIT Press, 1995.

Winnicott, D. W. "Mirror Role of Mother and Family in Child Development. In *Playing and Reality*. Harmondsworth, England: Penguin, 1967, 1980.

Yogman, Y. "The Father's Role with Preterm and Fullterm Infants." In *Frontiers of Infant Psychiatry,* vol. 2, ed. J. Call, E. Galenson, and R. Tyson. New York: Basic Books, 1984.

Acknowledgments

The preceding pages are the product of many good minds. At times, my job has seemed little more than that of bringing those minds together.

This book would never have come to light and life without my editor, Colin Harrison. He somehow found the shape within the stone that fell on his desk, and was my teacher and companion throughout. His presence is on every page, and yet his touch is so light, and so superb, that the work still feels like mine.

The thoughts found herein owe much to years of conversation, and friendship, with Jim Herzog. His contributions to this book and our understanding of fatherhood are inestimable.

Similarly my mind, my thinking, indeed my character, are indelibly shaped by my long and good friendships with Steven Cooper and Chris Lovett.

Paul Bresnick, my agent, was the best. He had the courage to believe that I had something worth saying, and the smarts and perseverance to get my words to where they needed to be gotten.

Tony Kris belongs in a category of his own. He is, quite simply, in my head.

The thoughtful literary touches of Beth Weisberger and John Kerr can be found throughout. Likewise, Jim Baldwin, Dot Potter, Enoch Callaway, Matt Stone, Polly Stone, Lori Potter, Tom Goodwillie, and Tesi Kohlenberg generously lent me their intelligence, their friendship, their critical analysis, and their support. Their sharing of themselves has been more valuable to me than they know.

Acknowledgments

Many other minds are imprinted in mine, to my great good fortune. All of them have found their unique way onto these pages: Bill Kenney, Donald Hanson, Bill Moriarty, Tony Elliot, George Stone, Jessie O'Hare, Ron Carlson, Jennifer Pride, Leni Herzog, Chuck and Penny Jarecki, Leslie O'Rourke, Jack Smith, Drew Hargrove, Marta Zurad, Julian Baird, Stephanie Jones, Darryl Mathews, Chris Potter, Bruce Potter, Norm Sanders, Michael Castellana, Bob Blitz, Chris Perry, Doug McNair, Jennifer Stone, Bill Kates, William Warshawsky, Paul Cotton, George Fishman, Gerry Adler, Himal Mitra, Laura Mason, Owen Renik, Matt Goodwin, Ries Vanderpol, Jill Lovett, Joanie Wheelis, and Silvia de Montserrat.

I acknowledge with deep gratitude all of my patients, and all of my other teachers. I have learned from each and every one.

I suspect that little in the world gets accomplished unless Sarah Knight lends a hand.

Fred Chase's and Dan Cuddy's remarkable attention to the text was invaluable.

And finally, a man is fortunate if he loves, and is loved by, a good woman. I have been twice blessed.

By my mother, whom I love and admire. Would that I will someday be as proud of my life as she should be of hers.

And by Alison Potter, my wife, my best friend, and my partner in time.

About the Author

Dr. Mark O'Connell received his doctorate in psychology from Boston University and his postdoctoral training in psychoanalysis from the Boston Psychoanalytic Institute. He lives in Newton, Massachusetts, with his wife, Alison, and their three children: Miles, Chloe, and Dylan. He has a psychotherapy practice of adults, adolescents, and couples, and serves on the faculty of the Boston Psychoanalytic Institute and the Harvard Medical School. He writes and speaks about fatherhood, family life, and masculinity.

107394